IMAGES
of America

WORTH COUNTY

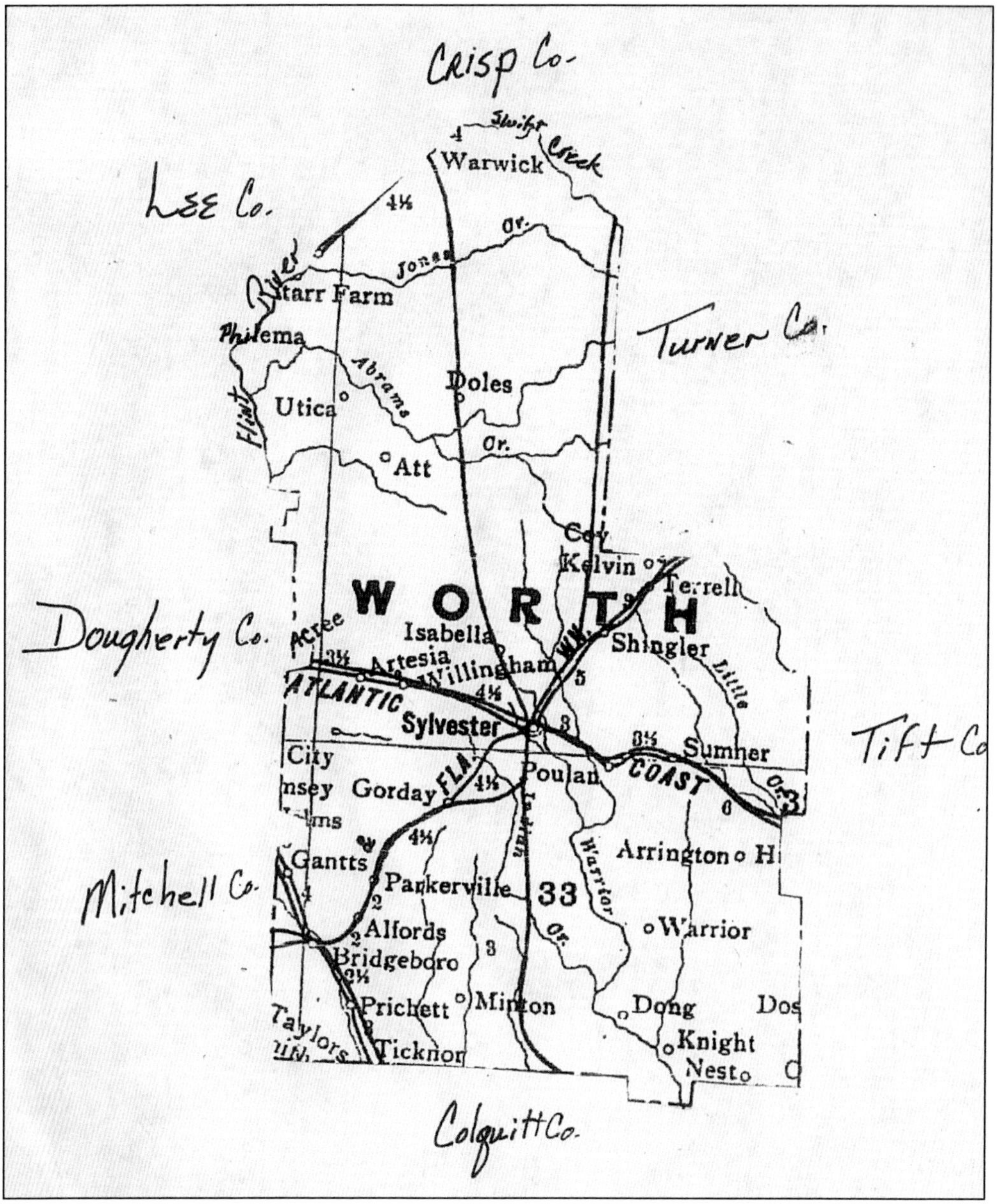

WORTH COUNTY, GEORGIA, C. 1915.

IMAGES
of America

WORTH COUNTY

Worth County Historical Society

ARCADIA
PUBLISHING

ISBN 978-0-07385-1538-0

Published by Arcadia Publishing
Charleston, South Carolina

Printed in the United States of America

Library of Congress Catalog Card Number: 2003105840

For all general information contact Arcadia Publishing at:
Telephone 843-853-2070
Fax 843-853-0044
E-mail sales@arcadiapublishing.com
For customer service and orders:
Toll-Free 1-888-313-2665

Visit us on the Internet at www.arcadiapublishing.com

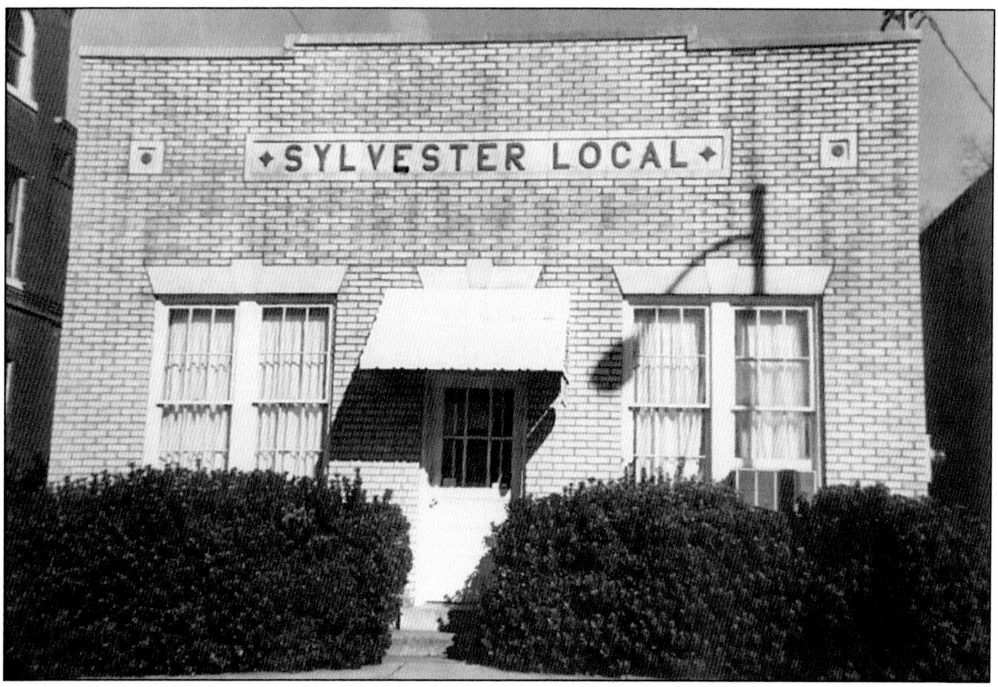

The Sylvester Local Office. This building was erected in the 1920s and houses the county's newspaper, which is the oldest continuous business in the county. It began in 1885 as the *Sumner Free-Trader.*

CONTENTS

ACKNOWLEDGMENTS

The Worth County Historical Society was organized in June 1993, with Add Lovejoy as its first president. Since 1996, Nell Deariso Thompson has served as president. The society's goals include promoting the study of Worth County and preserving its historical and cultural artifacts. Prior to the 1998 celebration of Sylvester's 100th birthday, members read old newspapers on microfilm in order to document the building of Sylvester's homes and businesses. This was great fun and we chased many rabbits, but along the way we learned a great deal about the early history of the town and county. In 2000, Sylvester celebrated the completion of her downtown beautification project and again the Historical Society provided information on the history of the buildings and businesses in the Downtown Historic District. An ongoing project of the society has also been to identify photographs taken during Worth County's Centennial in 1953.

After gathering all of this background information, we could hardly say no when we were contacted by Arcadia Publishing to judge our interest in a pictorial history of the county. In fact, it was just the impetus needed (read DEADLINE) to spur us into action. Months and many meetings later, this is the finished project.

We are most grateful to the following people who shared their photos and/or knowledge with us: Betty Perry Gibson, Jane Davis, Dot Anderson, Lynn Rouse Fowler, Mary King Givens, Matt Gammage, Marsha Young-Whitacre, Victor Gregory, Ann Poss, Laura Deariso, Pearson Golden, D.L. and Glenda Gammage, Ridley Monk, Otis Ulm, Charles Reynolds, Ray Jenkins, Doris Hinson, Jean Woolard, Runelle Moore, Sylvia Dinkel, Alston Banks, Alice Jones, Leigh Ford and the *Sylvester Local*, Nell Thompson, Theresa Harris, Elma Lee Champion, Doris Cochran, Thomas Latimer and Vicki Young, librarian of the Margaret Jones Public Library and her staff. If we have omitted anyone, we are very sorry and do appreciate your help in our endeavor. Royalties from the publication of this history will be used by the Worth County Historical Society to further its programs of preservation and documentation.

DISCLAIMER

The size restrictions (128 pages and no more than 240 images) have meant that many worthy photographs have been excluded. Some were too faint or damaged to include. Copies were made of all of these, however, and the Historical Society has these so they are not lost. Future plans include organizing these images also. We have tried to be as accurate as possible. Sources used to document names, places, and dates include, but are not limited to *History of Worth County, Georgia, 1854–1934* by Mrs. Lillian Grubbs; *History of Worth County, Georgia, Vol. II, 1934–1974* by the Barnard Trail Chapter, National Society Daughters of the American Revolution; the *Complete Cemetery Records of Worth County, Georgia* compiled by Catherine Fussell Wells, Worth County Tax Assessors Office; backfiles of the *Worth County Local* and the *Sylvester Local*; the 1911 and 1924 Sanborn Fire Insurance maps of downtown Sylvester; and the personal knowledge of those mentioned above. We apologize for any errors and ask that you notify us of them so that they may be corrected in our files.

INTRODUCTION

In 1540, nearly two centuries before Georgia received the charter from the Crown of England, the renowned adventurer, Hernando De Soto, and his 600 selected men were the first Europeans to set foot on Georgia soil. His itinerary shows almost positive proof that he passed through lands that would become Worth County. Also, Gen. Andrew Jackson passed through the northwest part of what is now Worth County when he was sent to put down the Seminoles who were massacring the settlers and Creek Indians in southwest Georgia.

Other travelers would use Thigpen Trail and Barnard Trail. The Thigpen Trail was a military road cut by James Thigpen for Col. James Moore for use in transporting supplies. It is the oldest military road in Georgia. Barnard Trail was blazed by Timothy Barnard to bring trade between his home in Macon County and the coast of Georgia. The local chapter of the Daughters of the American Revolution (DAR) adopted Barnard Trail as their chapter name.

The Native Americans of Worth County belonged to the Muscogees. The English named them Creeks because they were always found living near streams. There were two divisions: the Upper and Lower Creeks. The Muscogees of Worth County were Lower Creeks. After the Indian land cession in 1821, white settlers bought the village of Pinder Town from the Creeks. It became a town of considerable importance. For a long time, it was the only post office south of Macon between the Ocmulgee and Flint Rivers. The Stage Coach Road from Milledgeville to Tallahassee went through Pinder Town. All that is left of this settlement today are the ruts made by the stagecoach as it traveled through the countryside.

Worth County, Georgia was carved from two large counties, Irwin on the south and Dooly on the north, by an Act of the Legislature on December 20, 1853. Containing 569.8 square miles, it is one of the largest counties in the state.

Worth County was named for Maj. Gen. William James Worth, a distinguished soldier of the Mexican War, and a son-in-law of General Zachary Taylor. Maj. William A. Harris, the leader of the movement to organize the new county, fought under General Worth in this war, and he named the county in honor of him.

San Barnard was selected as first the county site when the county was created in 1853. Soon after Isabella was named as the county seat and remained so until 1904, when Sylvester became the county seat after an election that had voters choosing between Sylvester, Isabella, Sumner, and Poulan. Isabella was located three miles north of the railroad and it was hard to travel that far to reach the courthouse. Sylvester began as a depot named "Isabella Station" on the Brunswick and Albany Railroad (later known as the Atlantic Coast Line). The first record of "Sylvester" was as a post office established on June 17, 1882, at Isabella Station. This is Latin for "sylva" meaning *wood* and "vester" meaning *your*. The community was incorporated as a city by the Georgia Legislature on December 21, 1898.

Earning a living off the land has been the mainstay of the county. Many early settlers came to this area for the abundant pine forests. Sawmills, lumberyards, and turpentine stills provided the living. Corn, wheat, rye, sorghum, cattle, swine, cotton, peanuts, soybeans, tobacco, watermelons, cantaloupes, peaches, grapes, and pecans all played a part. Agriculture and agribusiness are still the backbone of the county.

Two festivals mark the importance of agriculture: the Georgia Peanut Festival in Sylvester and the Annual Grits Festival in Warwick. Worth County boasts of being the Peanut Capital of the World. Every jar of Peter Pan Peanut Butter is processed here. The Peanut Festival is held the first weekend in October. The Grits Festival is held each April. Georgia Code 50–3–78 recognizes grits as the official prepared food of the State of Georgia and the Georgia House of Representatives approved a resolution naming Warwick as "The Grits Capital of Georgia".

We hope you enjoy this look at the county's distant and not-so-distant past.

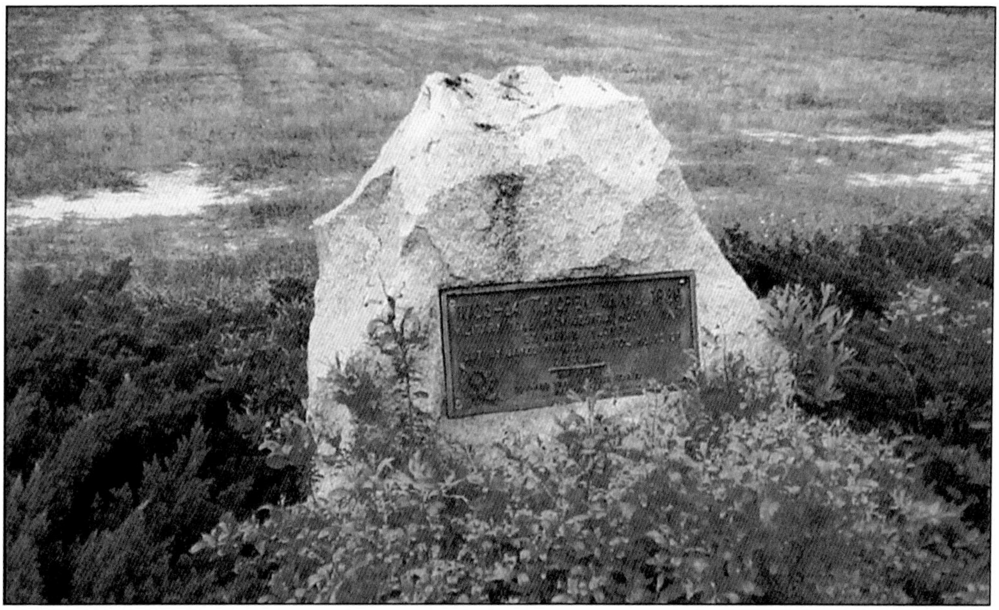

1703–1704 Thigpen Trail 1929. The marker was erected by the Barnard Trail Chapter of the NSDAR in 1929. The Trail followed a well beaten path of the Native Americans from the mountains to the sea. Beginning in South Carolina above the Broad River, the trail follows the Chattahoochee water divide to the Gulf of Mexico, avoiding all swamps and great rivers. The English claimed the territory as Carolina while the Spanish claimed it as Florida. Colonel Moore led the English in an attack down Thigpen Trail and "made Carolina as safe as the conquest of the Spanish and Appalachee (Indians) can make it." (Georgia Historical Commission.) nd its buccounts indicate Front Street. Most of Front Street buildings had been completed by 1905 with the exception of the old Bank of Worth County structure (1912). Isabella had a few buildings before 1910, but most were erected 1910–1920.

One

Sylvester

Sylvester's downtown and its businesses developed along the railroad. Early newspaper accounts indicate that the corner of Main and Front Streets was built first, followed by growth north up Main Street and west on Front Street. Most of Front Street buildings had been completed by 1905 with the exception of the old Bank of Worth County structure (1912). Isabella had a few buildings before 1910, but most were erected 1910–1920.

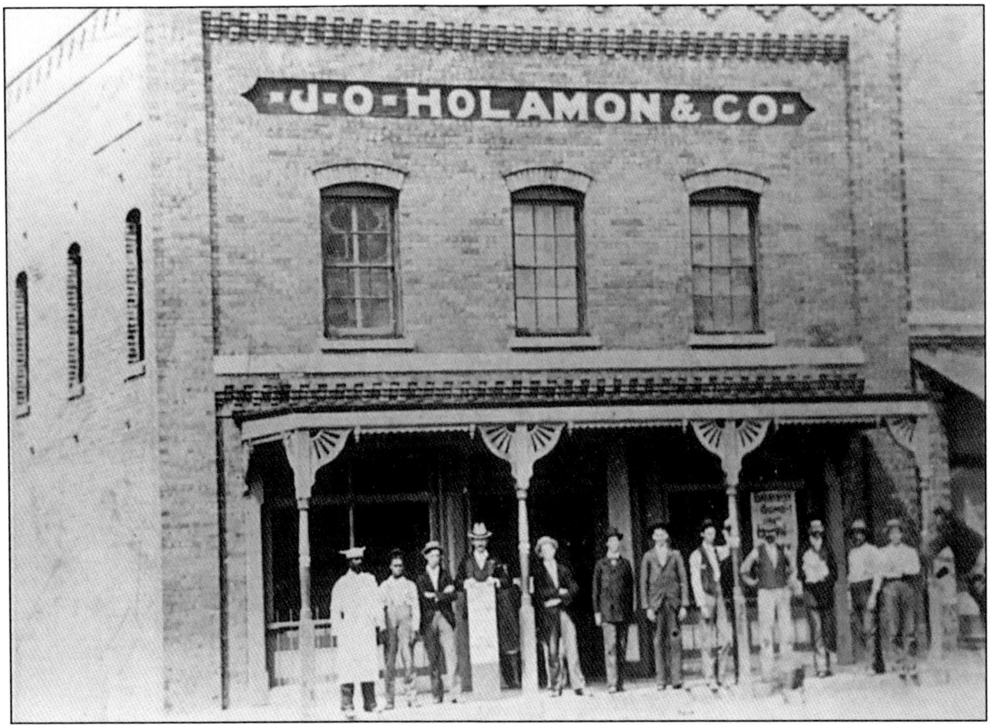

J.O. Holamon & Co. The company opened for business on May 6, 1898 in the building formerly occupied by J.S. Westberry & Co. It was located on the corner of Main and Front Streets and is the present site of the Sylvester City Hall.

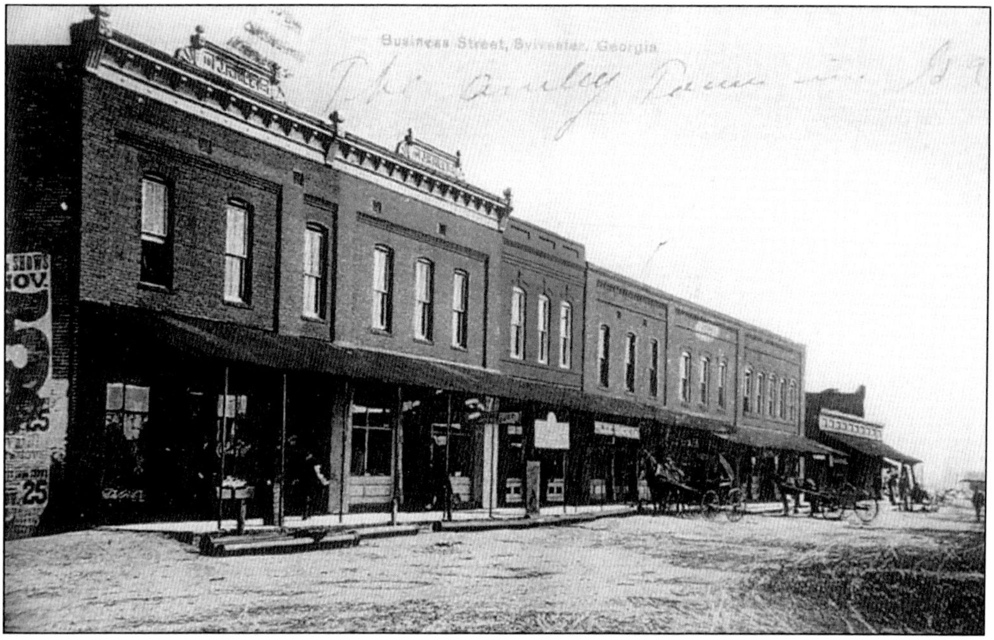

FRONT STREET. This view is from west to east and shows the two Hill buildings, which were built between 1902 and 1905.

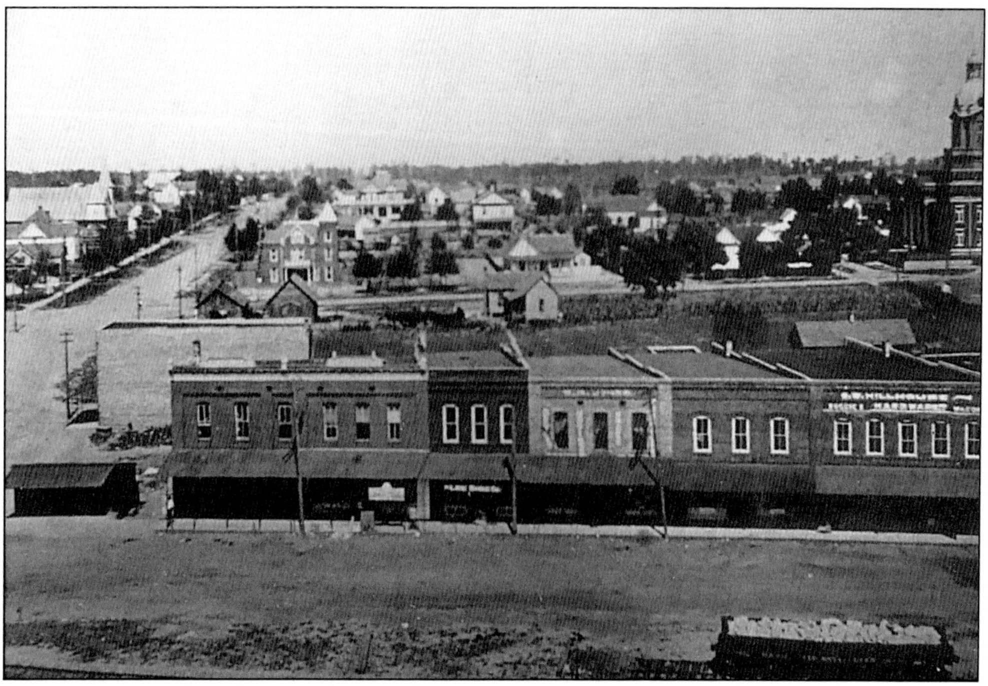

FRONT STREET. This photograph was taken from the water tower and shows Front Street as it looked between 1906 and 1910.

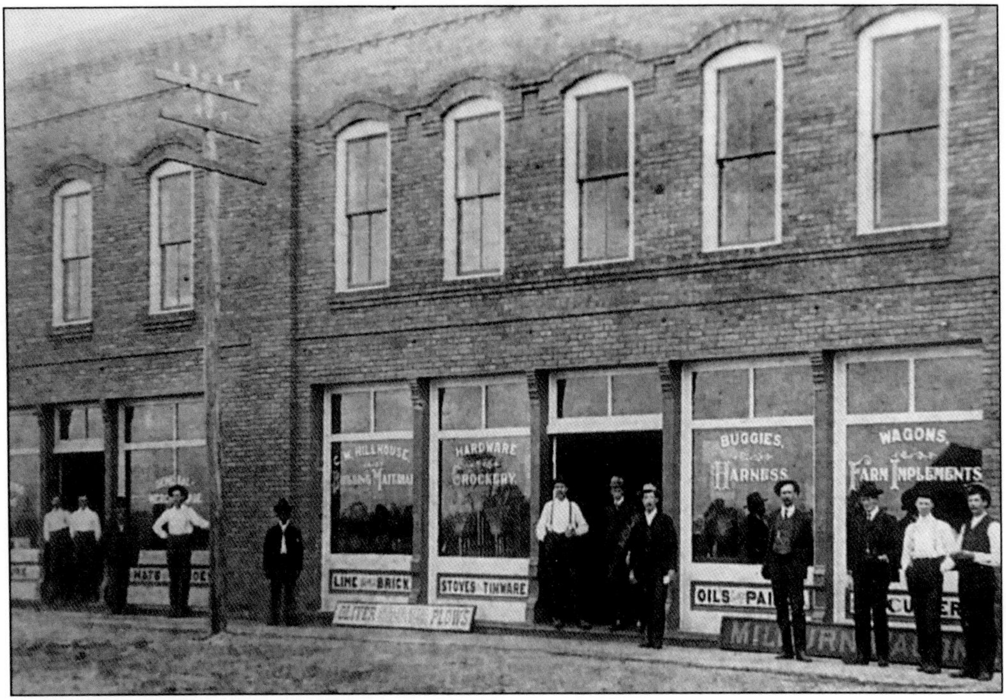

Front Street. The C.W. Hillhouse Hardware store was built in 1902.

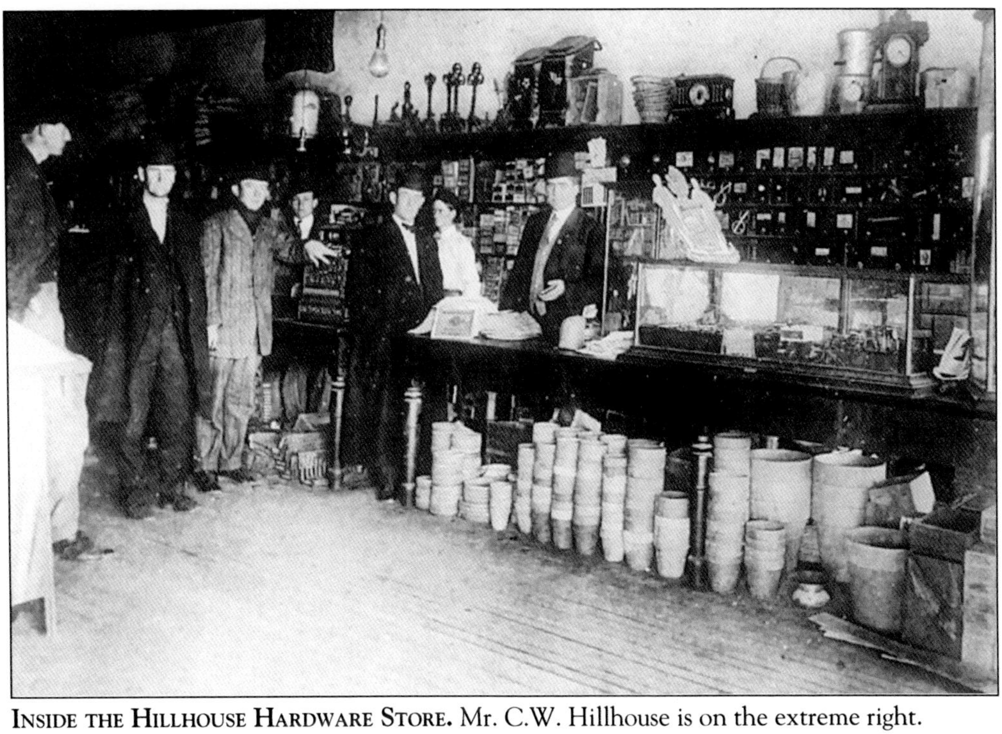

Inside the Hillhouse Hardware Store. Mr. C.W. Hillhouse is on the extreme right.

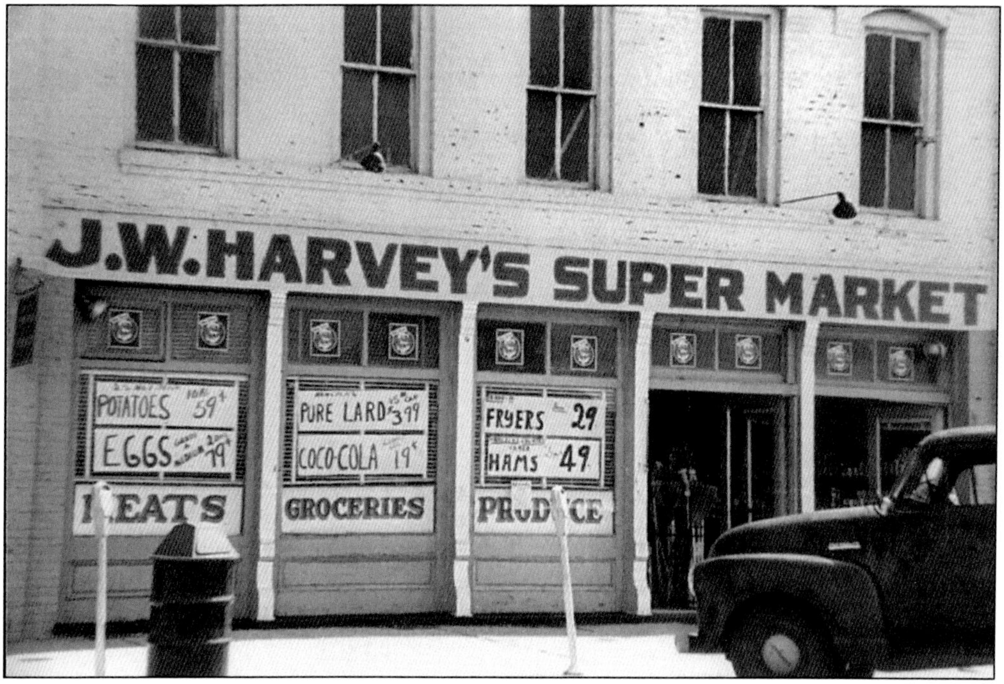

J.W. Harvey's Super Market on Front Street, 1950s. Harvey's later moved to Kelly Street and is now located on U.S. Highway 82.

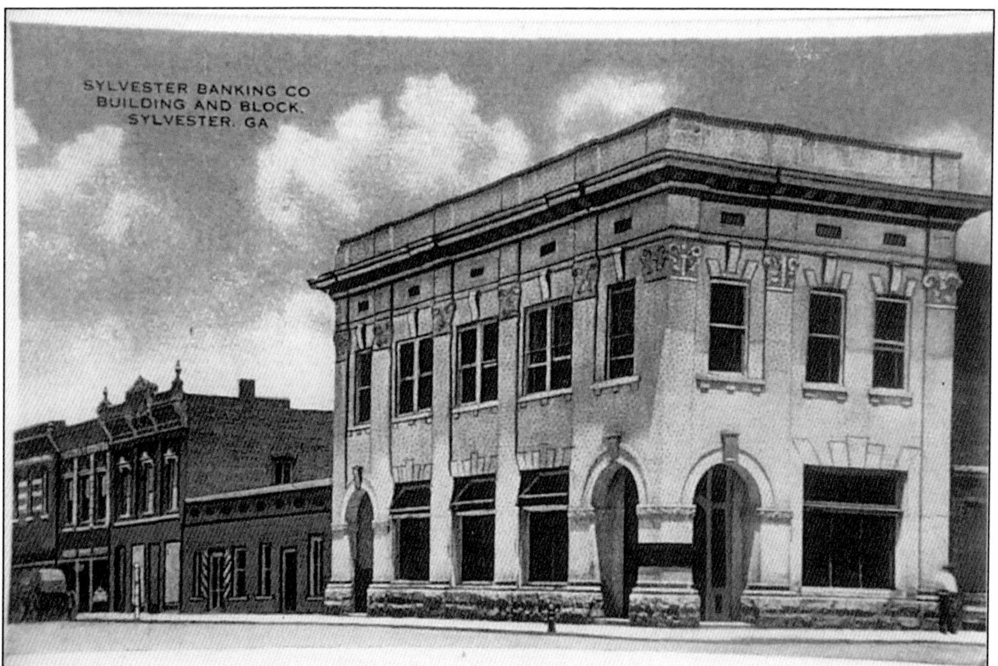

Sylvester Banking Company. The bank was built in 1910; it is now the home of the Sylvester City Hall.

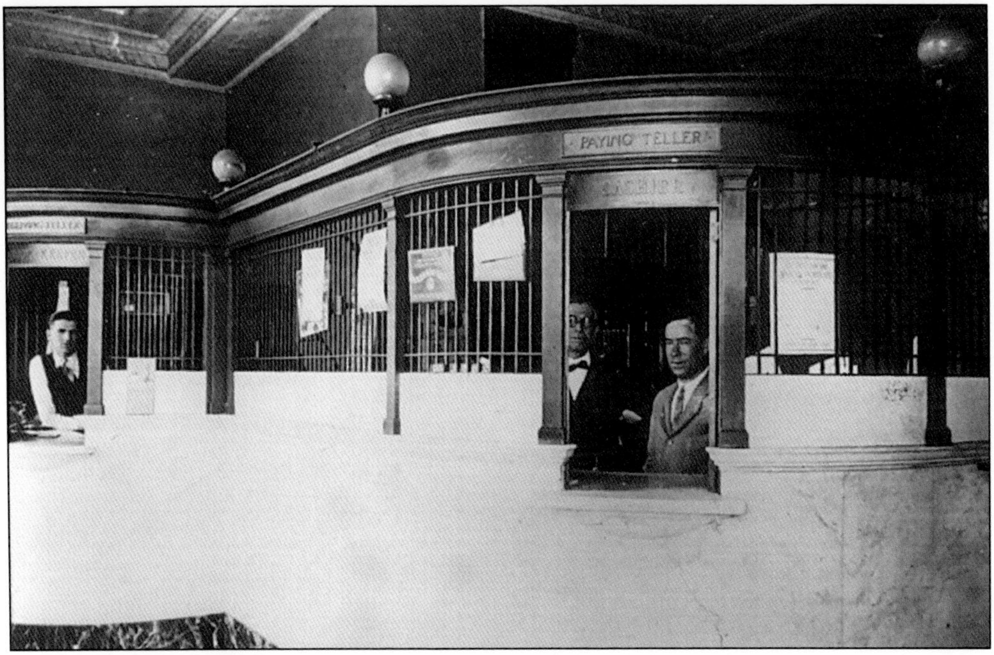

Inside the Sylvester Banking Company. Pictured from left to right are J.H. Westberry Jr., J.H. Westberry Sr., and Tom M. Purdom.

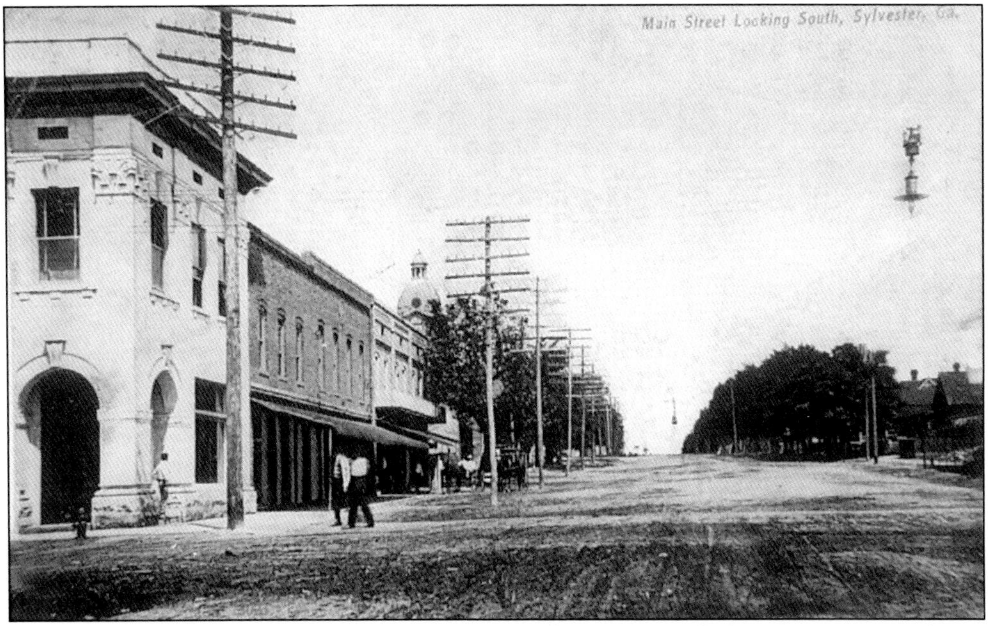

Main Street. This is a postcard of Main Street with a view north from Front Street, dating between 1910 and 1920.

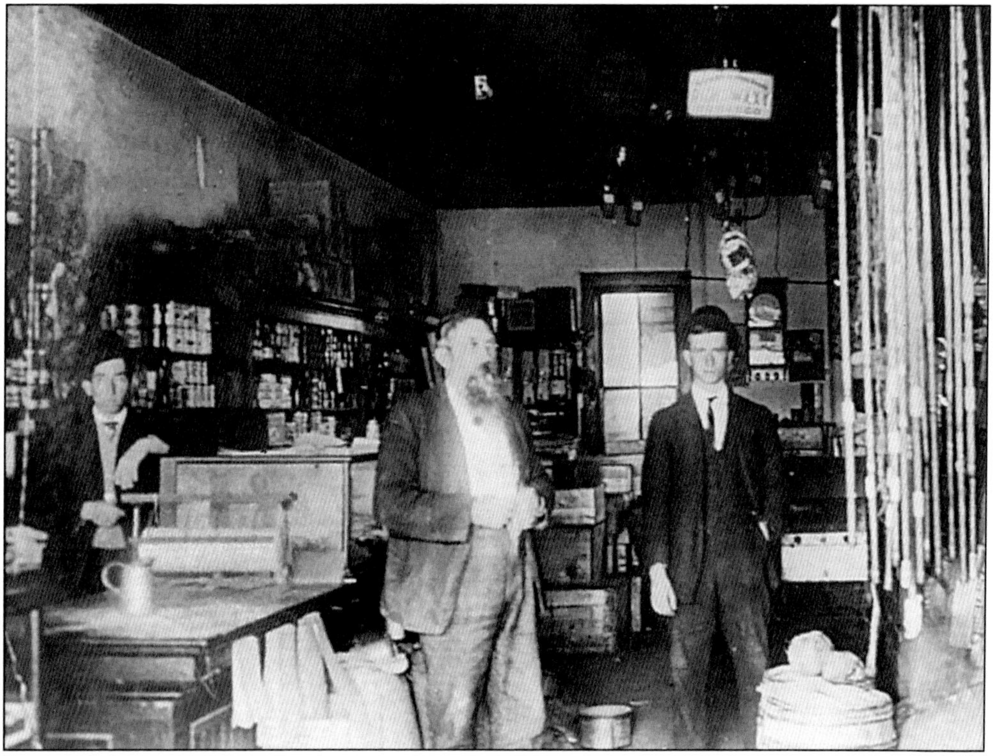

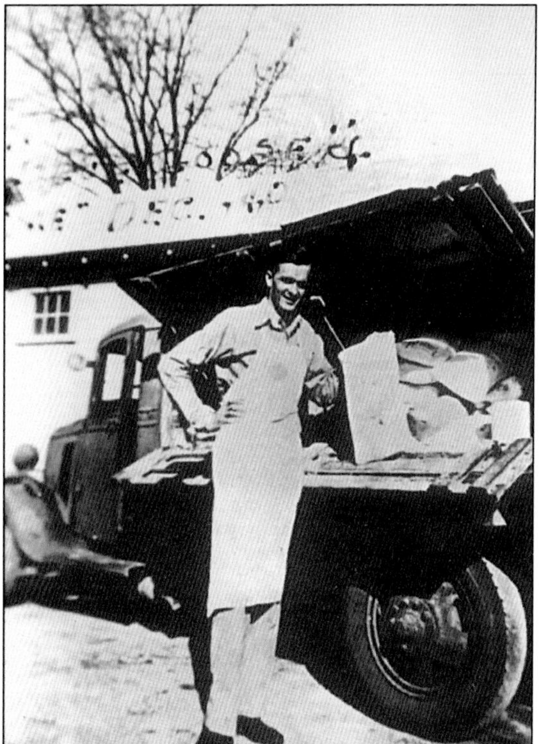

INSIDE N.M. RHODES STORE. This store was located on the west side of Main Street in the 100 block. Pictured, left to right, are Norbert Mayes Rhodes, Eldred Jasper Rhodes (Norbert's father), and an unidentified customer.

ROLLING GROCERY STORE. Herman Gregory and the "Blue Goose" are pictured here in December 1940. This store came to your door and was vital to those in the county that could not always make a trip to town.

DERISO DRUGS IN THE 1950S. First owned by Fred Deariso, it was later sold to a distant cousin, Frank, who spelled his last name without the "a."

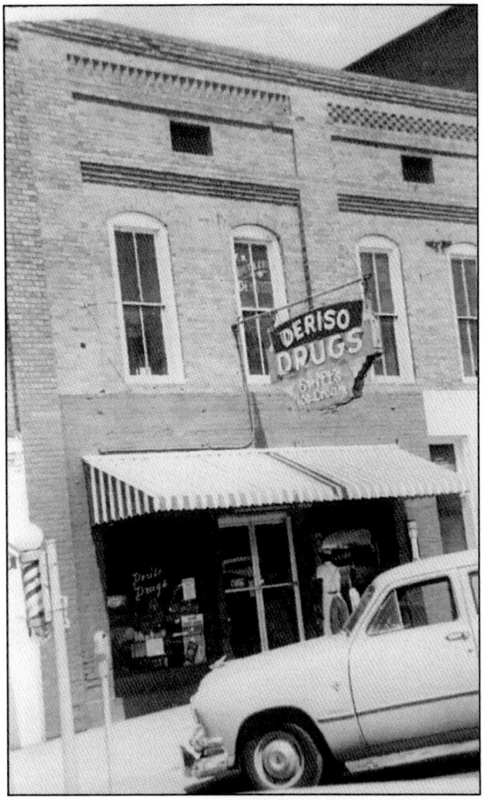

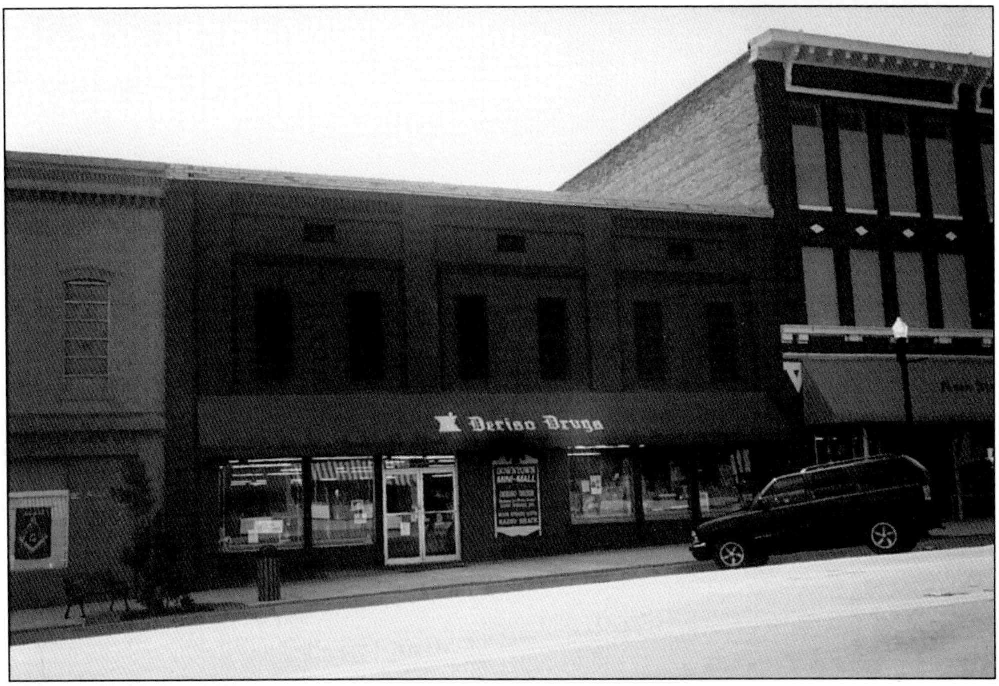

MAIN STREET IN 2000. The three-story Alford Building, erected c. 1911, is pictured on the extreme right.

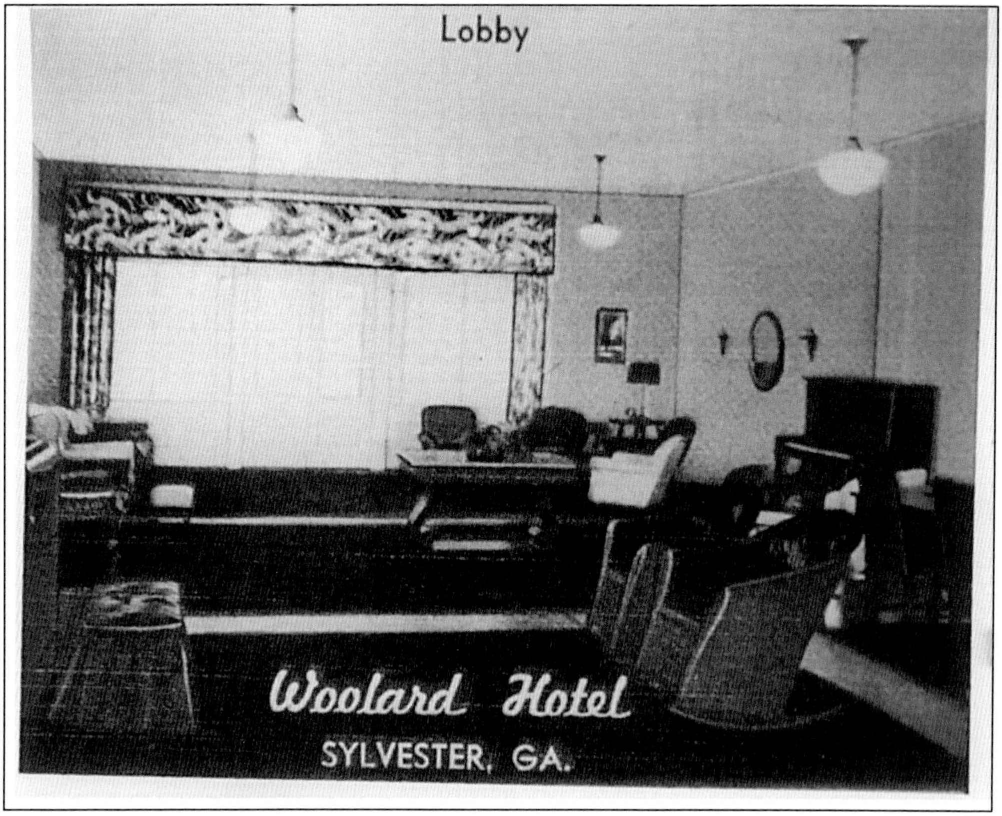

THE LOBBY OF THE WOOLARD HOTEL. This building was erected in 1900 as the Dr. W.L. Sikes Drug Store.

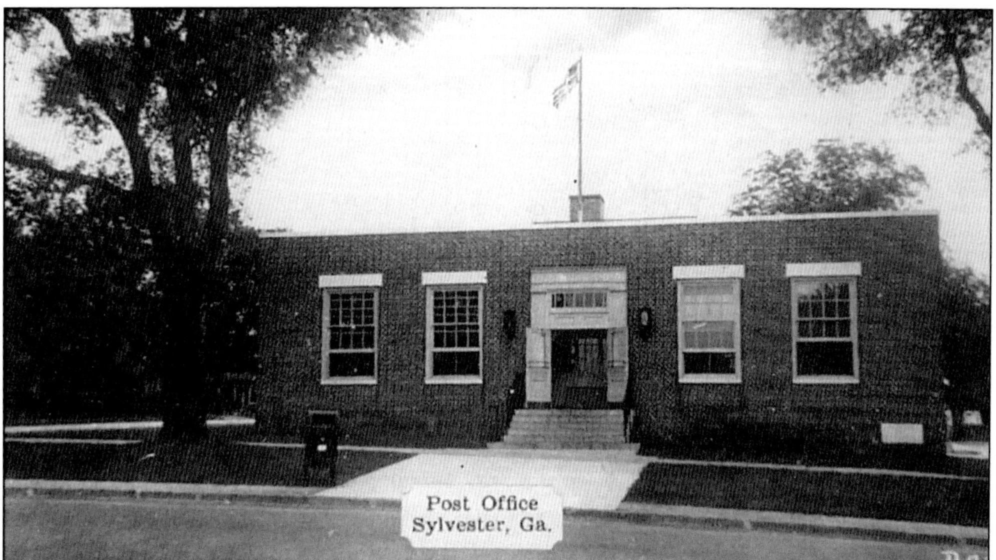

WORTH COUNTY BUILDING ON MAIN STREET. Built in 1937, as the Post Office at a cost of $65,000, the Worth County Building on Main Street was on the site of the residence of Col. T.R. Perry.

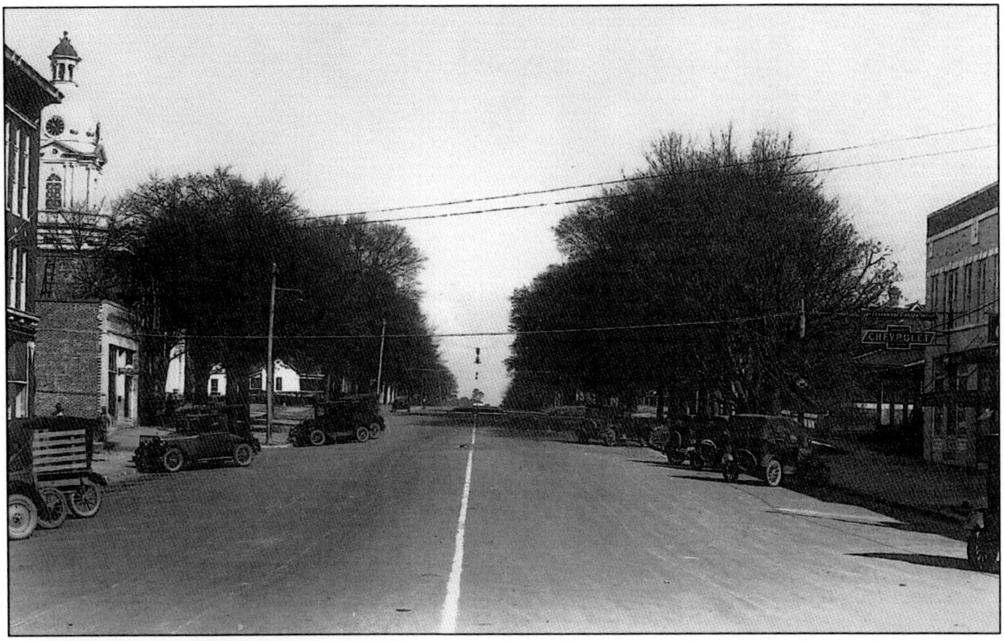

MAIN STREET, C. 1920S. Located on the west side of the street is the Post Office and across from it is J. Stewart's Chevrolet.

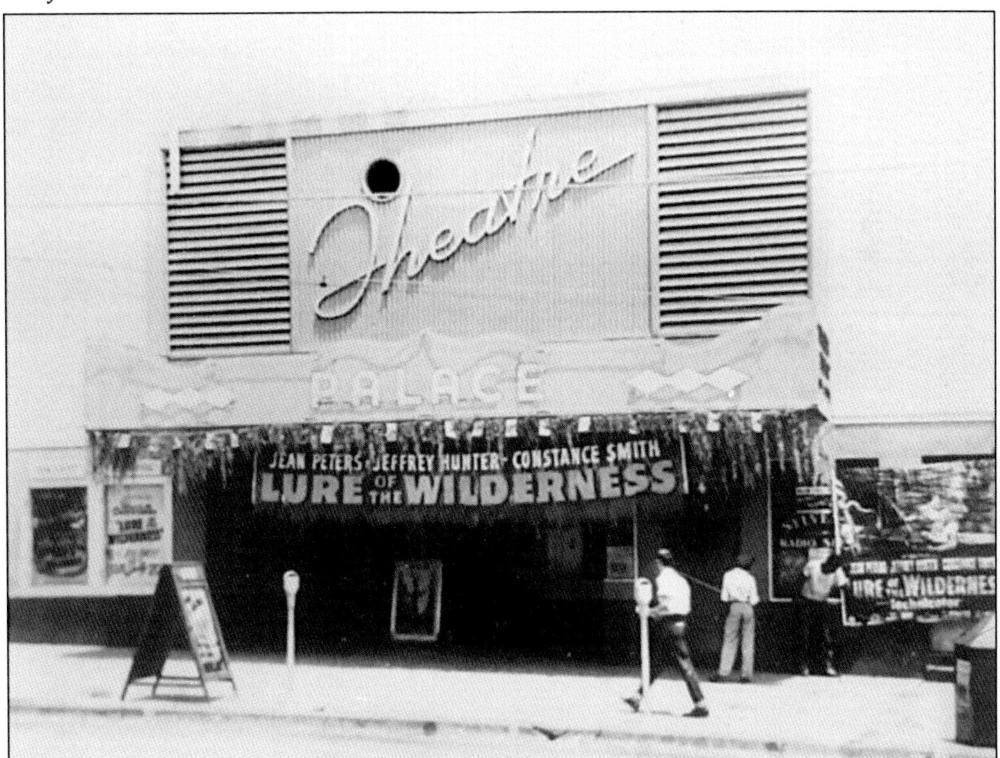

PALACE THEATRE ON MAIN STREET, 1953. Who can forget Saturday afternoon at the picture show? This is now the site of Jessie's Salon.

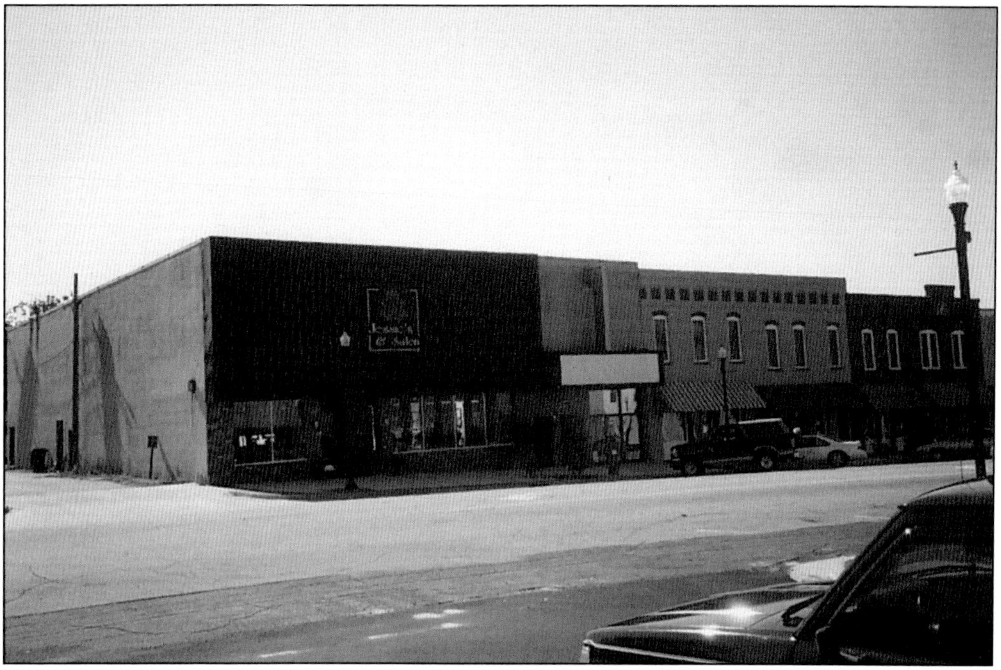

MAIN STREET 2000. The buildings shown were erected between 1900 and 1925. The earliest block of five were built from 1900–1903 and were known as the Gillis Block, after Mrs. W.D. Gillis who owned them. These were later called the Woolard Hotel Complex and were purchased and renovated by Hal and Priscilla Carter in the 1990s.

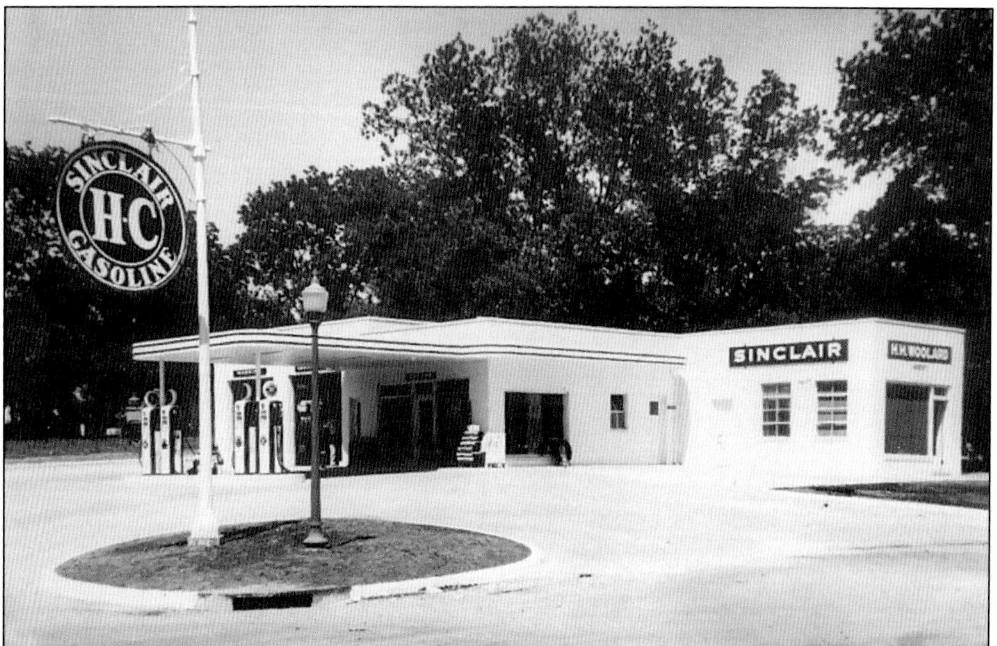

H.H. WOOLARD SINCLAIR STATION. The Sinclair Station was located on the corner of Kelly and Main Streets, which was the site of the old Sylvester Inn.

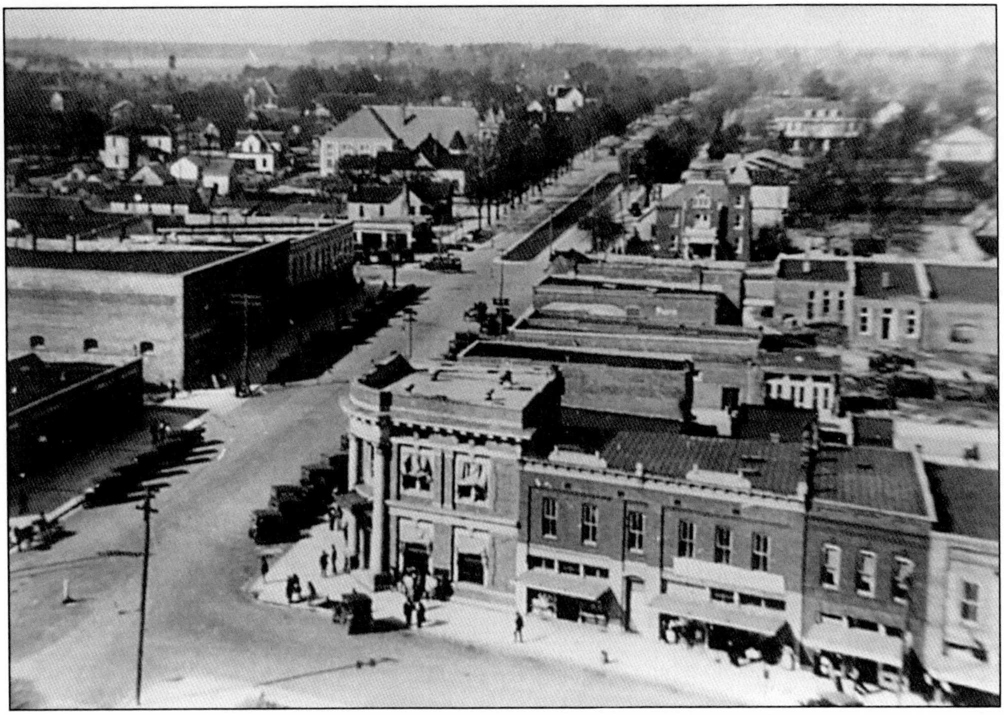

Isabella Street, c. 1920s. This view from the water tower shows the median from Kelly Street northward.

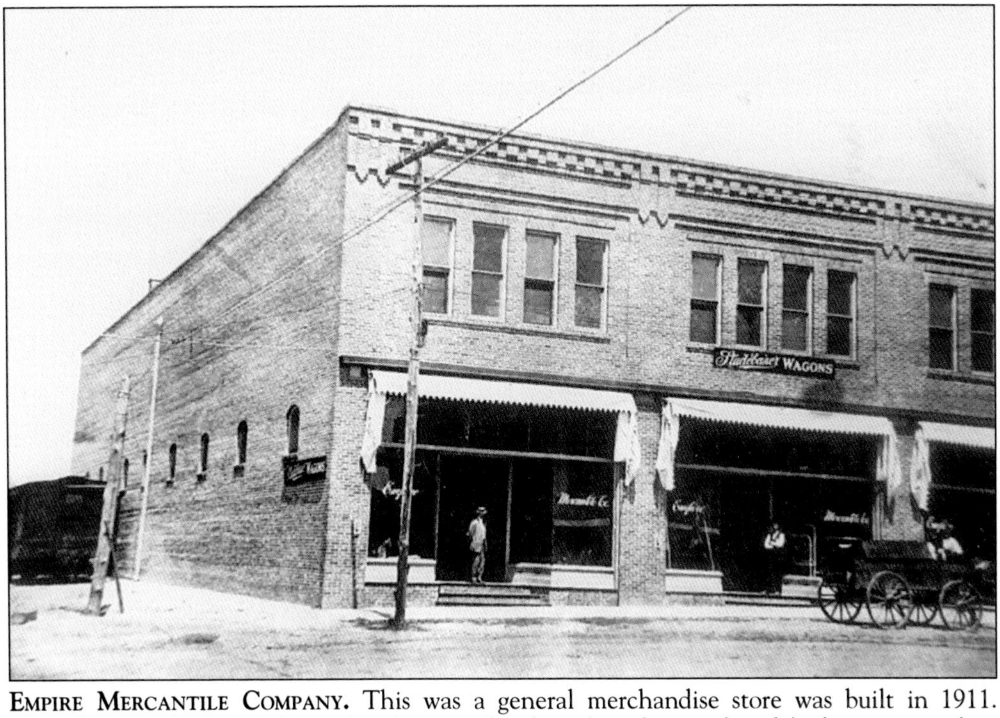

Empire Mercantile Company. This was a general merchandise store was built in 1911. The photograph shows the railroad car and siding (on the south side) that was used to transport materials.

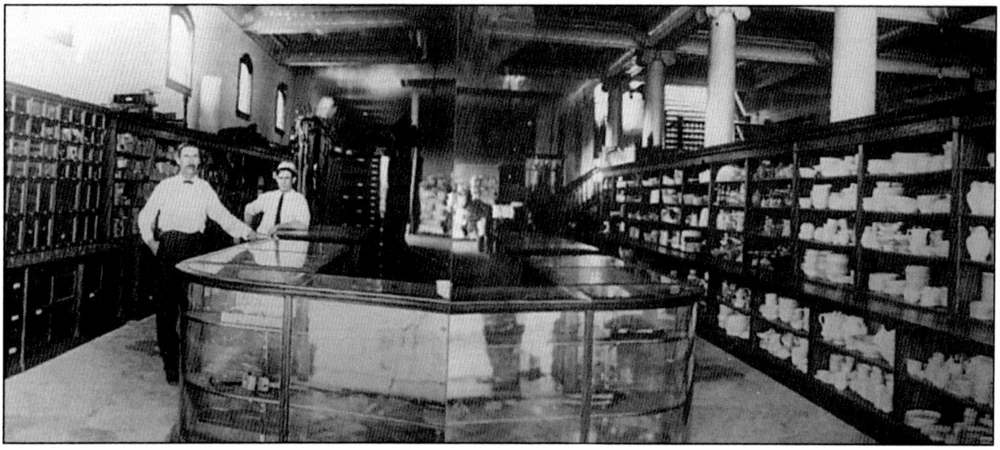

INSIDE EMPIRE MERCANTILE COMPANY, HARDWARE SECTION, 1914–1915. Shown are C.W. Hillhouse and Charlie Russel Hancock. On top of the display cabinet is a sign for Kabo corsets and umbrellas.

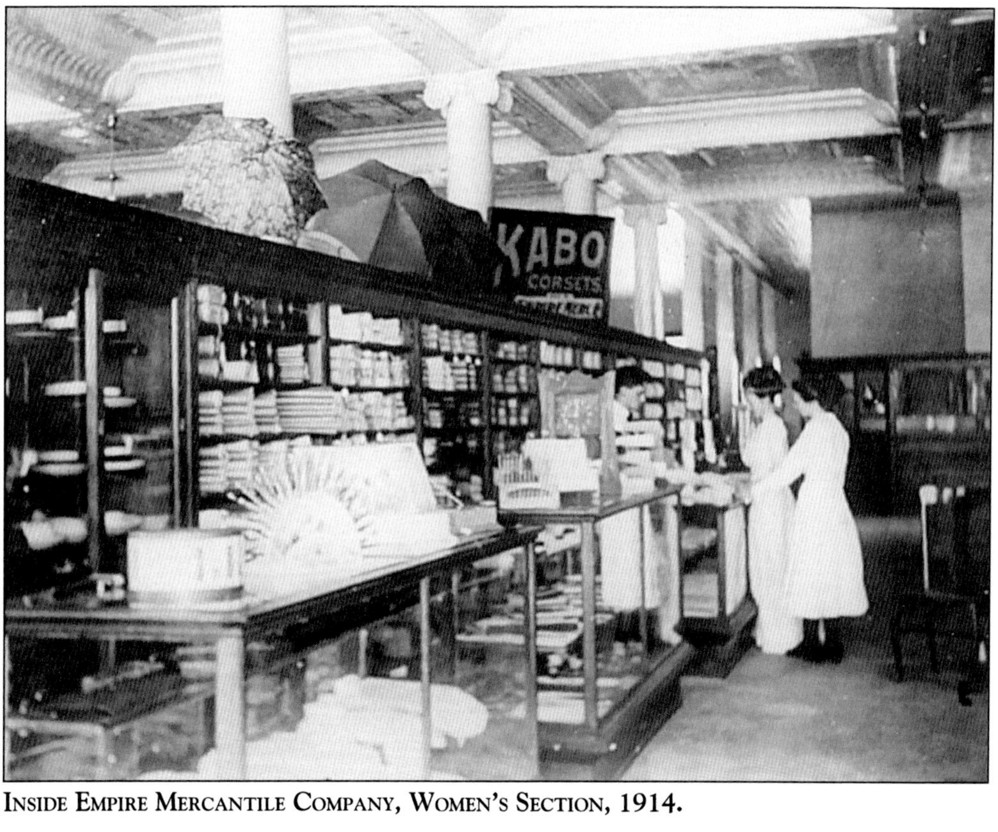

INSIDE EMPIRE MERCANTILE COMPANY, WOMEN'S SECTION, 1914.

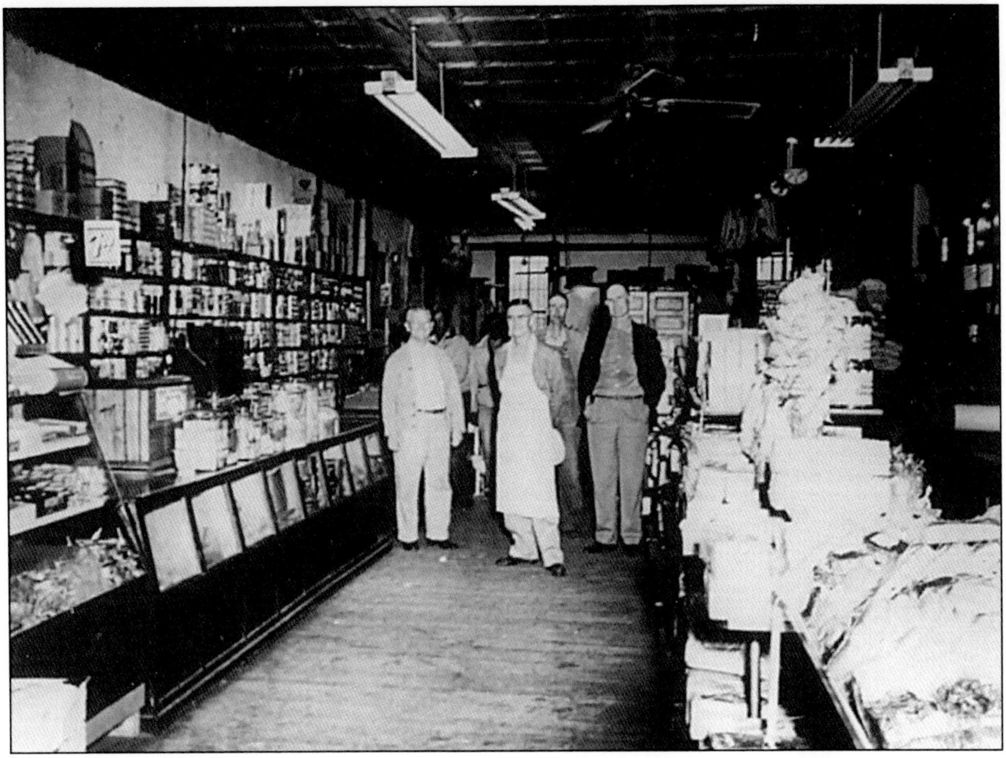

MACK PARK'S GROCERY IN THE LATE 1940S. The building was erected in 1907.

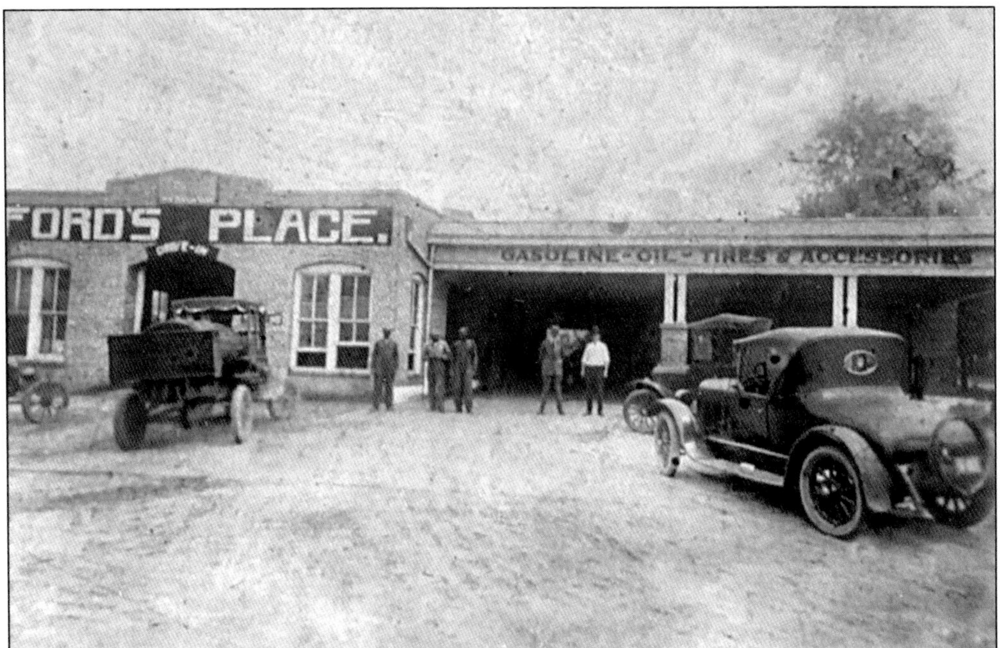

E.J. FORD'S PLACE. This service station was located on the corner of Kelly and Isabella Streets, the current location of the SunTrust Bank.

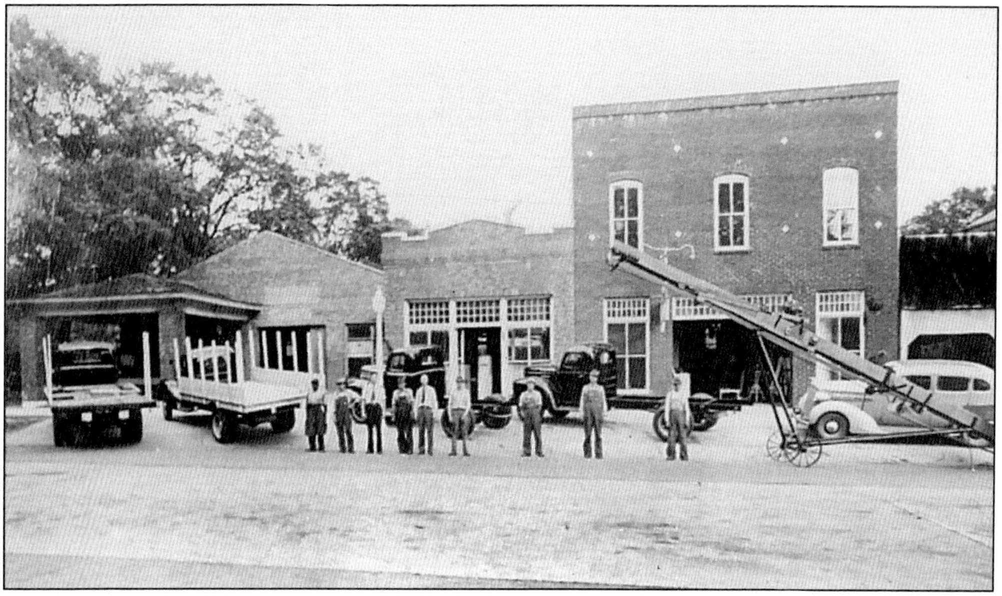

Isabella Street, 1941. Photograph shows the Park Variety Works which was later the Park Built Body Shop. It was located behind the old jail on the east side of Isabella (now a parking lot). The conveyor belt in front was used for loading peanuts. The belts were built and sold here. Shown, left to right, are Arthur "Hambone" Knight, Tom Snipes, Earl Park, S.L. Helms, Cortez Reynolds, Joe Aultman, Joe Jones, Evan Priest, and Mr. Hood.

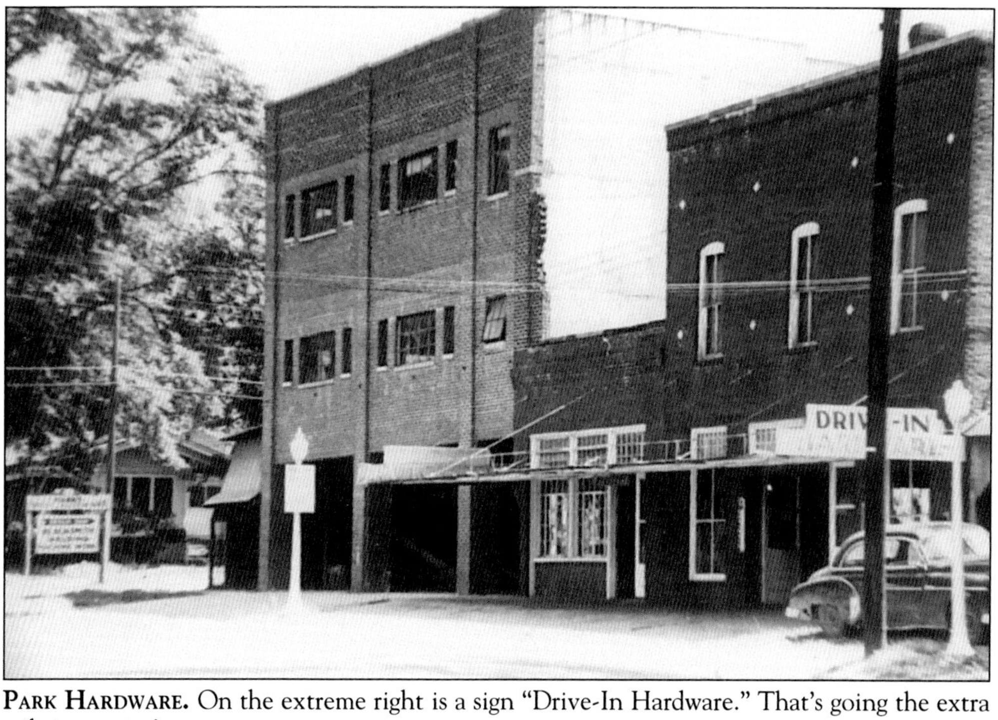

Park Hardware. On the extreme right is a sign "Drive-In Hardware." That's going the extra mile in service!

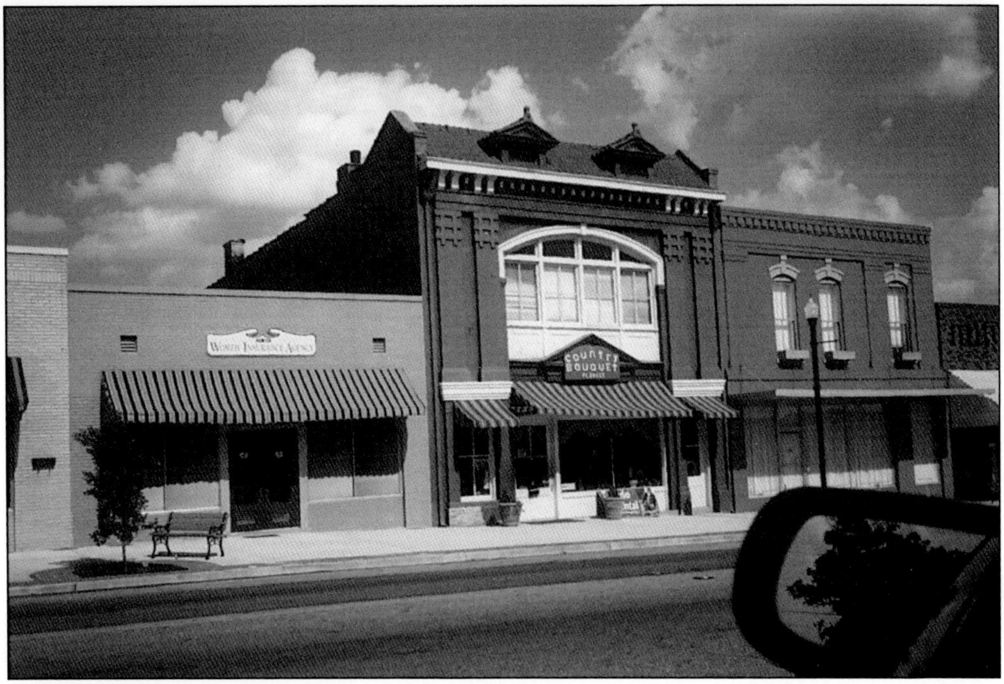

ISABELLA STREET, 2000. Shown are the Worth Insurance Agency building (*c.* 1949); the Country Bouquet building (1911), home to the *Worth County Local* before its move to Kelly Street; and the Daniel Building (*c.* 1911).

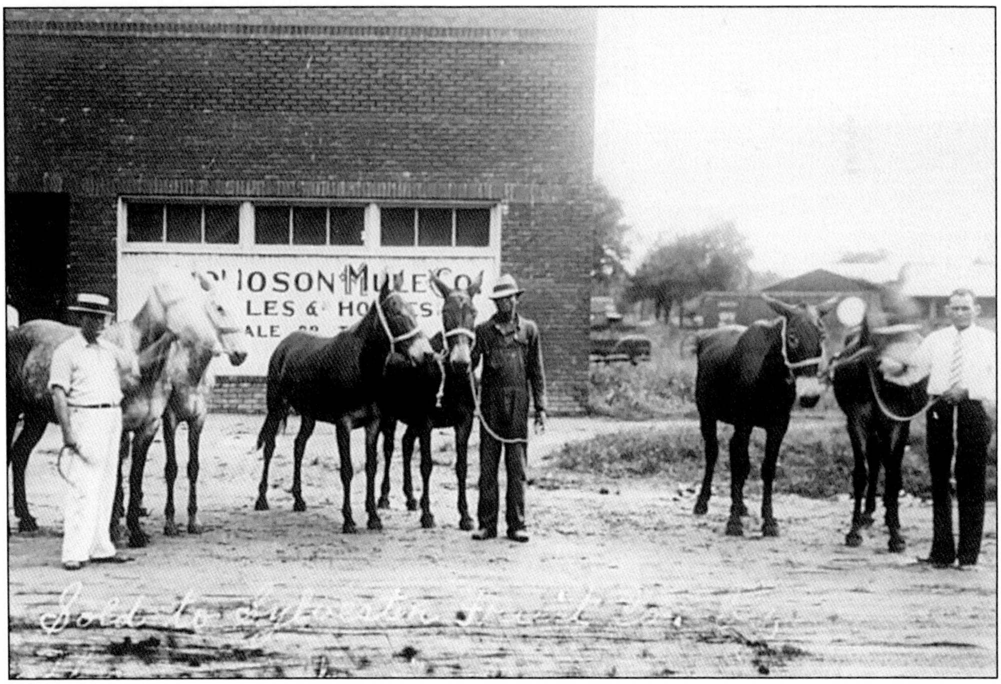

KELLY STREET, C. 1937. Pictured is the Thomoson Mule Company, which was owned by Clint Thomoson. Charles Strangward, on the far right, is buying mules for the Sylvester Fruit Company.

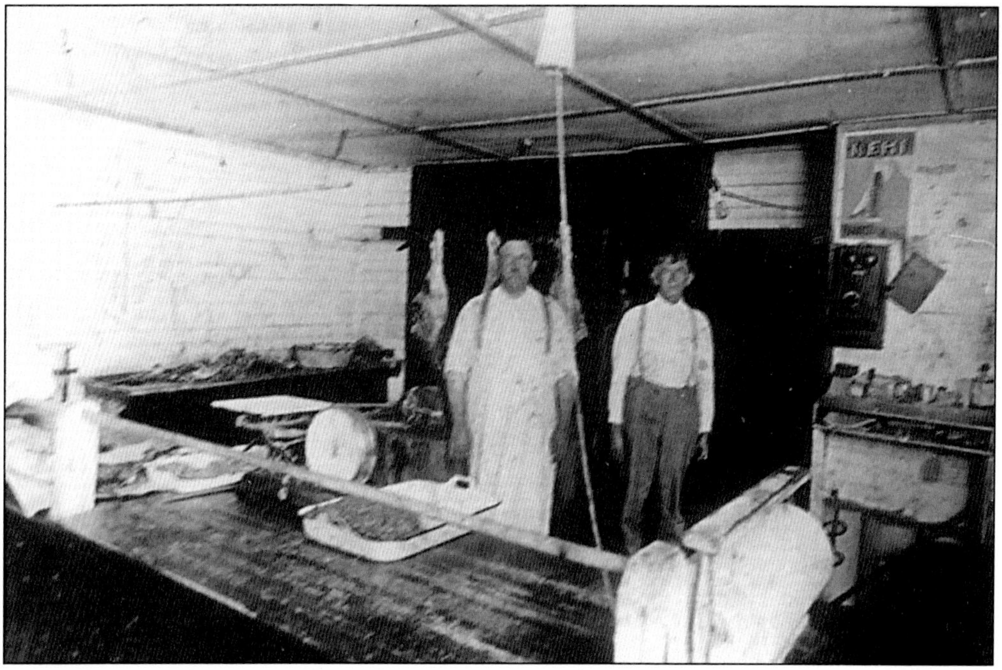

INSIDE BRIDGES MARKET ON KELLY STREET, C. 1919. Shown left to right are R.H. Bridges and W.W. Tomberlin. The cord hanging from the ceiling was used to tie packages.

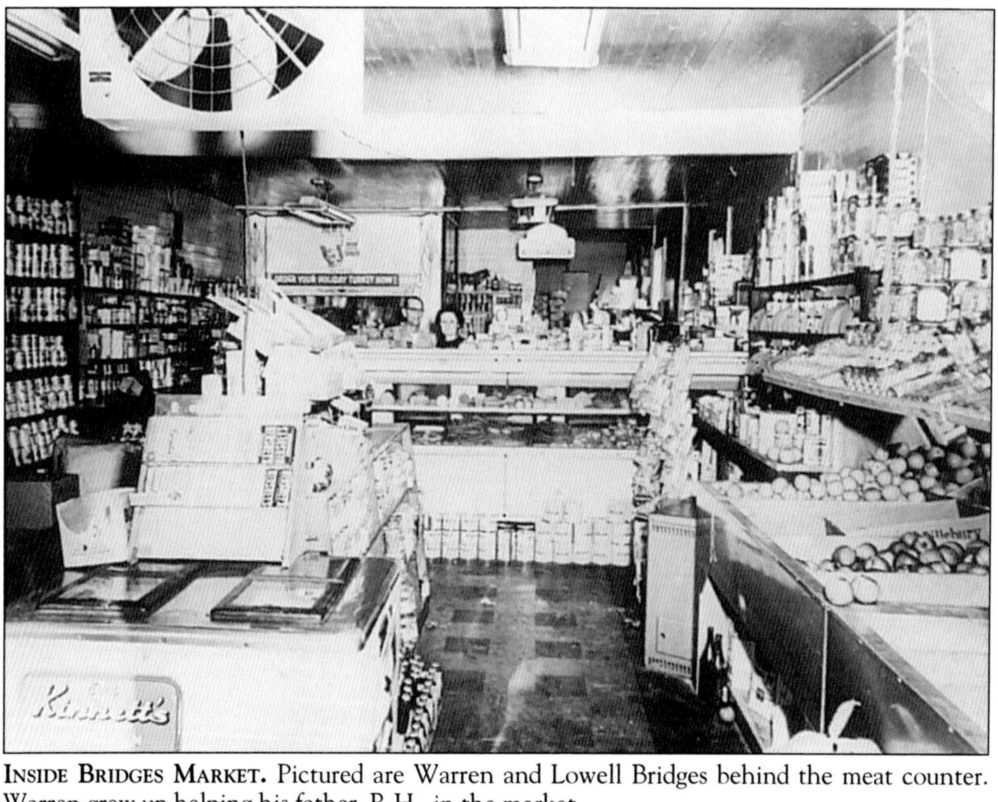

INSIDE BRIDGES MARKET. Pictured are Warren and Lowell Bridges behind the meat counter. Warren grew up helping his father, R.H., in the market.

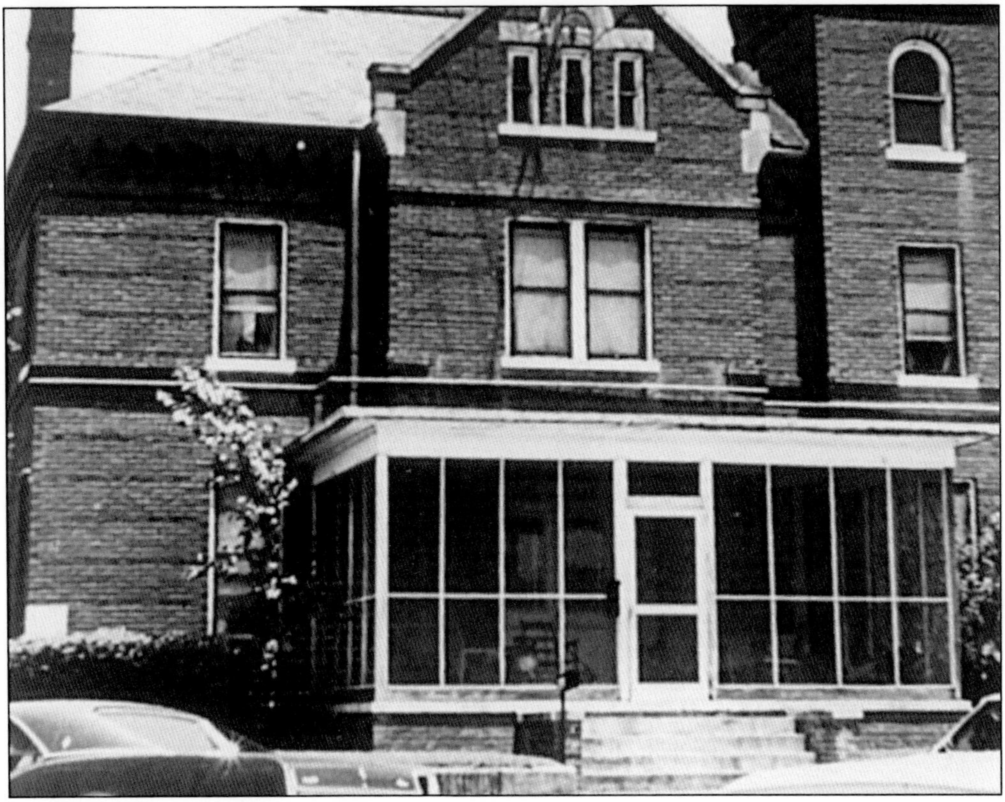

Old Jail. The old jail was located on the corner of Kelly and Isabella Streets and is now a parking lot.

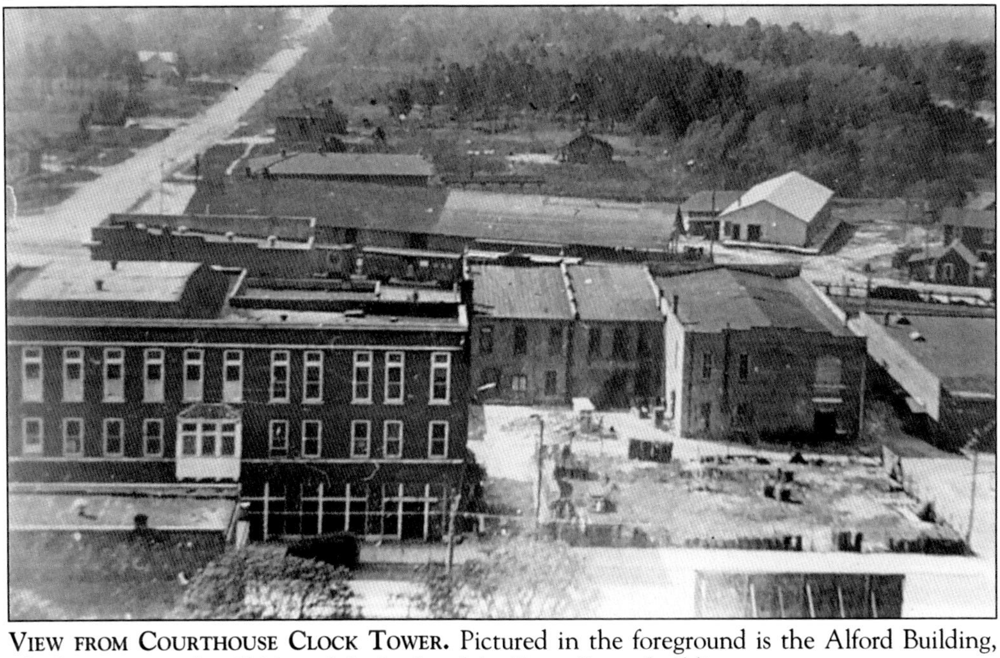

View from Courthouse Clock Tower. Pictured in the foreground is the Alford Building, which was erected *c.* 1911, and the backs of the Front Street buildings.

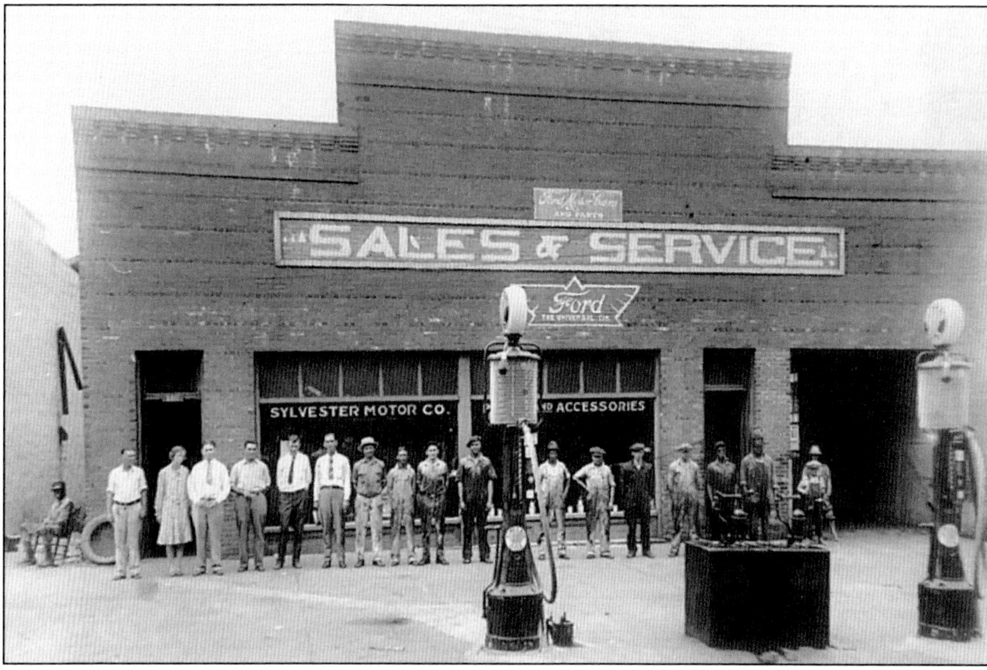

KELLY STREET. The Sylvester Motor Company building was erected by 1911.

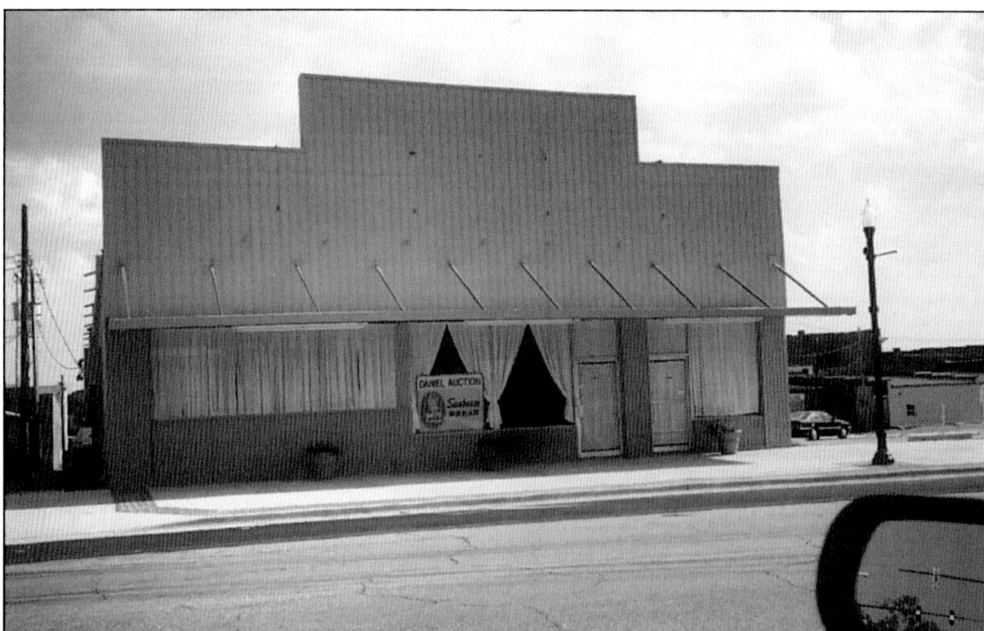

KELLY STREET, 2000. Pictured is Daniel Auction. Between its years as the Sylvester Motor Company, and an auction house, this building was a grocery store, dollar store, etc.

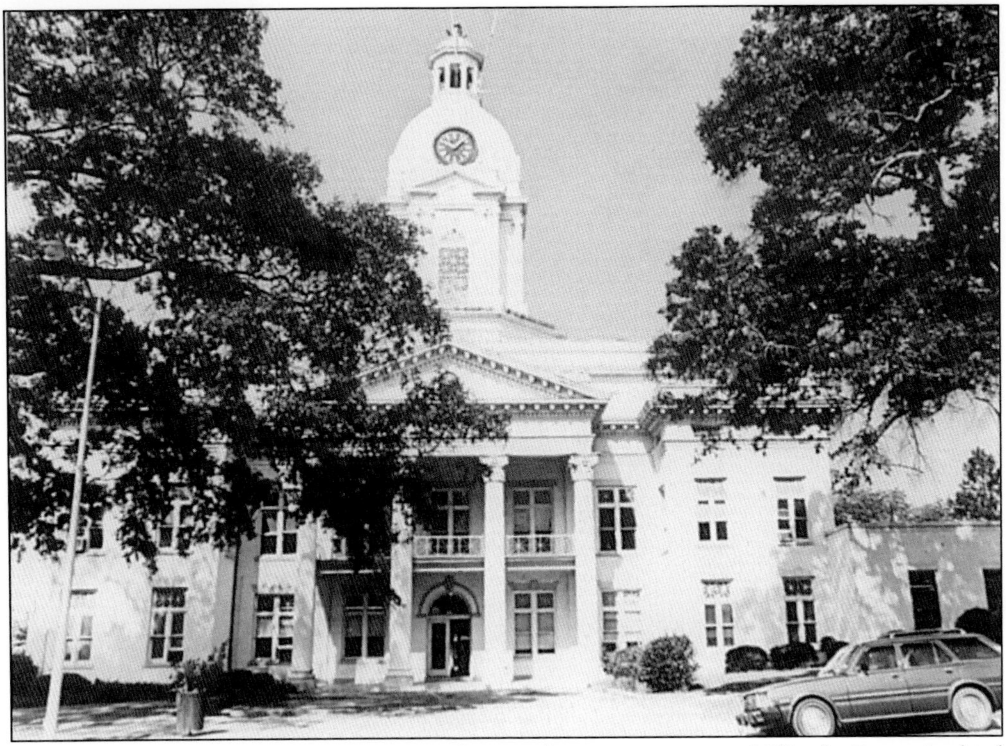

WORTH COUNTY COURTHOUSE. A view depicts the east entrance of Worth County's third courthouse, which was built in 1906.

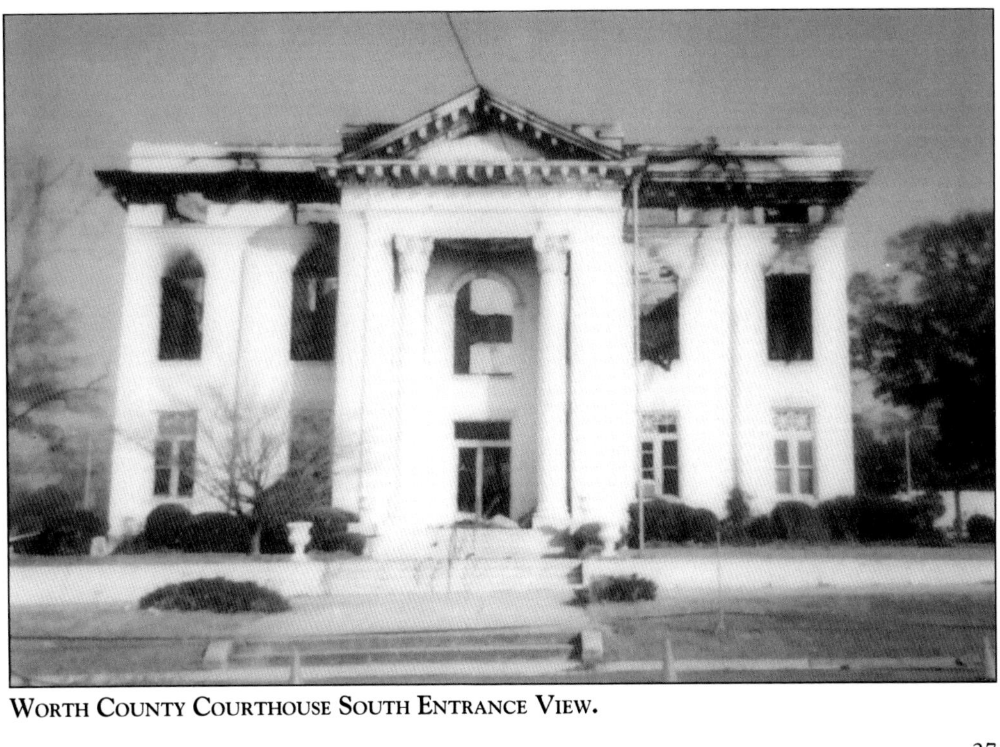

WORTH COUNTY COURTHOUSE SOUTH ENTRANCE VIEW.

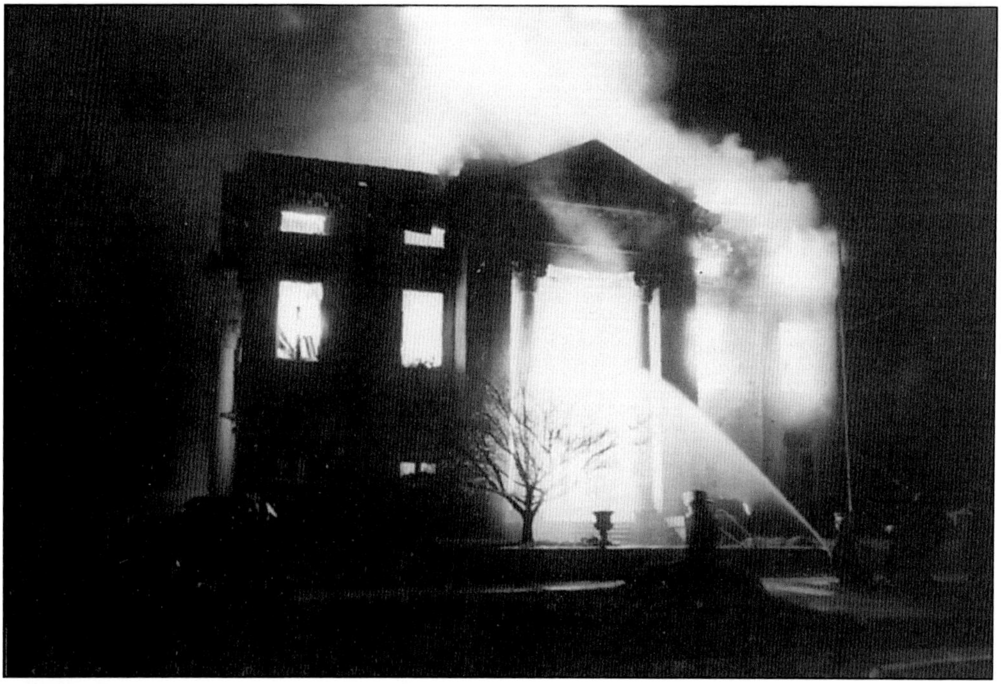

Worth County Courthouse in Flames. The fire, which was a result of arson, was on Wednesday, January 27, 1982. Pictured are the efforts to put out the fire.

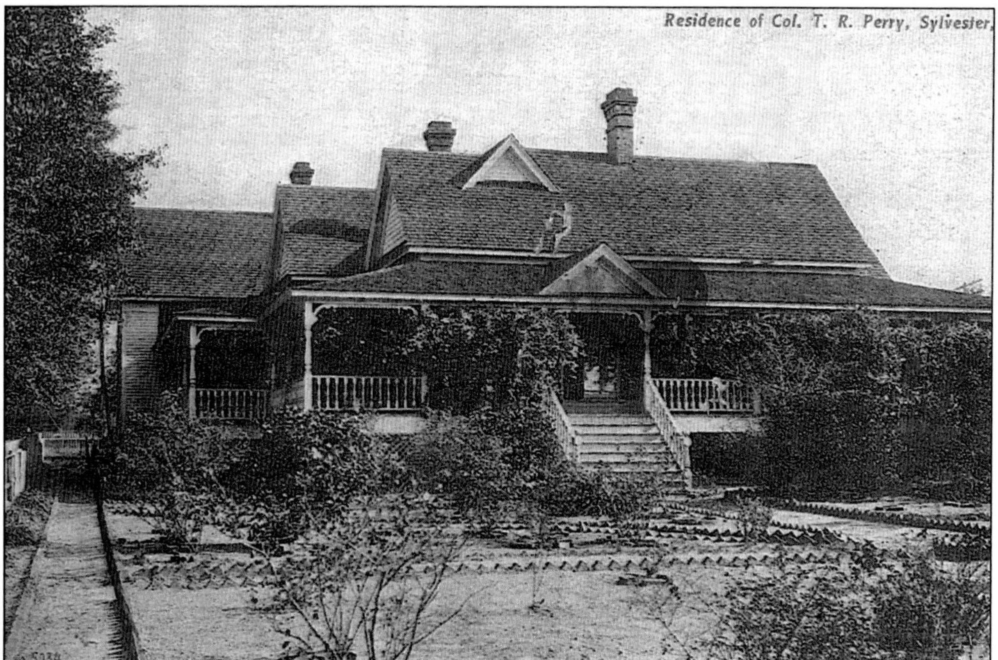

Residence of Col. T.R. Perry. Built in 1898, by C.W. Hillhouse, on the corner of Main and Kelly Streets, this home faced Main. A tennis court was on its south side and next to that was the law office of Colonel Perry. It was moved back and faced Kelly Street when the post office was erected on this site in 1937.

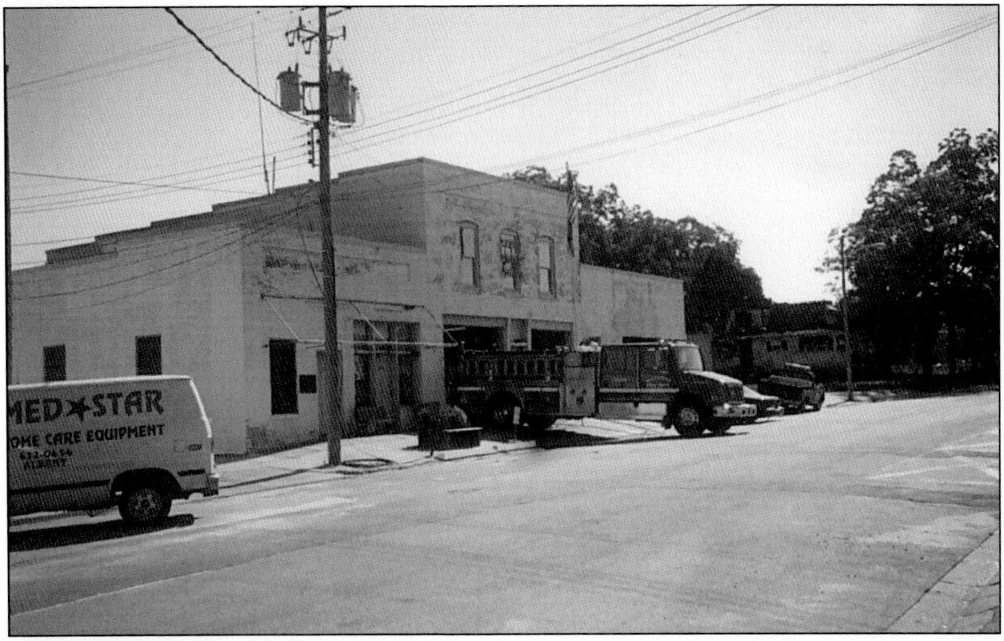

SYLVESTER FIRE DEPARTMENT ON FRONT STREET, 2000. These buildings were erected before 1911. Sylvester Bottling Company (Chero-Cola) was in the two-story center building. The left side housed Joe Gong's laundry and on the right was Dr. Sutton and Howard Daniel's tractor business.

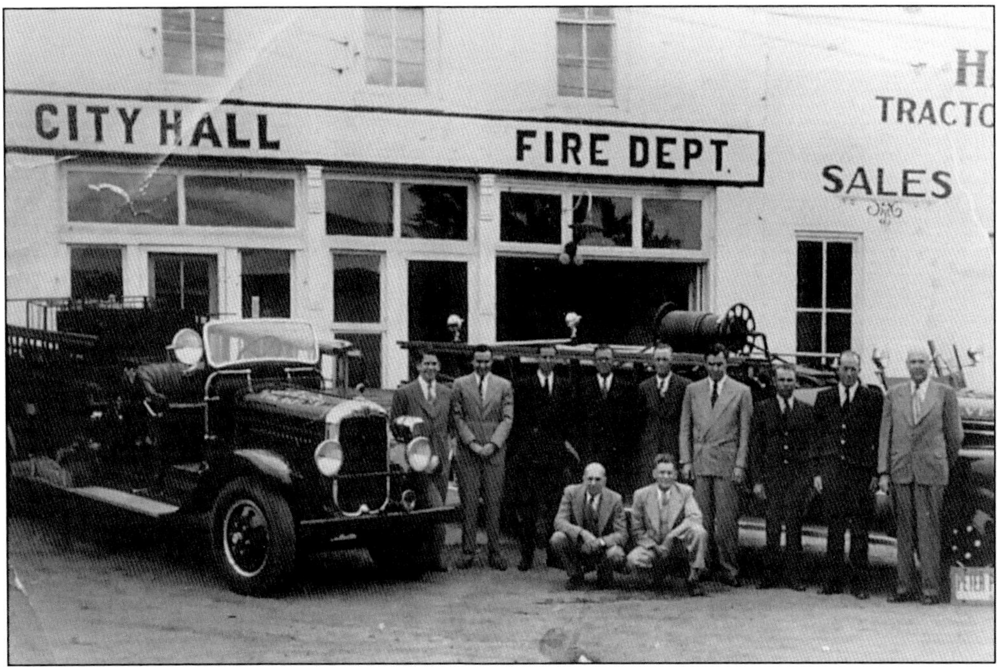

CITY HALL AND FIRE DEPARTMENT, 1945. Shown from left to right are Reese Conoly, Everett Clayton, Gus Luke, Bob Nelms, Ralph Callaway, Billy Allison, Alton Carter, Fire Chief Albert Surrency, and Mayor Fred Deariso. Kneeling are volunteer firemen Pat Collins and Delmar Nance.

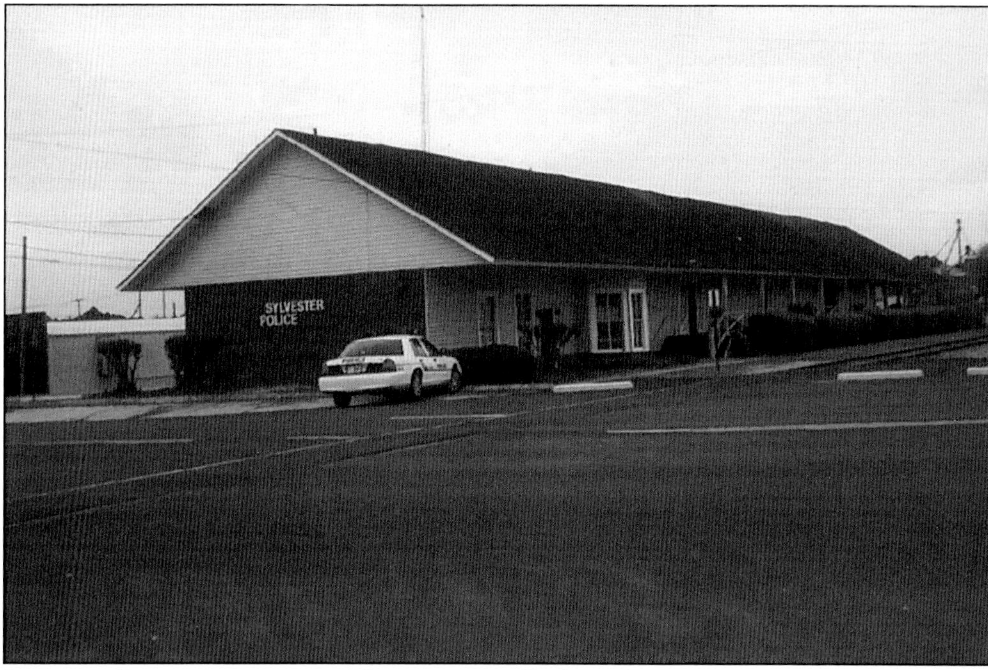

SYLVESTER POLICE DEPARTMENT. This was originally the Atlantic Coast Line Depot.

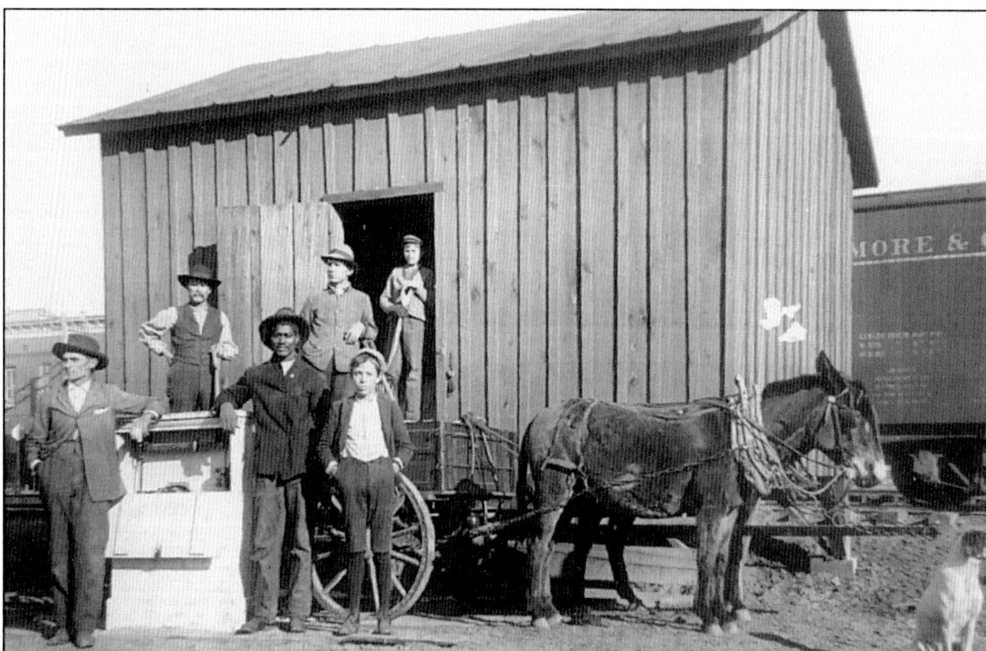

FREIGHT HOUSE AT THE DEPOT. Tim Jennings is on the far left. This was located to the west of the Atlantic Coast Line depot.

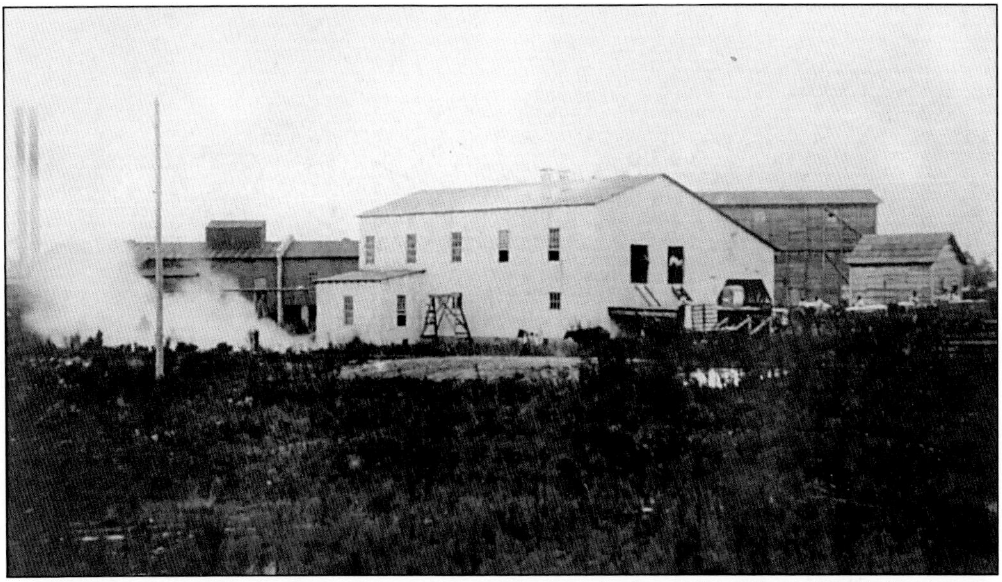

C.W. Hillhouse's Steam Run Cotton Gin. This was built south of the railroad about 1900. His son, Bryon, was killed when he was 18 years old when his new overalls were caught in the machinery.

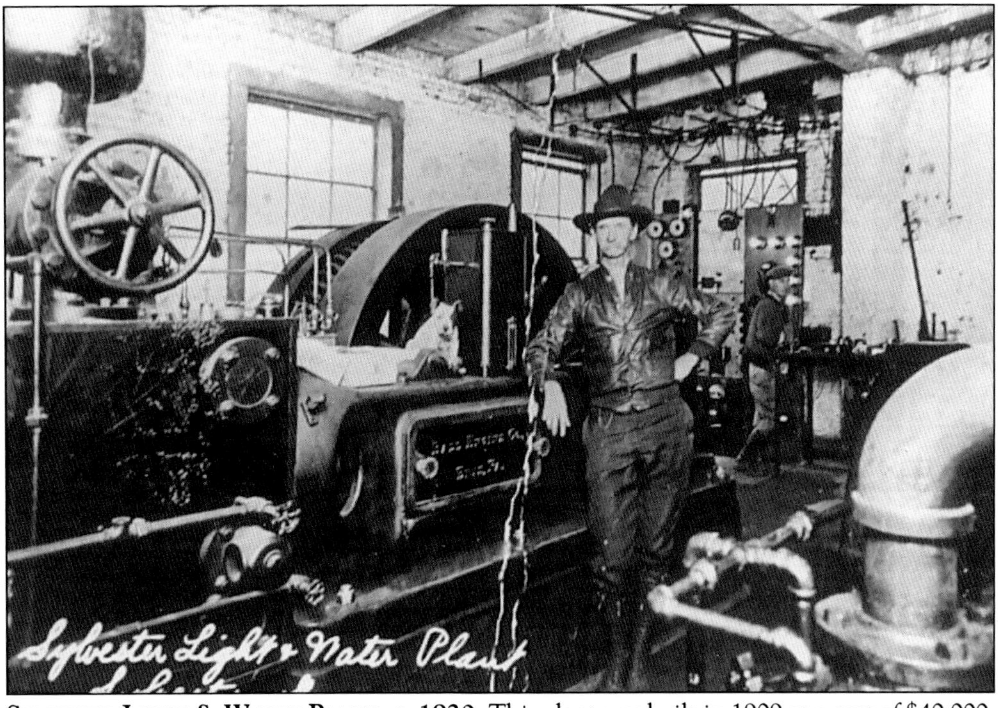

Sylvester Light & Water Plant, c. 1920. This plant was built in 1909 at a cost of $40,000. Pictured in the background is Floyd Jones and in the foreground is Jim Jones with his dog who provided security for the plant.

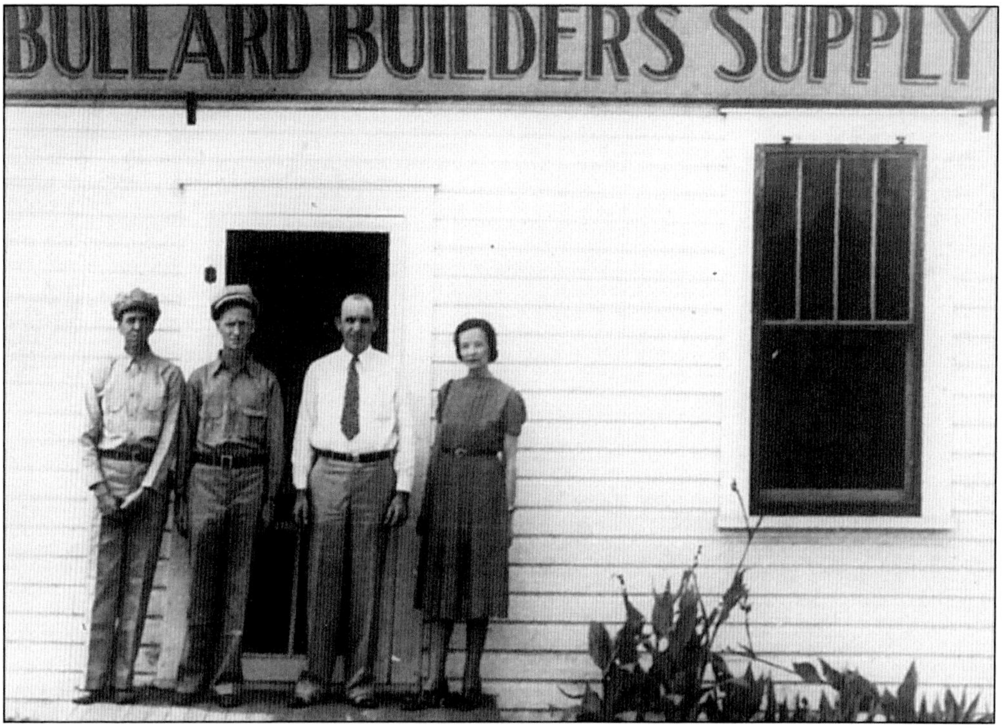

BULLARD BUILDERS, C. LATE 1930S–EARLY 1940S. Located just south of the Atlantic Coast Line railroad and depot, it is now known as Short & Paulk. Pictured are William Floyd, Mr. Glover, W.H. Hawkins, and Mrs. J.M. Bullard.

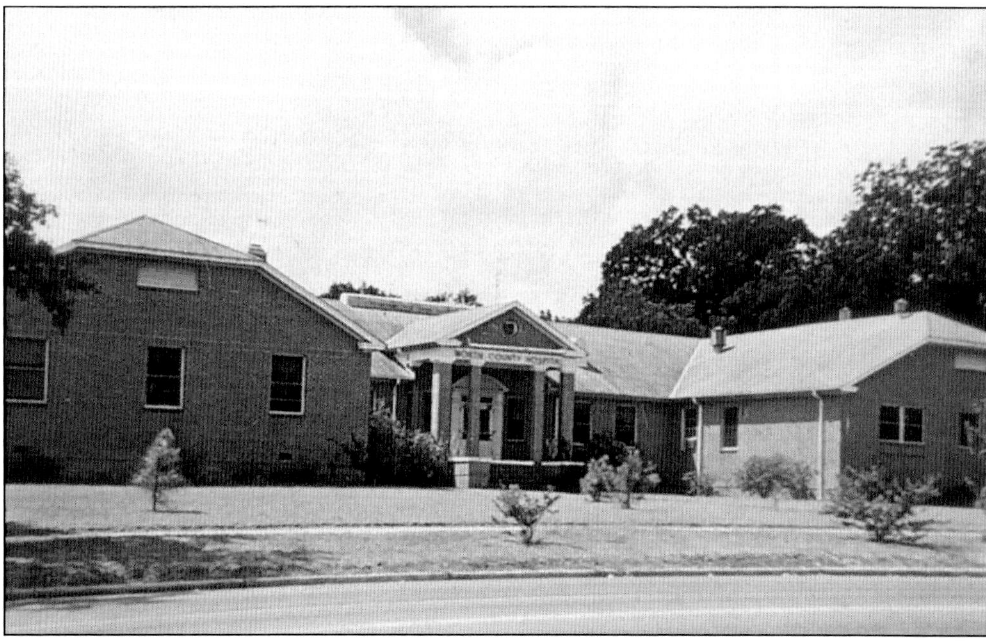

FRANKLIN STREET (US HIGHWAY 82). The old Worth County Hospital was built in 1950 at a cost of $293,000 on land donated by Dr. T.C. Jeffords. It now serves as the Worth County Governmental Building.

Two

COMMUNITIES

Worth County, created in 1853 and containing more than 500 square miles, was dotted with many small communities and towns. Travel was difficult and roads had to be hacked out of the timbered lands. The communities grew around the stagecoach road, turpentine stills, sawmills, gristmills, waterways, and railroads. A couple of stores and businesses, a post office, a church, and a school would be built and a certain level of self sufficiency would be obtained. As travel became less arduous, some of these communities faded away. Some of the old names are Att, Artesia, Egypt, Pinder Town, Utica, Dong, Willingham, Gintown, and Alford's Switch. These may be a distant memory now or perhaps a road sign.

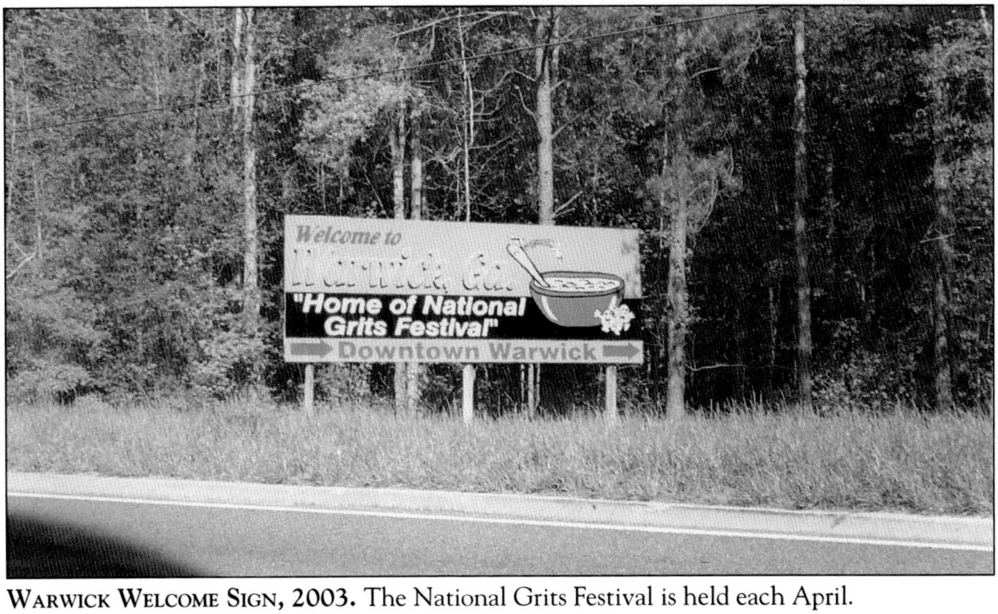

WARWICK WELCOME SIGN, 2003. The National Grits Festival is held each April.

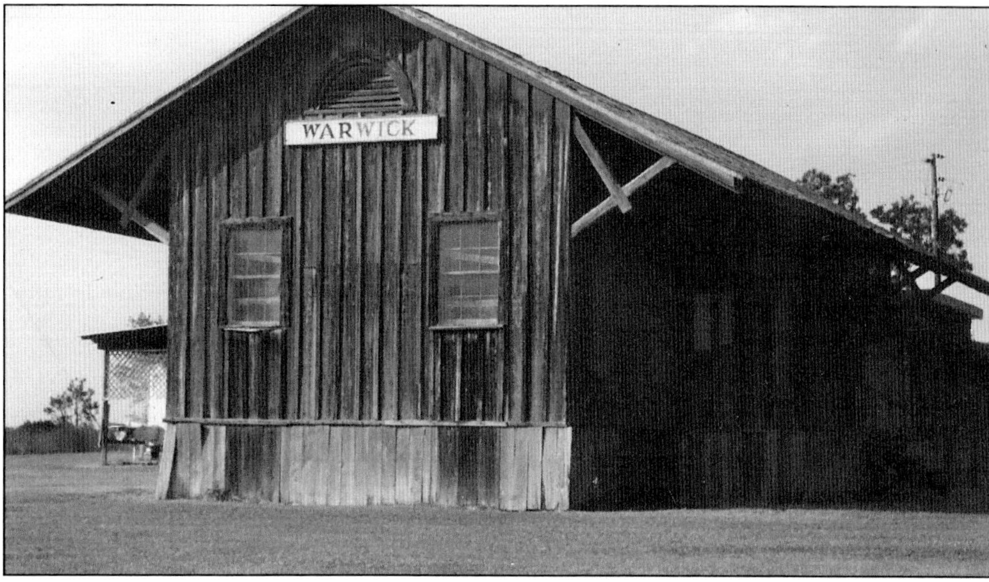

TRAIN DEPOT IN WARWICK. Because of the railroad, the town of Warwick is located at its present site. Prior to this railroad, the community was centered at Fort Early.

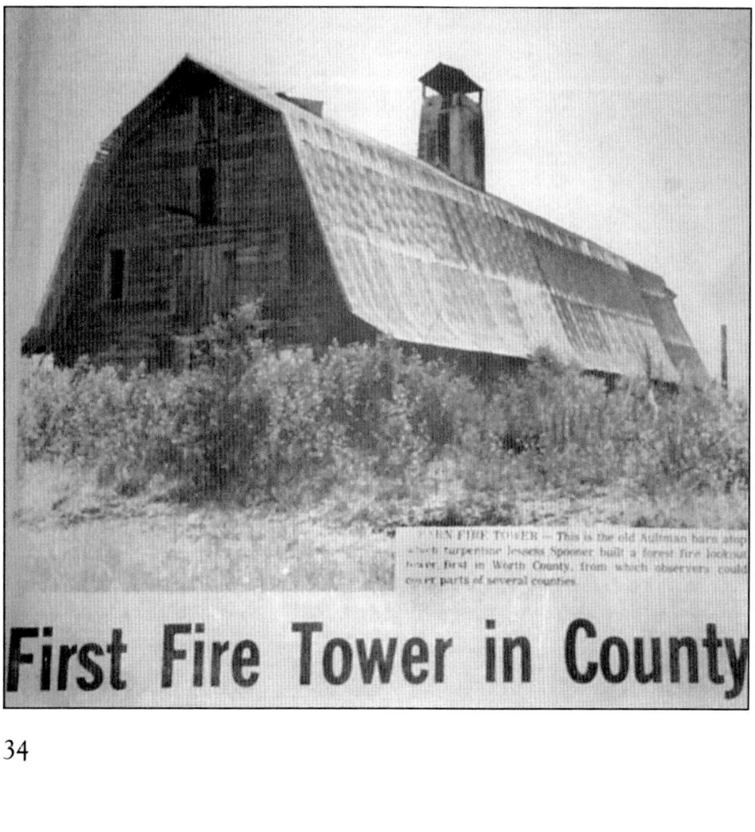

FIRST FIRE TOWER. This is the old Aultman barn where turpentine leasee Spooner built a forest fire lookout tower from which observers could cover parts of several counties.

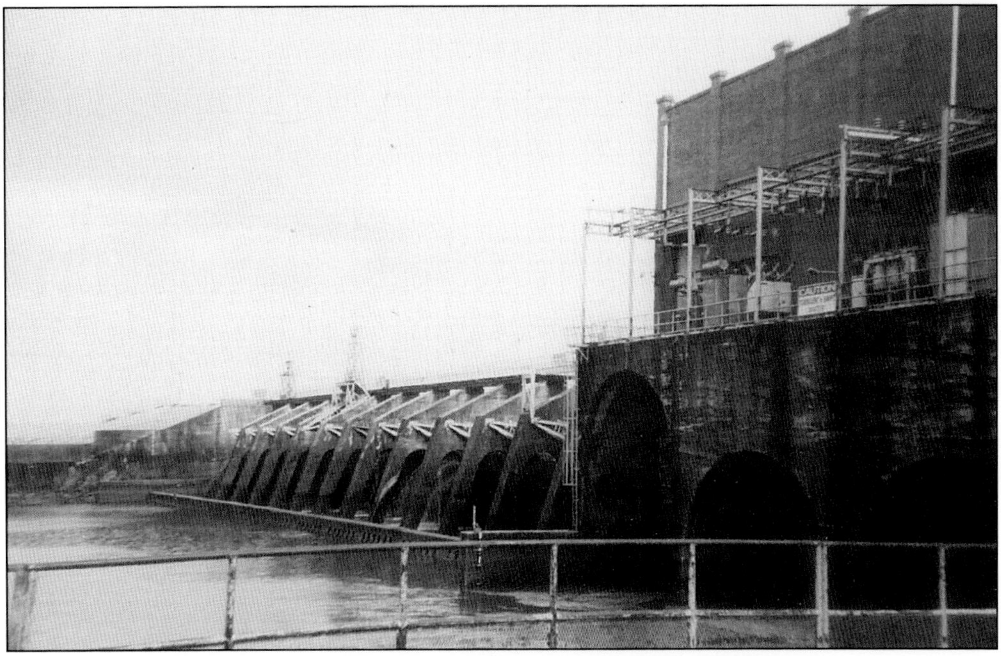

POWER DAM IN WARWICK. The Flint River backwaters form Lake Blackshear.

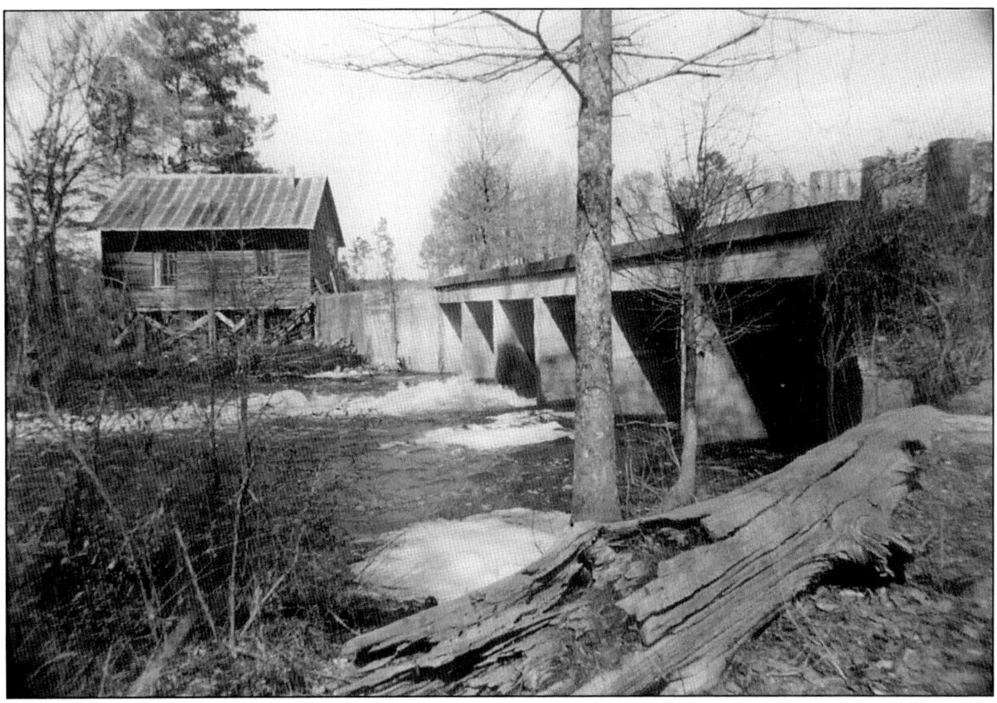

OLD DAVIS MILL. The mill, which was built in 1879, was donated in 1975 to the Agrirama in Tifton, Georgia.

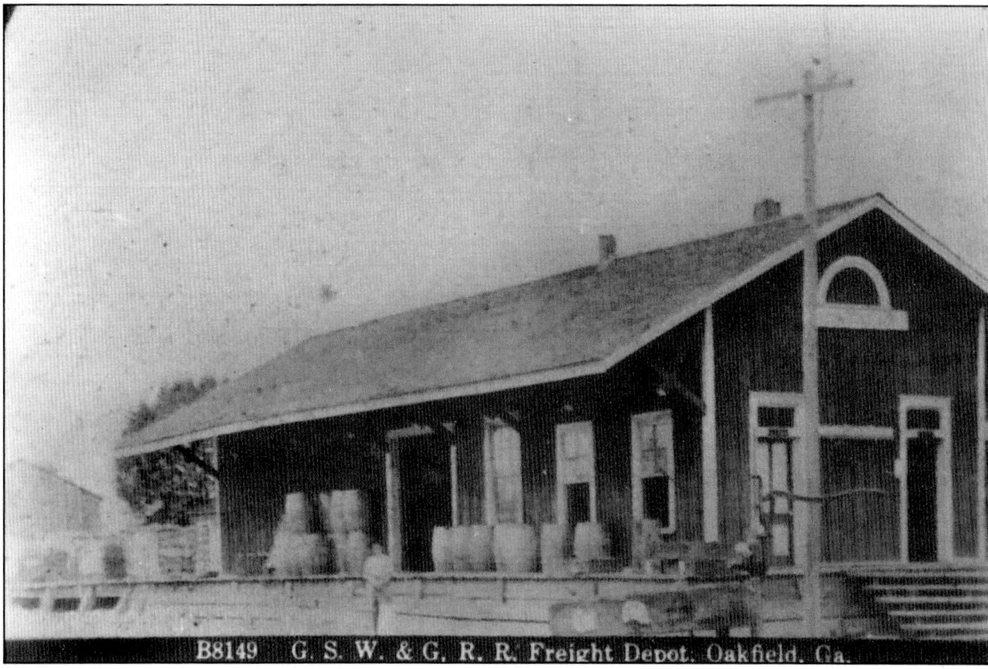

Freight Depot at Oakfield. It was built on the old Stagecoach Road (off Georgia Highway 300). In earlier days, Oakfield had 2 churches, schools, a large ginnery, turpentine still, 5 or 6 businesses, and about 500 citizens.

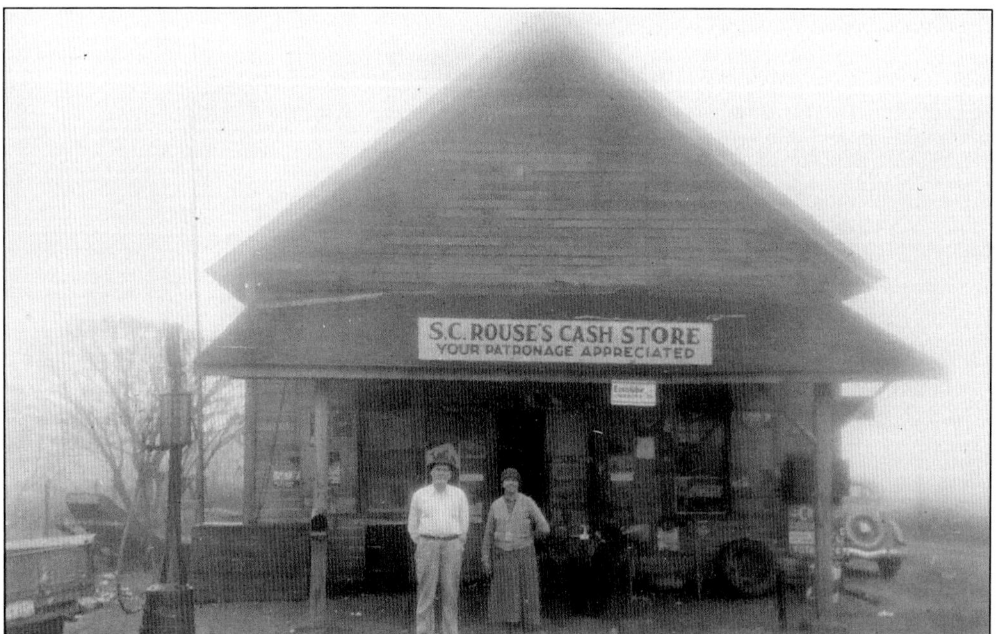

Rouse's Store at Red Rock. Red Rock is a community located about 10 miles northwest of Sylvester.

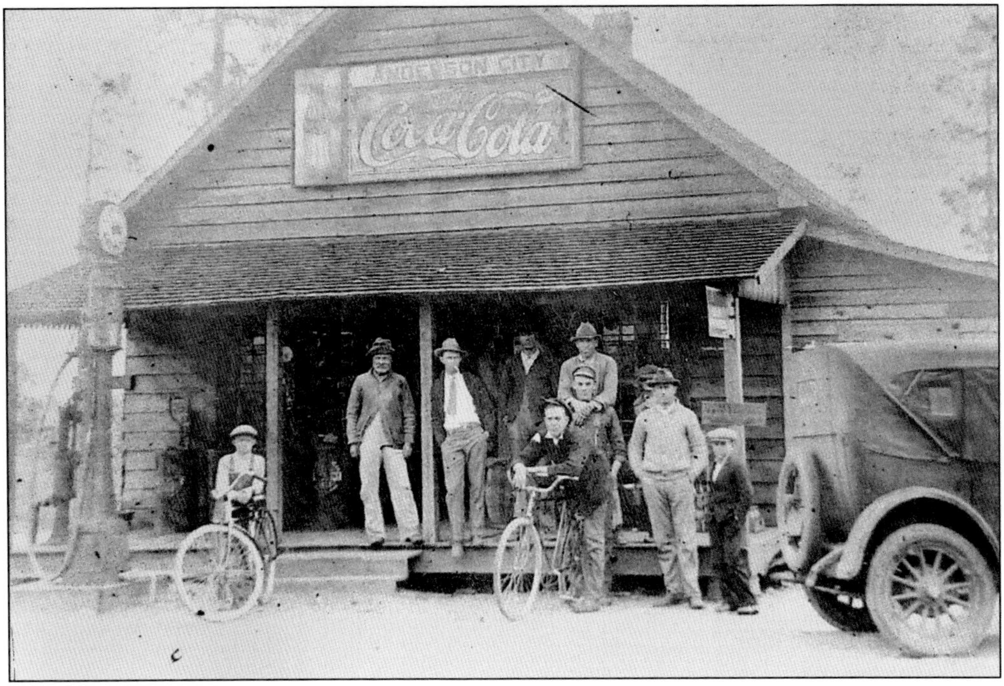

ANDERSON CITY STORE. Anderson City is located about 10 miles south of Sylvester on Georgia Highway 33.

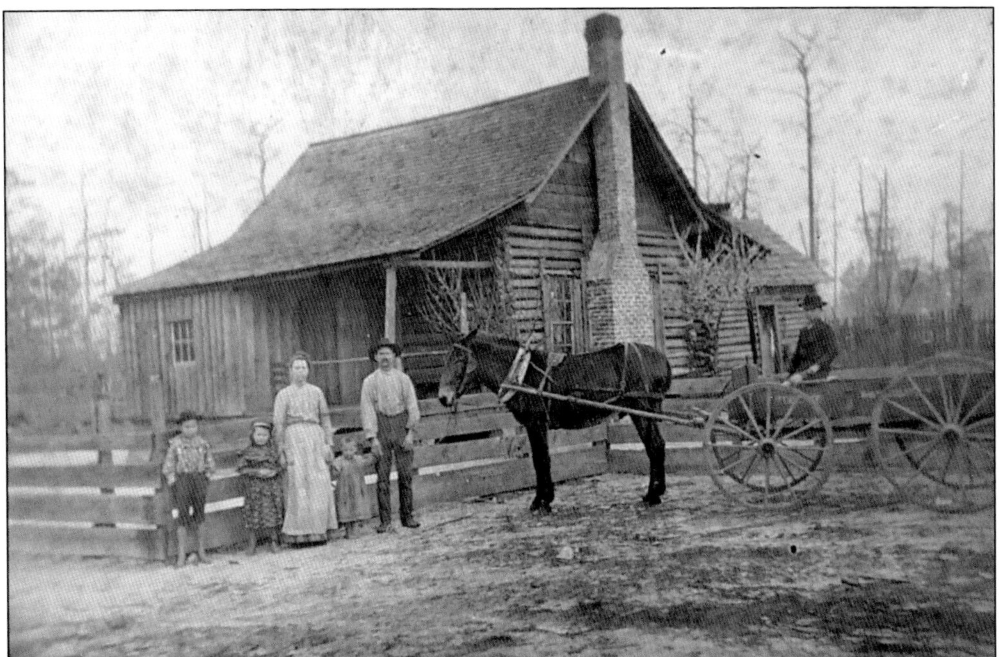

G.W. TURNER FAMILY AT COVERDALE. This was the second house built in the community, formerly known as Holtzwitch.

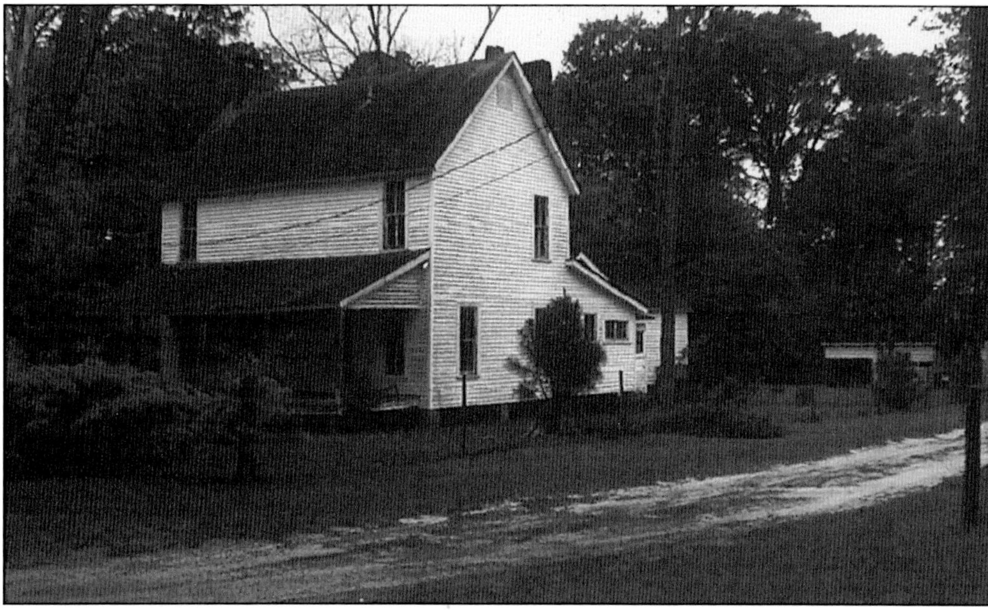

POSSUM POKE OF POSSUM LANE, POULAN. Shown is the Hunting Lodge of Chase Salmon Osborn (1860–1949) who was a dynamic Reform governor of Michigan, naturalist, philosopher, newspaperman, author, statesman, and world traveler. He came to Worth County in 1926 and fell in love with the people and surrounding country. He adopted Worth County as his winter home and gave 810 acres to the Boy Scouts to be used as a camp (Camp Osborn).

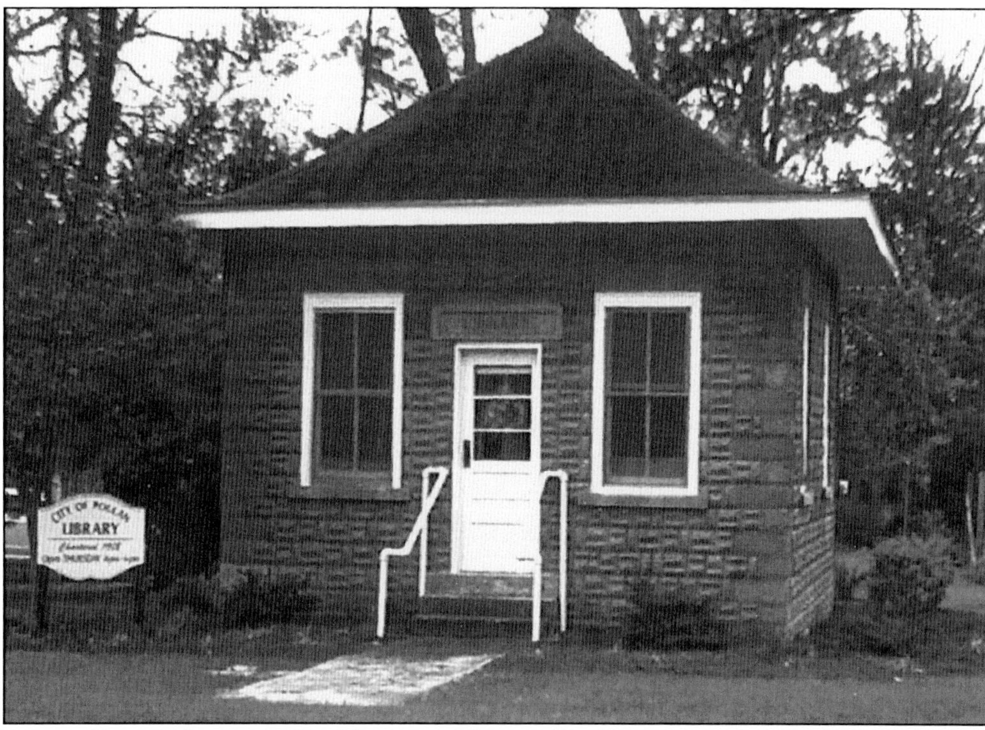

CITY OF POULAN LIBRARY. This library was chartered by the Superior Court of Worth County on April 27, 1908, and has been officially recognized as "the smallest city library in Georgia."

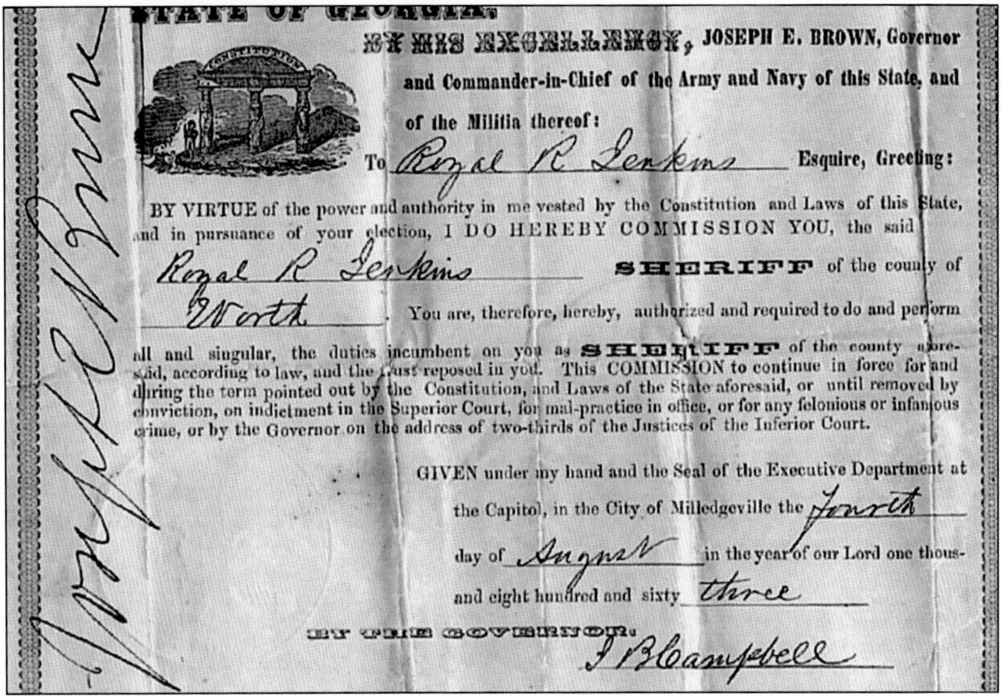

STATE OF GEORGIA,

BY HIS EXCELLENCY, JOSEPH E. BROWN, Governor and Commander-in-Chief of the Army and Navy of this State, and of the Militia thereof:

To Royal R Jenkins Esquire, Greeting:

BY VIRTUE of the power and authority in me vested by the Constitution and Laws of this State, and in pursuance of your election, I DO HEREBY COMMISSION YOU, the said Royal R Jenkins SHERIFF of the county of Worth. You are, therefore, hereby, authorized and required to do and perform all and singular, the duties incumbent on you as SHERIFF of the county aforesaid, according to law, and the trust reposed in you. This COMMISSION to continue in force for and during the term pointed out by the Constitution, and Laws of the State aforesaid, or until removed by conviction, on indictment in the Superior Court, for mal-practice in office, or for any felonious or infamous crime, or by the Governor on the address of two-thirds of the Justices of the Inferior Court.

GIVEN under my hand and the Seal of the Executive Department at the Capitol, in the City of Milledgeville the fourth day of August in the year of our Lord one thousand eight hundred and sixty three

BY THE GOVERNOR:

J B Campbell

Joseph E Brown

Royal R. Jenkins's Sheriff Commission. This appointment as sheriff of Worth County was signed in 1863 by Gov. Joseph E. Brown.

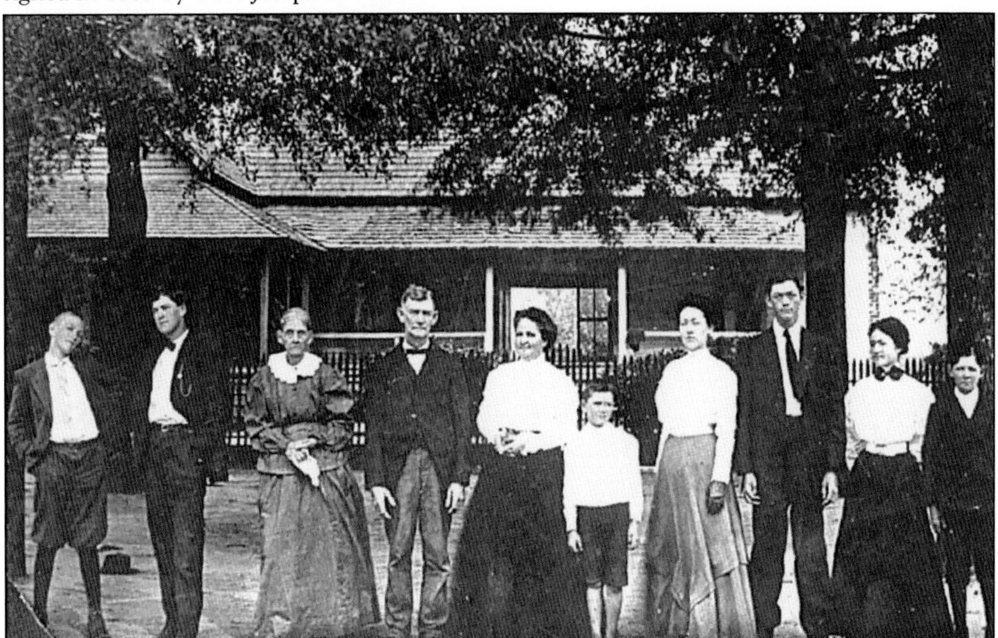

Charles Jones Jenkins Family of Bridgeboro, c. 1907. Pictured from left to right are Herbert Jenkins, Charlie Early Jenkins, Mary Ann Martha Daniel Jenkins, Charles J. Jenkins, Laura Celestial Bowles Jenkins, Wallace Jenkins, Berta Lee Jenkins, Cyrus Jenkins, Annie Jewel Jenkins, and Paul Jenkins.

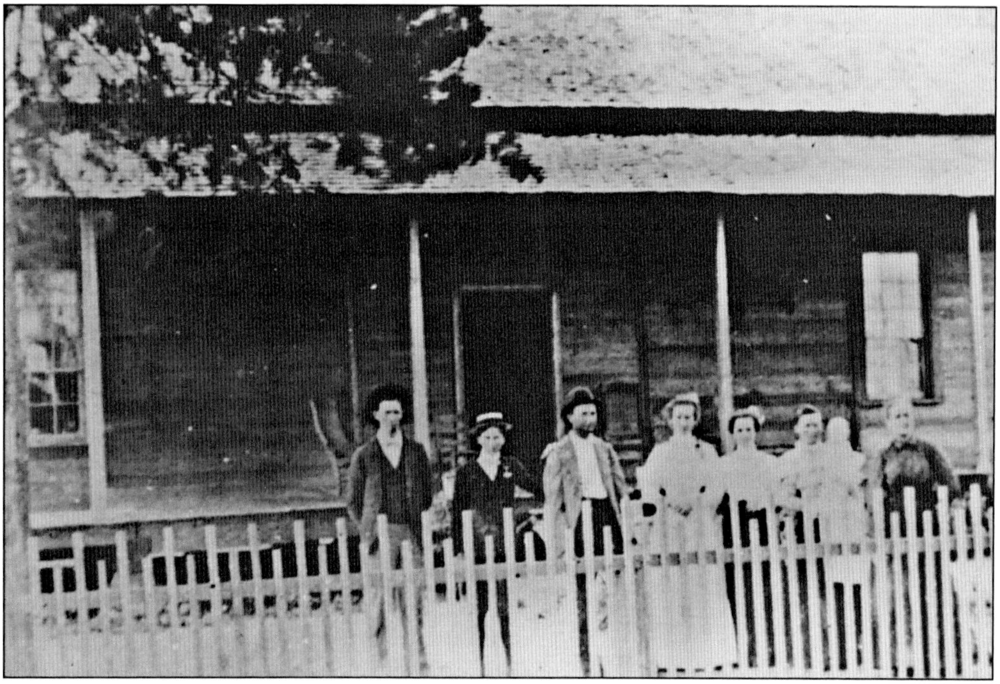

WILLIAMS HOUSE AT ISABELLA, C. 1900. Shown from left to right are Elzie J. Williams, Preston F. Williams, William Custer Williams, Ina Mae Williams (later Blizzard), Elizabeth Williams (later Warren), Jackie W. Gregory holding Mamie, and Mary Ford Williams. This home was moved to Sylvester in 1973 by Herman and Ann Poss and is now owned by Victor A. Gregory.

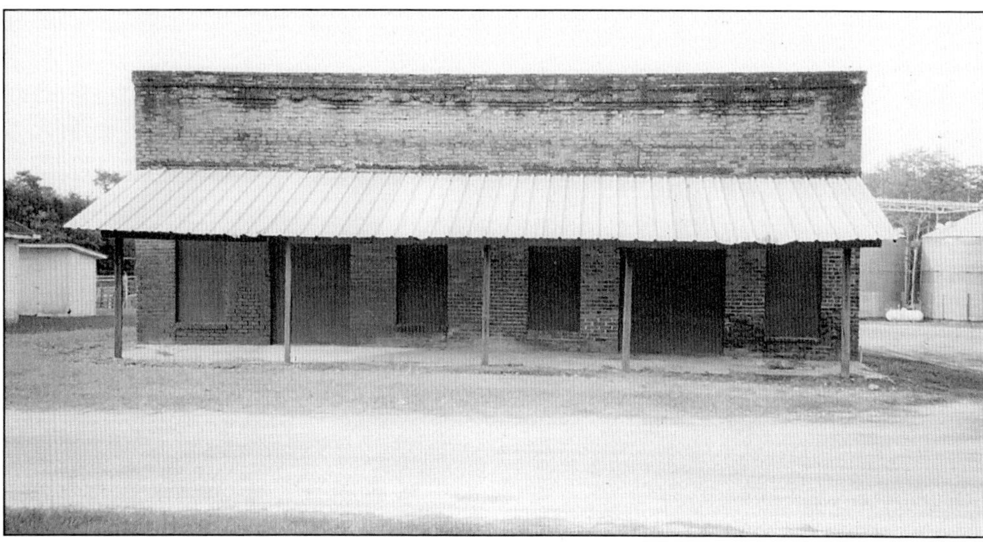

OLD HOLLINGSWORTH STORE AT BRIDGEBORO. Bridgeboro is situated 16 miles southwest of Sylvester on Georgia Highway 112 South.

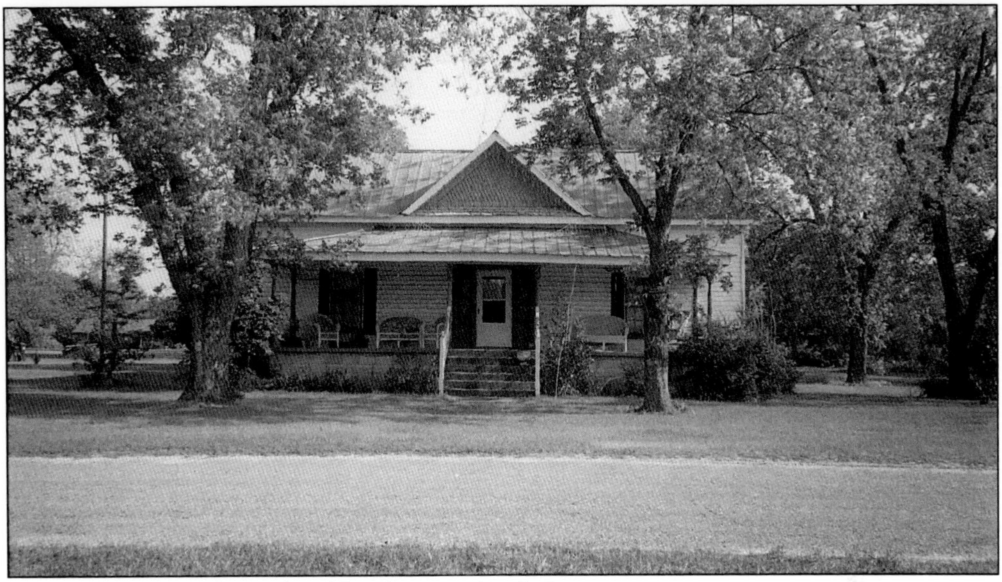

Hornsby House. This is the oldest house in Bridgeboro.

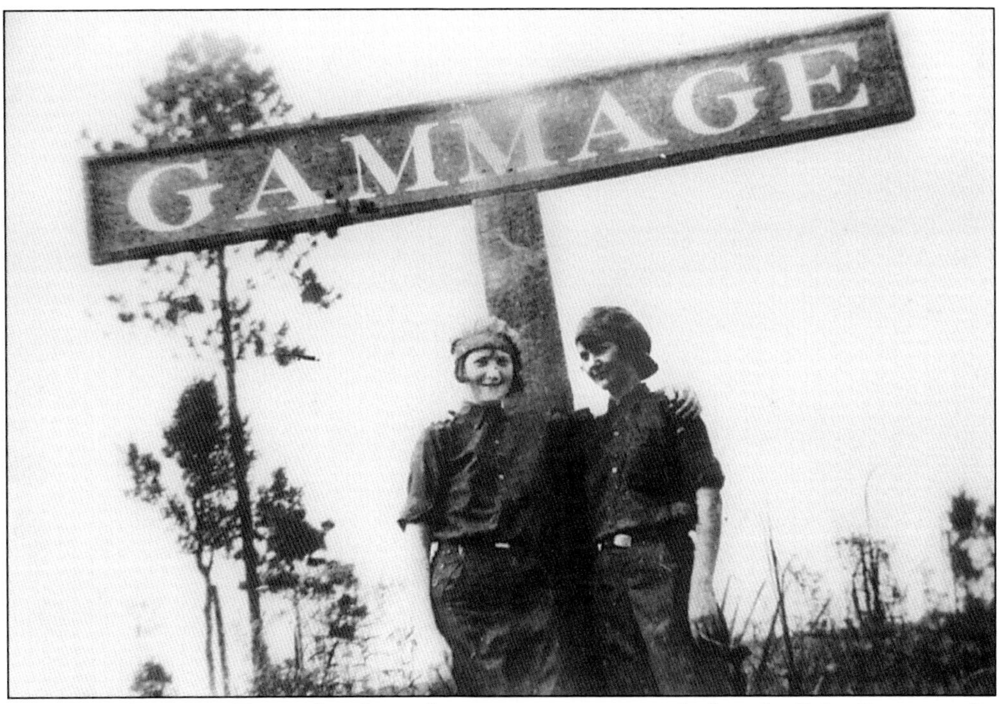

Gammage Station. This railroad switching station was named after the D.L. Gammage Sr. family that lived nearby. It was approximately three miles west of Sylvester and was built during the Atlantic Coast Line strike *c.* 1926. From left to right are Ella Mae (Sister) Gammage and Berta (Mrs. Willie Frank) Gammage.

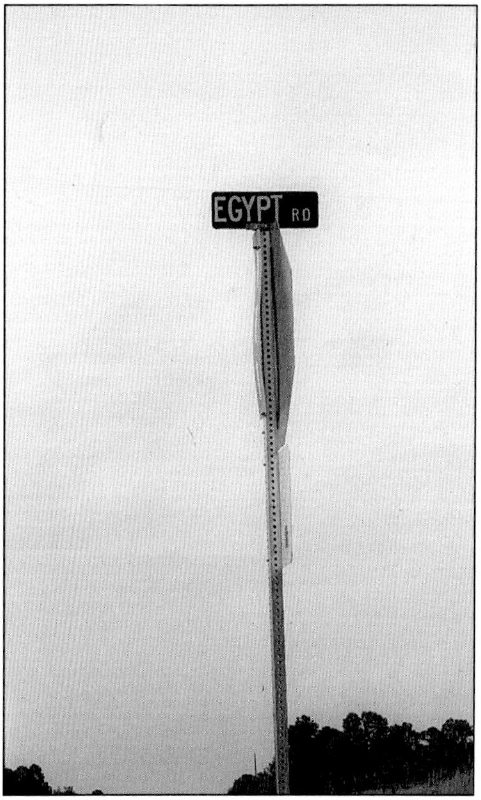

Egypt Road Sign. This sign marks the community of Egypt, which was located about 15 miles northwest of Sylvester.

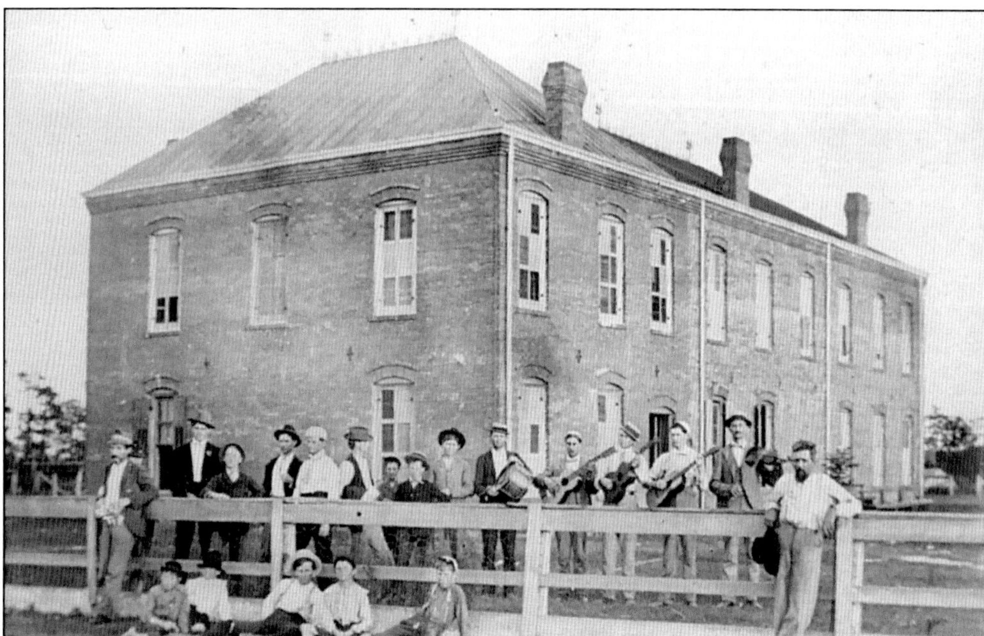

A Gathering at the Courthouse At Isabella, Before 1900. The presence of guitars and a drum indicates a celebration.

Three

CHURCHES

Churches of many faiths dot the countryside, Mt. Horeb being the oldest. The people of Worth County take pride in their country and city churches. Many are over 100 years old. Religion is a vital part of the county's heritage and reflects the deeply religious nature of its people.

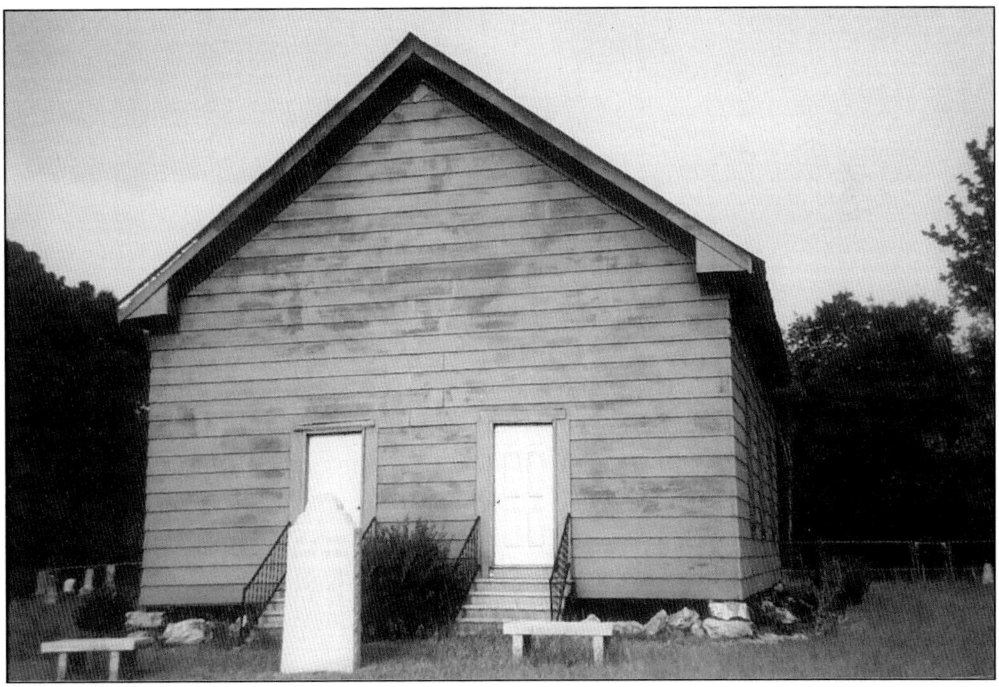

MT. HOREB BAPTIST CHURCH. Constituted in 1848 in Dooly County (now Worth), it was first built on the banks of the Flint River. In 1868, the congregation moved to its present location. The land was given by Mrs. C.E. Buckalew. At the time, the deacons were H.W. Vines, David Ridley, T.W. Tison. Services are now held on the fourth Sunday in August each year.

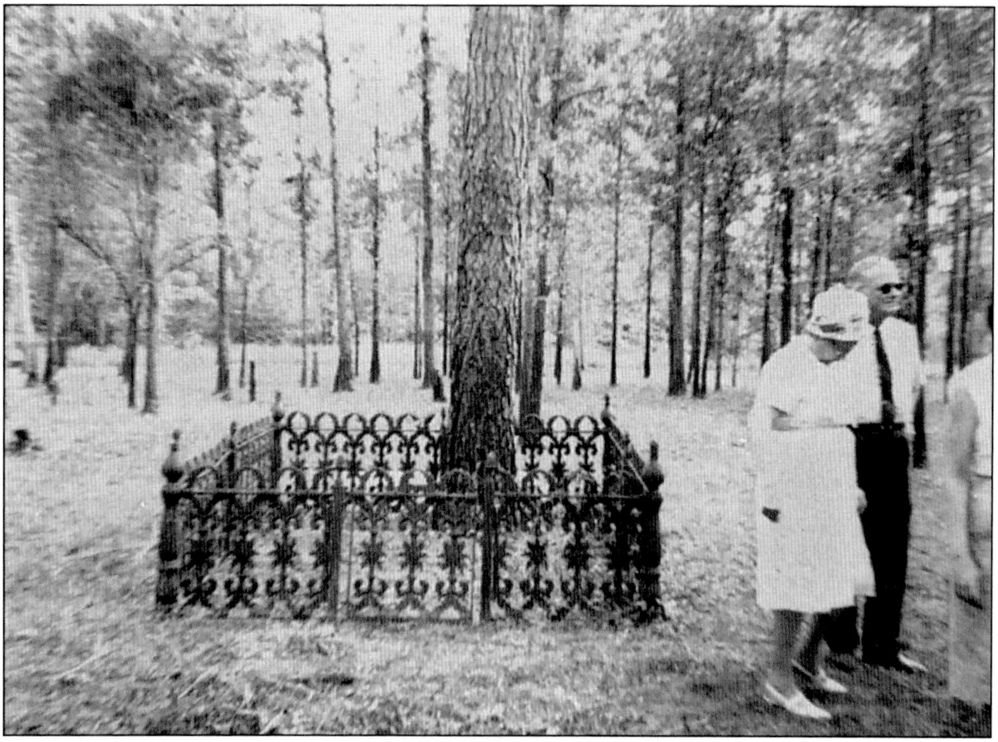

Wrought Iron Fence in Old Mt. Horeb Cemetery. This was removed by unknown persons in the 1950s and no longer marks this plot.

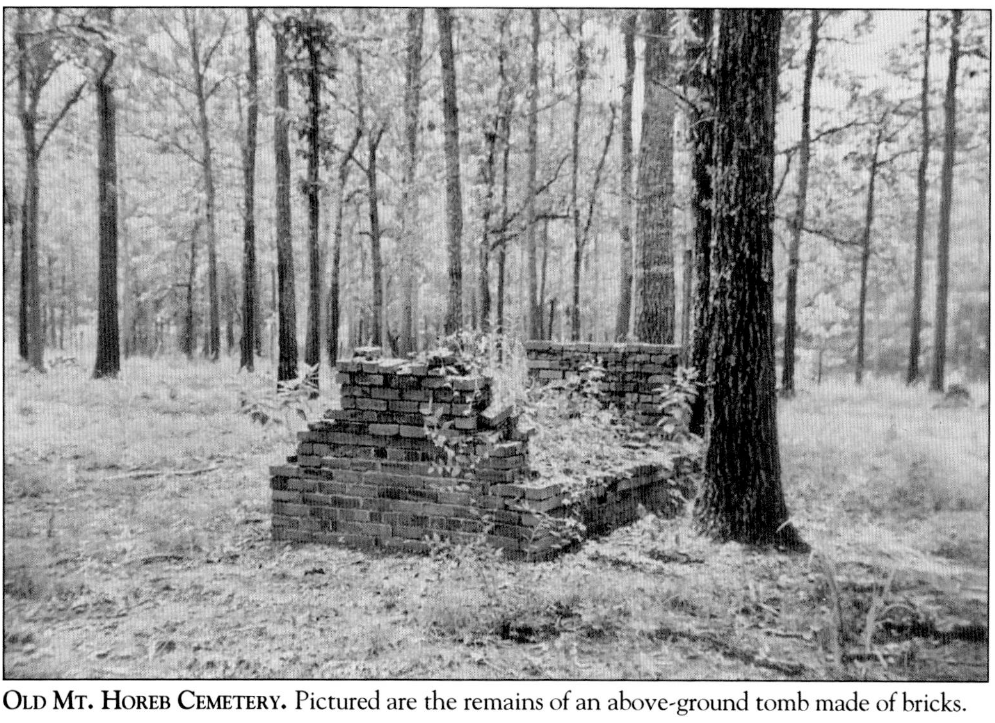

Old Mt. Horeb Cemetery. Pictured are the remains of an above-ground tomb made of bricks.

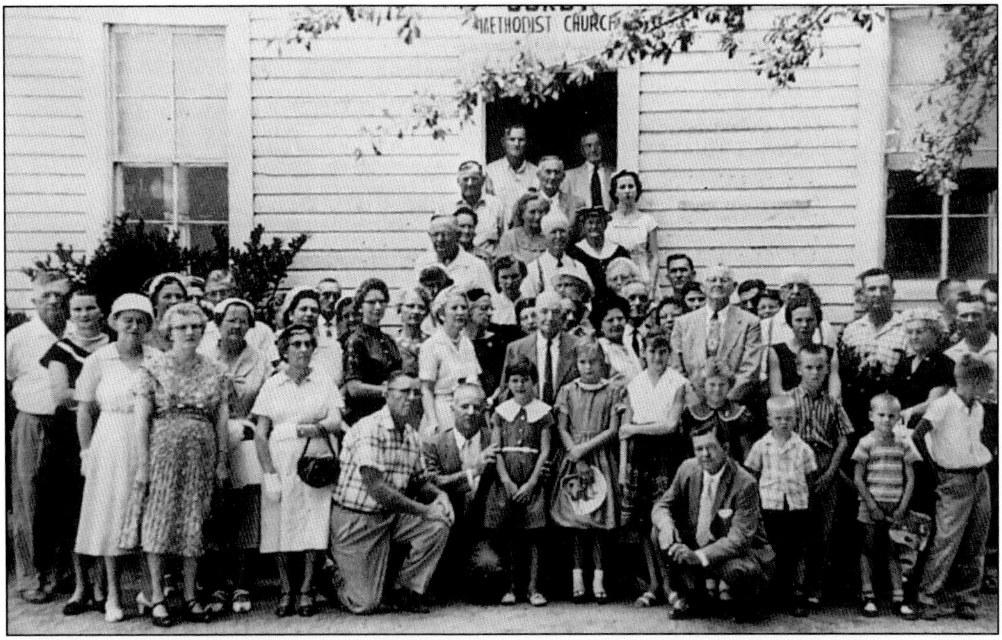

GORDY METHODIST CHURCH, C. 1950S. Gordy is located four miles southwest of Sylvester. The church is no longer active.

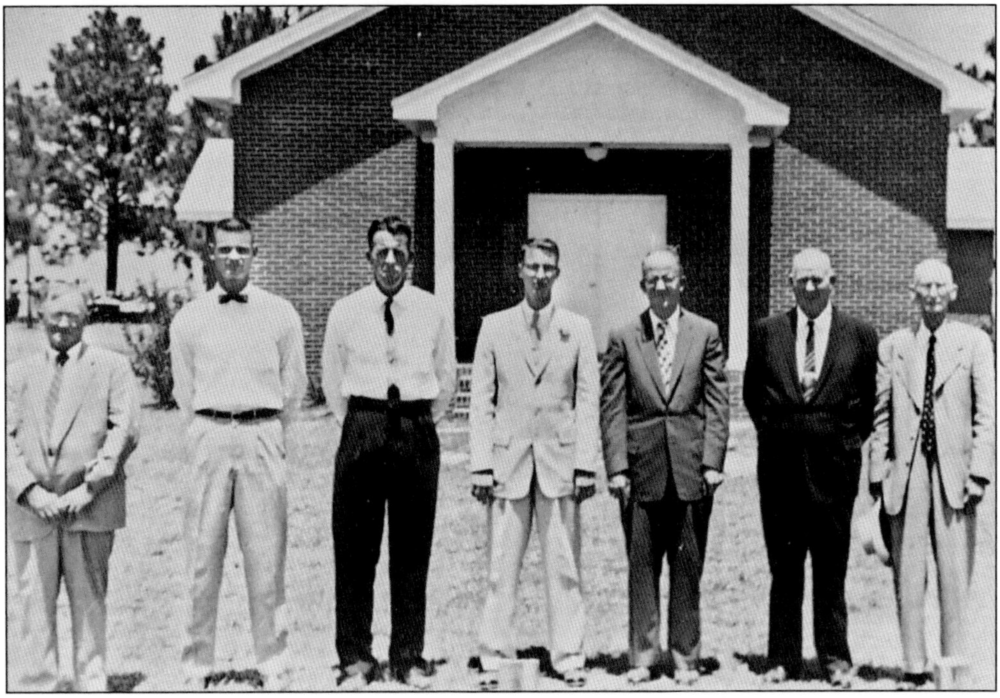

PINE FOREST BAPTIST CHURCH. Organized in 1894, the congregation first met at the Hobby Schoolhouse until a church could be built. When that church was destroyed by fire in 1909, a new one was erected in 1910. Due to growth in membership, a new sanctuary was erected in 1958. Pictured from left to right are deacons D.J. Chester, Rex Jenkins, and Talmadge Elliott; and pastors Glenn Hobby, Dexter Wilson, T.W. Matthews, and D.C. Rainey.

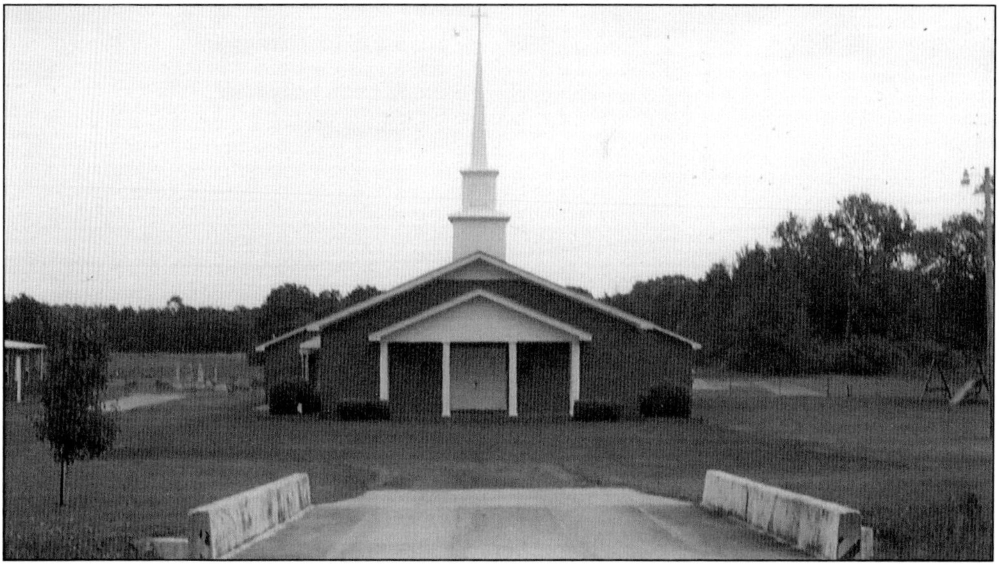

Bethel Baptist Church. Founded in the early 1860s, the members first met under a shelter and used pine straw for seats. Services were held only on the third Saturday and Sunday of the month, weather permitting. Charter members were Fulton and Belle Shiver, Frank and Sarah Braswell, J. Hue and Lizzie Shiver, John and Emily Waters, Tom and Mattie Waters, Henry and Malvina Rouse, Wesley and Rebecca Faircloth, Shack and Mollie Shiver, and Jake and Roxie Shiver. The brick sanctuary was constructed in 1965.

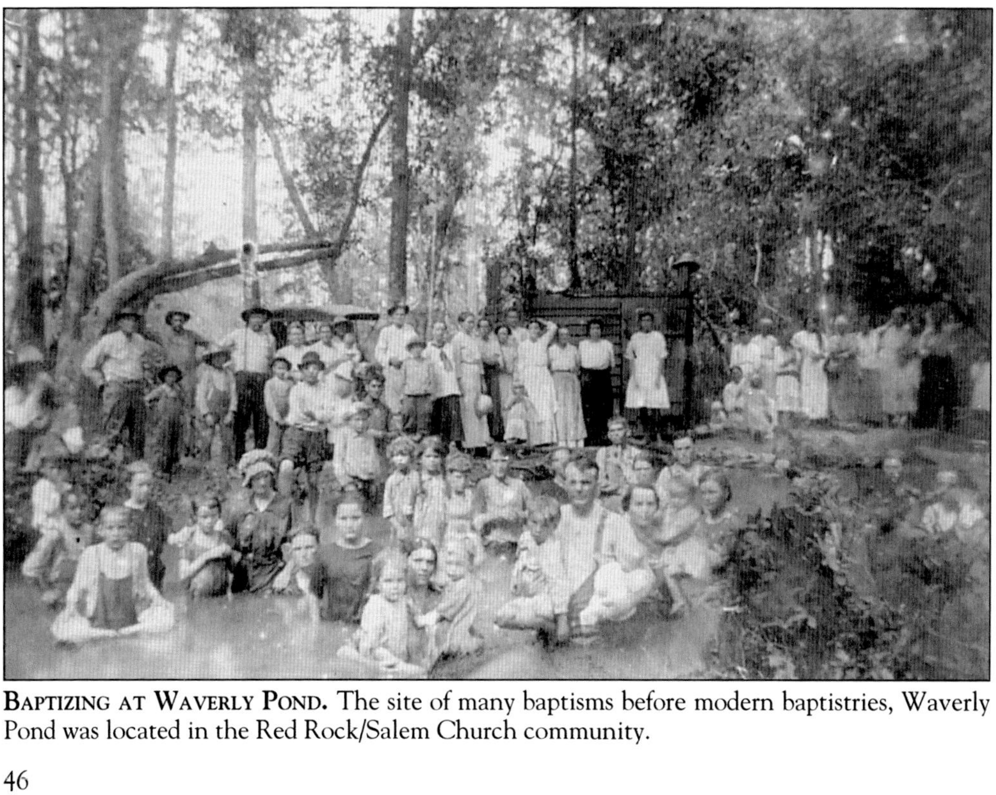

Baptizing at Waverly Pond. The site of many baptisms before modern baptistries, Waverly Pond was located in the Red Rock/Salem Church community.

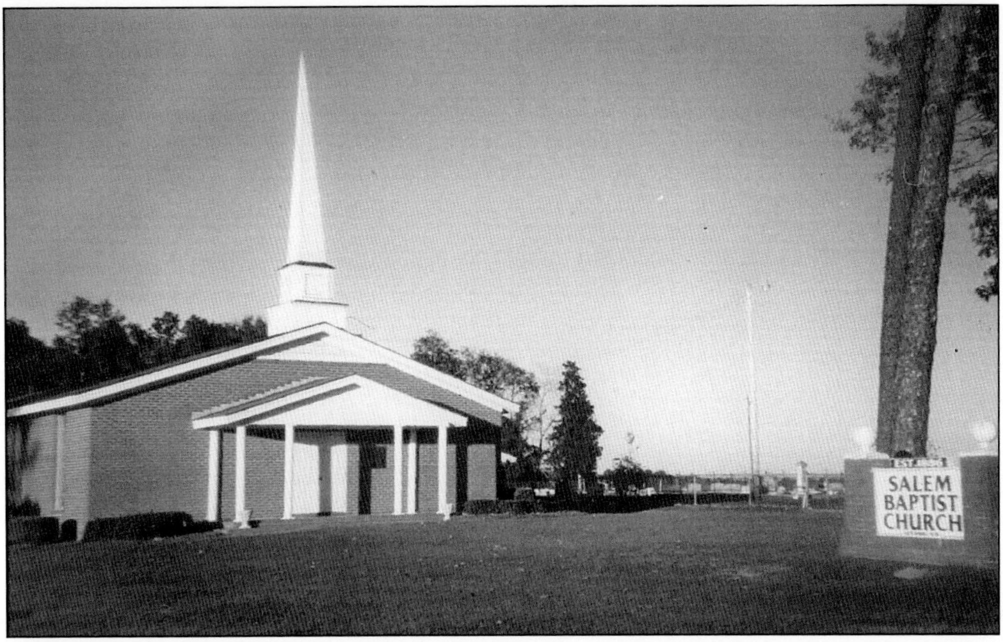

Salem Baptist Church. Located in the Red Rock community, the church was constituted September 18, 1886, under the presbytery of Ike Hobby and J.H. Champion. The first services were held in a two-room building about a mile east of the present church. This brick sanctuary was built in 1962.

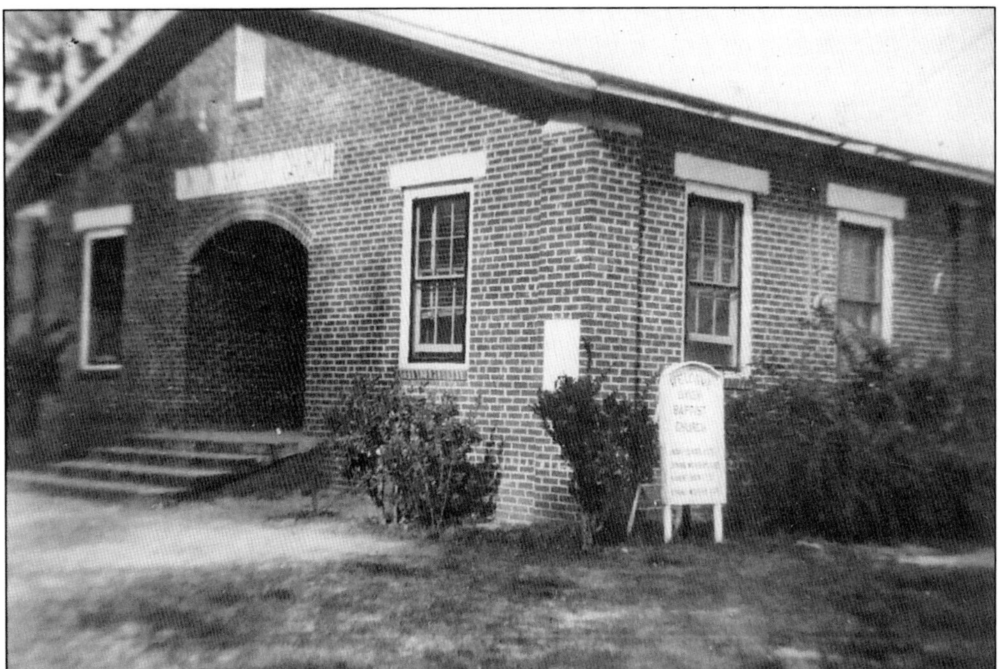

Union Baptist Church, Anderson City. It was organized in 1862. The building pictured was erected in 1943.

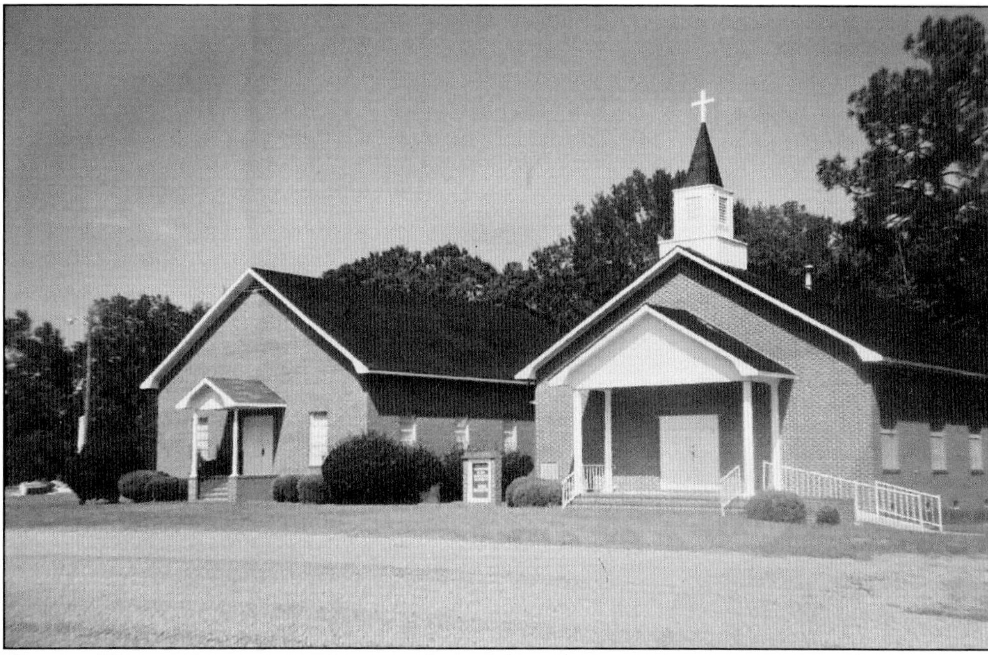

KIMBALL UNITED METHODIST CHURCH. Located in the Minton Community and named after F.C. Kimball, who donated the land for a new church in 1886, its history actually begins in 1816. At that time, a small log structure was used for a church and a school and was served by traveling preachers. It linked preachers between Brunswick and Camilla.

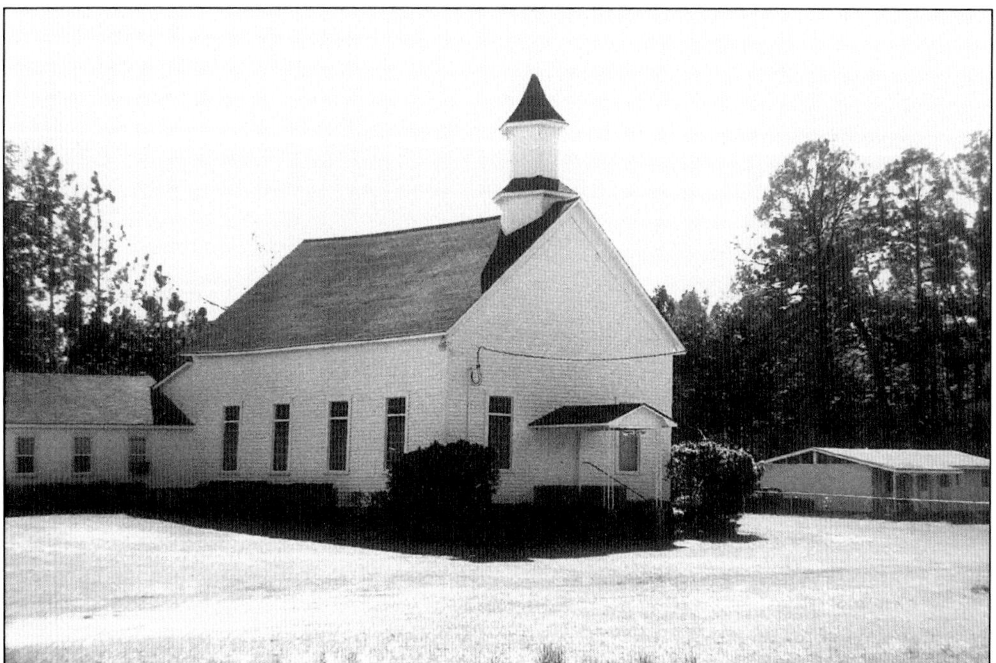

SUMNER BAPTIST CHURCH. Constituted on the fourth Sunday in May 1881. The regular meeting days were established as the fourth Saturday and Sunday in the month and the Rev. J.C. Bass was called to preach.

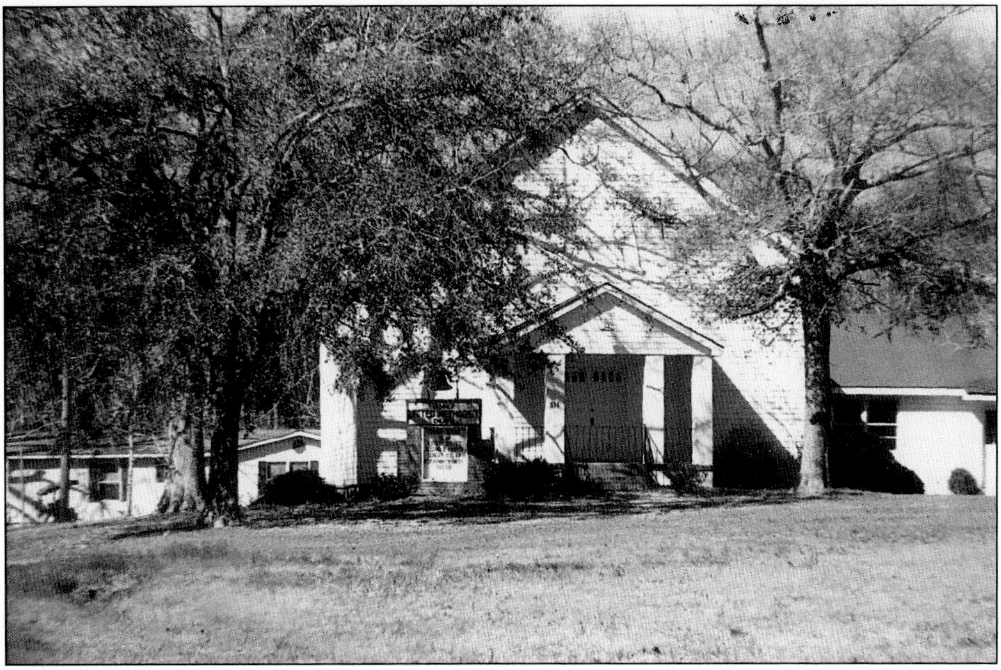

SUMNER METHODIST CHURCH. The first Methodist Church in the county was organized in 1839 at a site northeast of Sumner. The present church was built about 1880 and enlarged and remodeled in 1956.

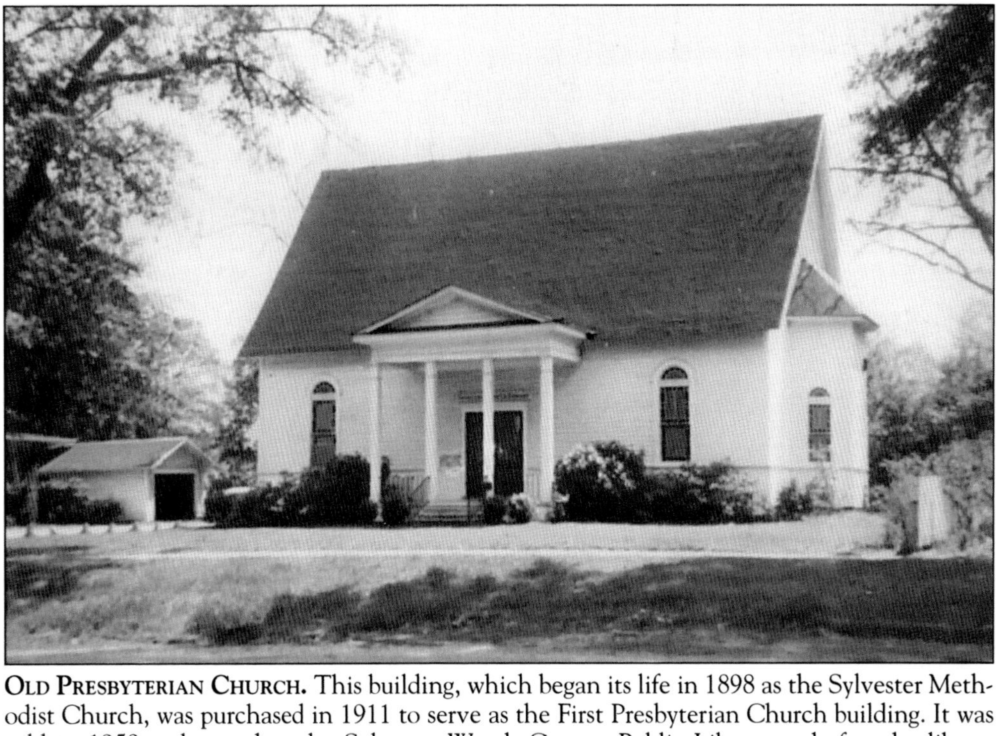

OLD PRESBYTERIAN CHURCH. This building, which began its life in 1898 as the Sylvester Methodist Church, was purchased in 1911 to serve as the First Presbyterian Church building. It was sold in 1959 to be used as the Sylvester-Worth County Public Library and after the library moved into its new building, it housed Brown's Interiors. It is currently vacant.

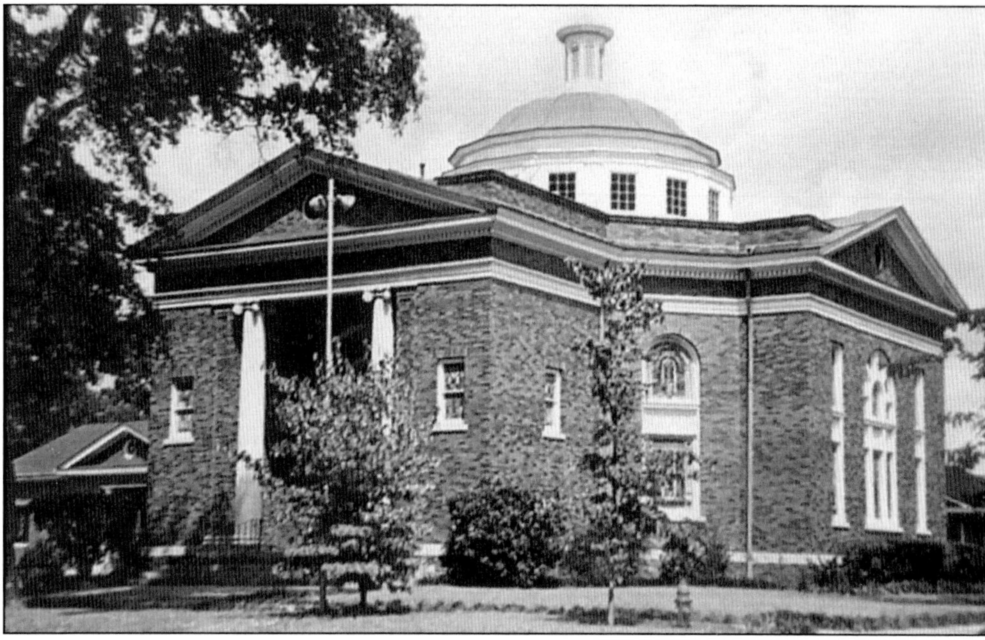

PINSON MEMORIAL UNITED METHODIST CHURCH. The church was organized in 1894. Early members were Dr. and Mrs. Crockett, Mrs. John C. Priest (later Mrs. E.E. Hicks), Mrs. Belle Ford (later Mrs. A.H. Overton), Mr. and Mrs. W.A. Allen, and Mrs. W.H. McPaul (later Mrs. T.C. Jeffords). This building was erected in 1910.

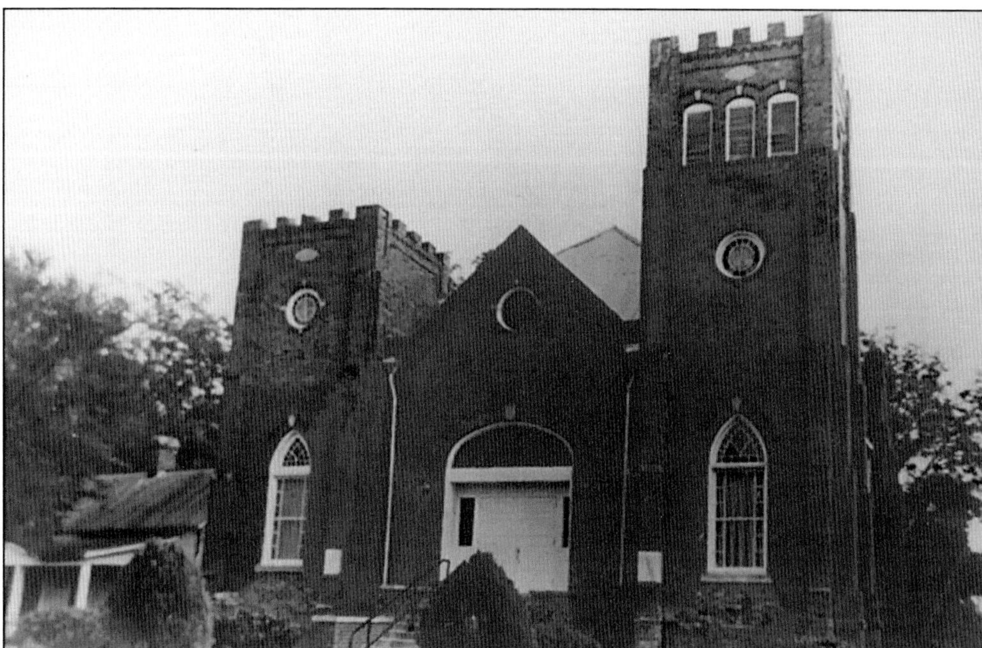

JONES CHAPEL AFRICAN METHODIST EPISCOPAL CHURCH. The church began in a frame building in 1900 and the present church building was erected in 1916 on the corner of Railroad and Livingston Streets. The architects and builders were Ed Lockette (member of Jones Chapel), Theo. S. Ayers, and James T. (Jim) Ayers.

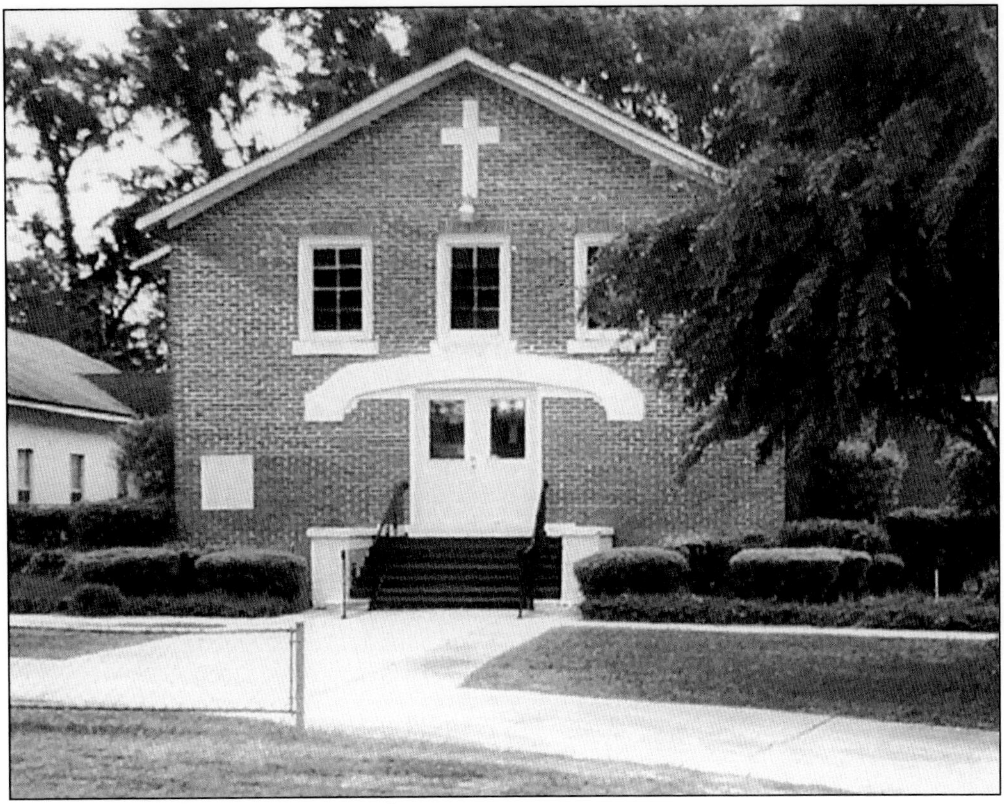

FIRST AFRICAN BAPTIST CHURCH. The church was organized around 1880 as Brooks Chapel Baptist Church and its name was changed to First African Baptist in 1900. This brick sanctuary was built in 1928 on the site of an earlier wooden building that burned. The builders were James T. (Jim) Ayers and Richard Braswell, both deacons in the church and skilled carpenters and bricklayers.

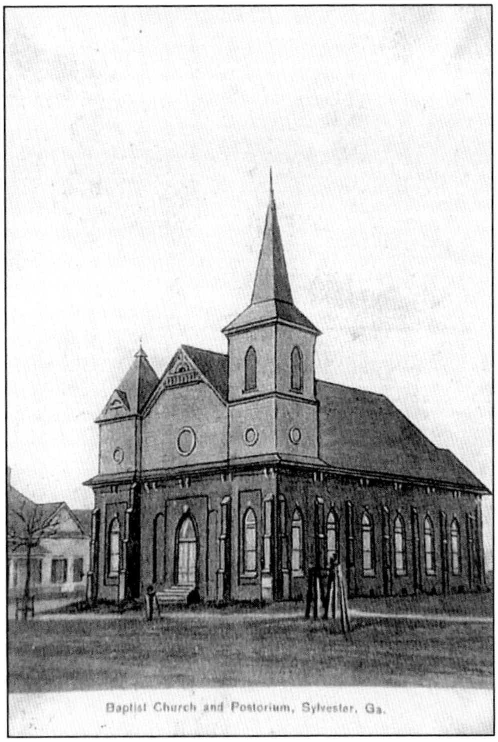

FIRST BAPTIST CHURCH. Built in 1900 for $7,000 with C.W. Hillhouse as the building contractor, it contained a vestibule and auditorium with a small room on each side but no Sunday School rooms. The pastorium was built in 1905.

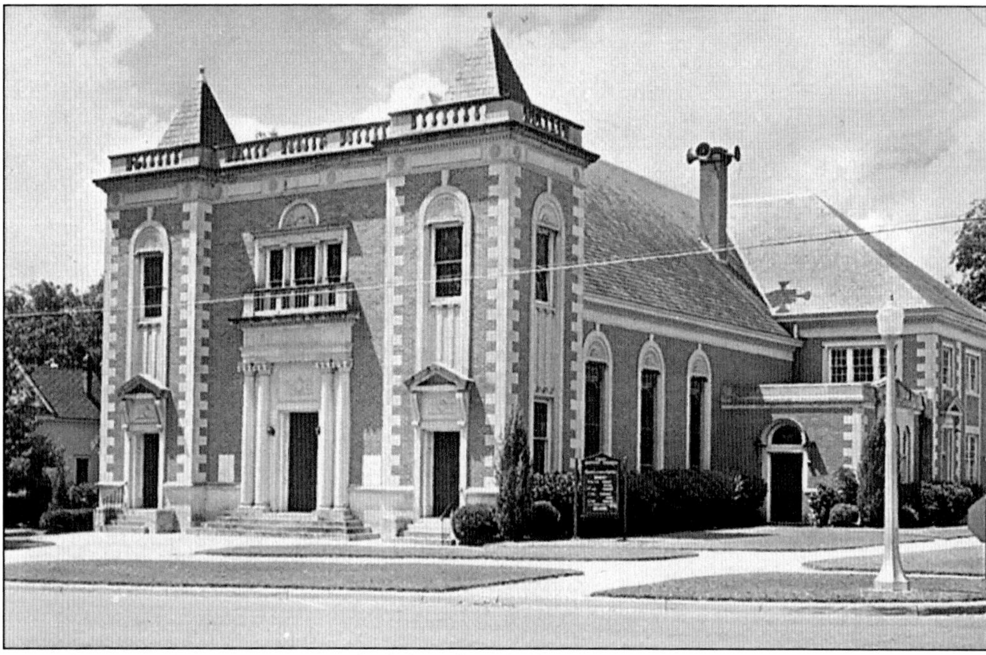

First Baptist Church. Postcard of the church that was made before the Annex was built in 1960. In 1919, the original brick structure was enlarged to add Sunday School facilities and departments.

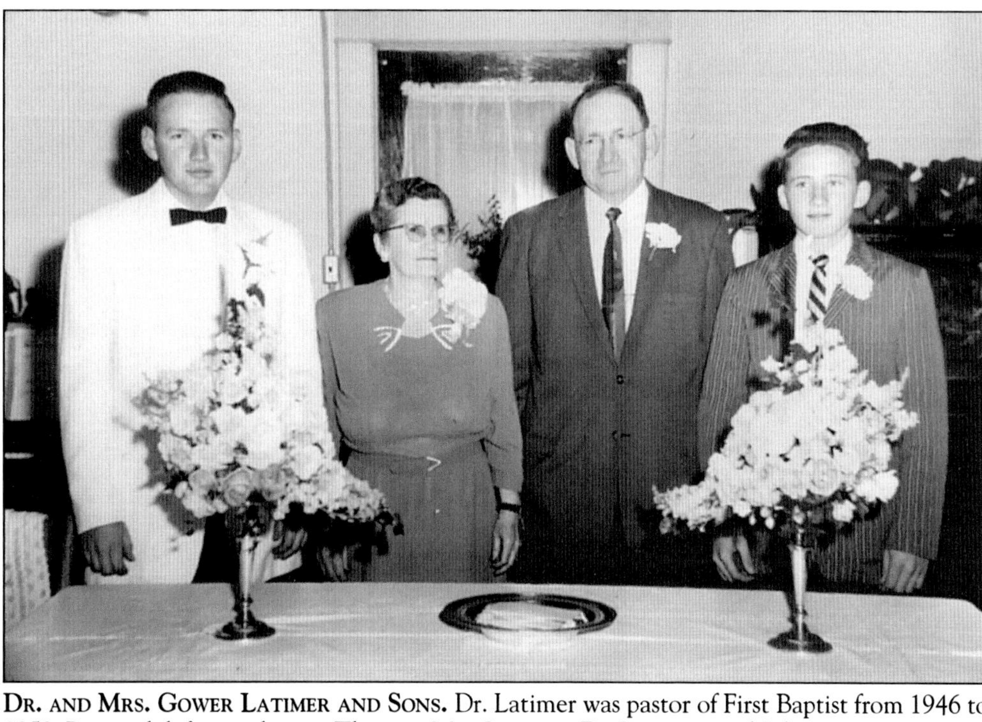

Dr. and Mrs. Gower Latimer and Sons. Dr. Latimer was pastor of First Baptist from 1946 to 1959. Pictured, left to right, are Thomas, Mrs. Latimer, Dr. Latimer, and John.

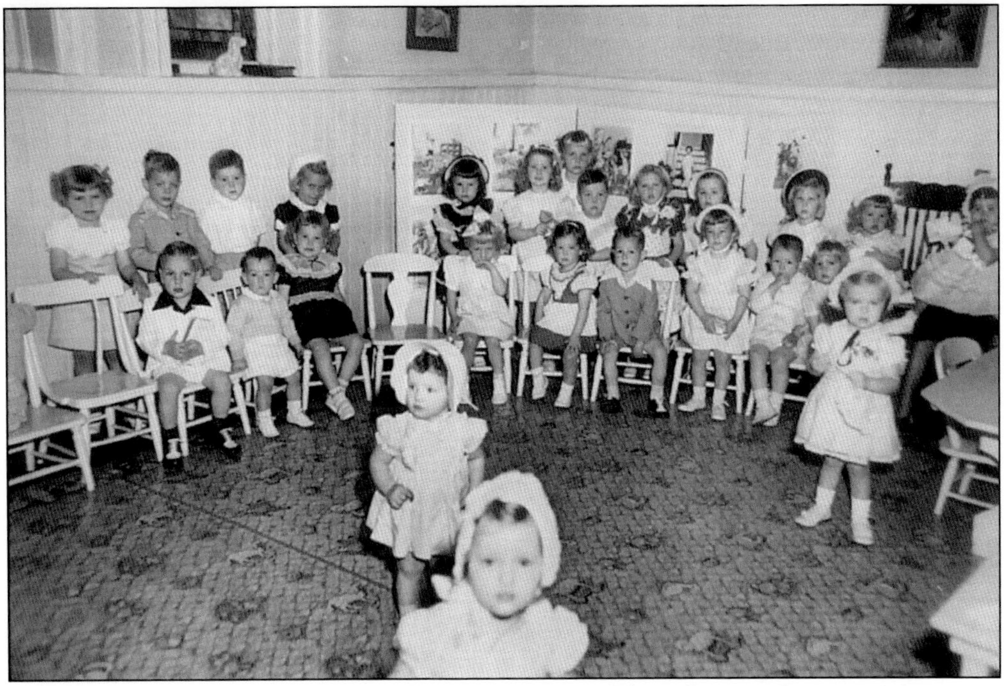

First Baptist Church Nursery Class, c. 1950. This photograph was made on an Easter Sunday.

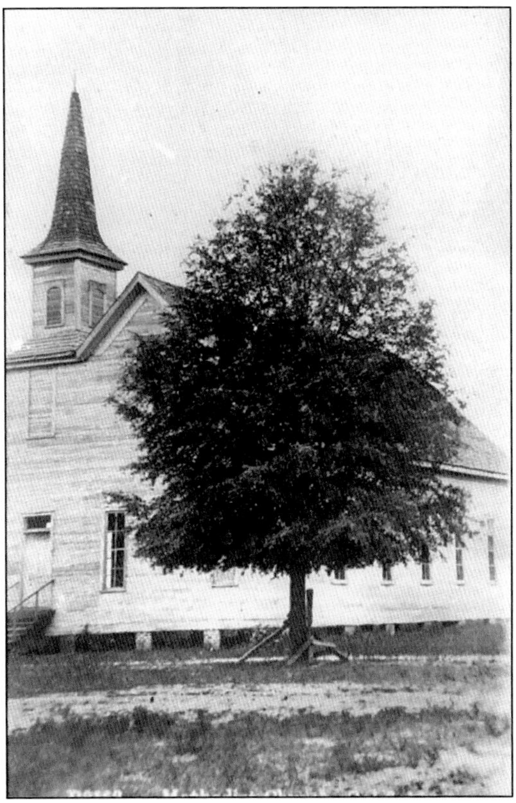

Methodist Church at Oakfield. Oakfield is one of the oldest communities in the county.

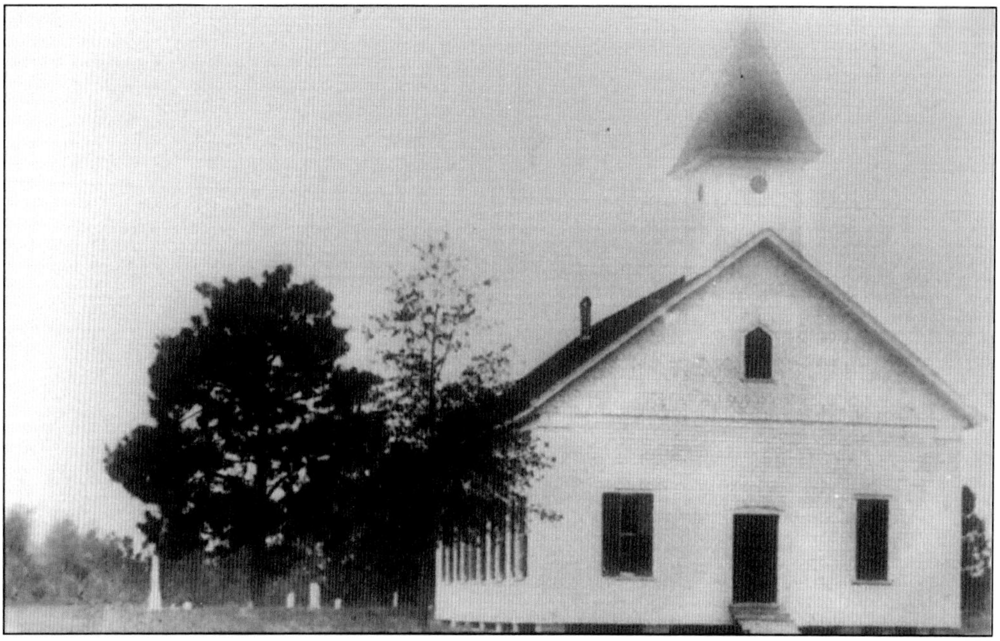

OAKFIELD BAPTIST CHURCH. Oakfield is located on the banks of the Flint River and on part of the Old Stage Coach Road.

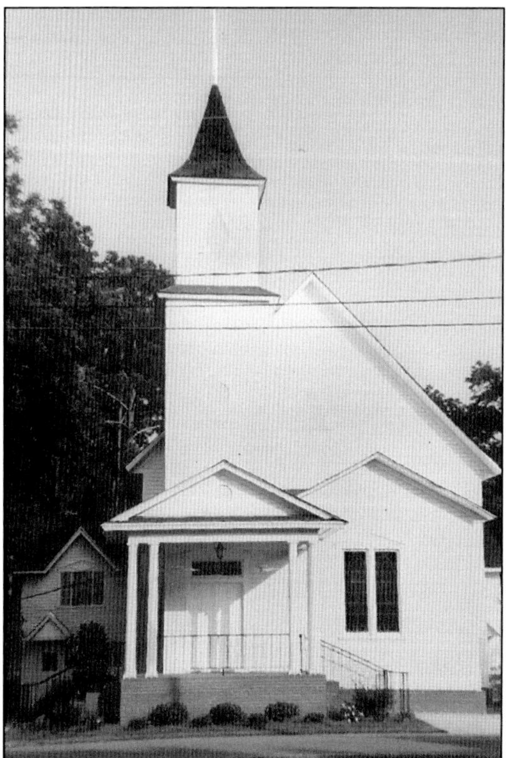

FIRST BAPTIST CHURCH AT WARWICK. Beginning as the Fort Early Baptist Church on the old Stage Coach Road in 1838, the renamed First Baptist Church in Warwick moved to its present location in 1896 when this building was erected. Classrooms were added in 1958 and 1961; a pastorium built in 1965; and the sanctuary was renovated in 1970.

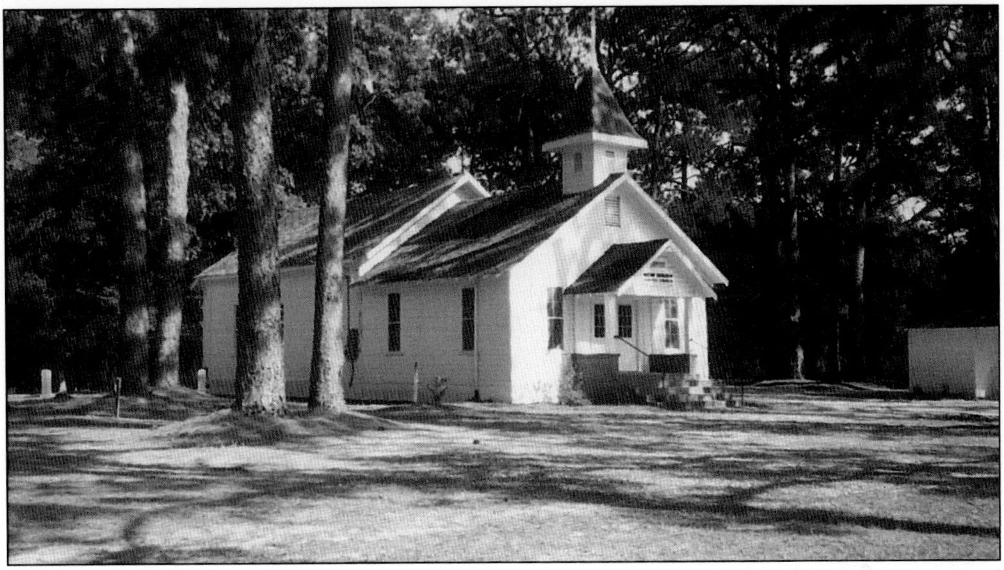

New Union Baptist Church. Located between Doles and Warwick, this church was organized in 1898. In 1902, two acres of land were given by Mr. D.H. Davis for a church building, a school, and a cemetery. The church was remodeled in the 1940s and 1950s.

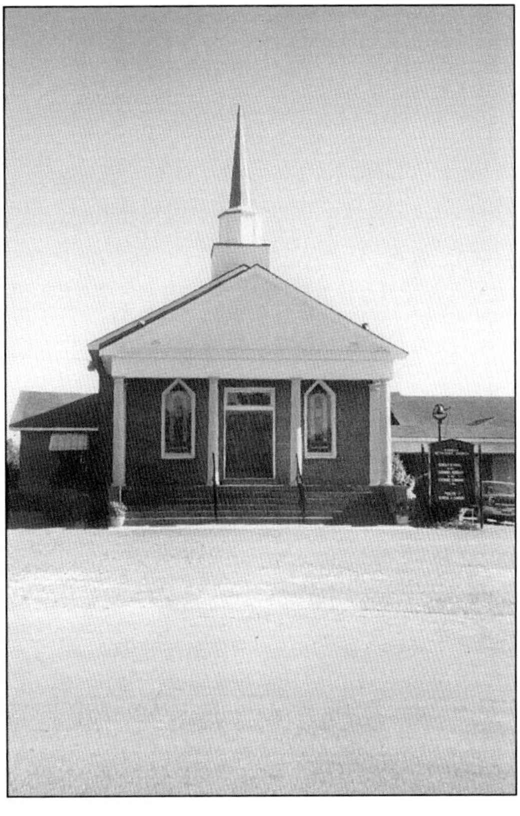

Warwick United Methodist Church. This church was founded in April 1913 with seven charter members: Charles W. Ansley, Mrs. M.S. Aultman, Mr. and Mrs. W.D. Etheridge, Mr. and Mrs. W.J. Murphy, and Mrs. John Wise. The first services were held in a brush arbor with a wooden structure erected about a year later. In 1947, this building was damaged by fire and rebuilt on the same site.

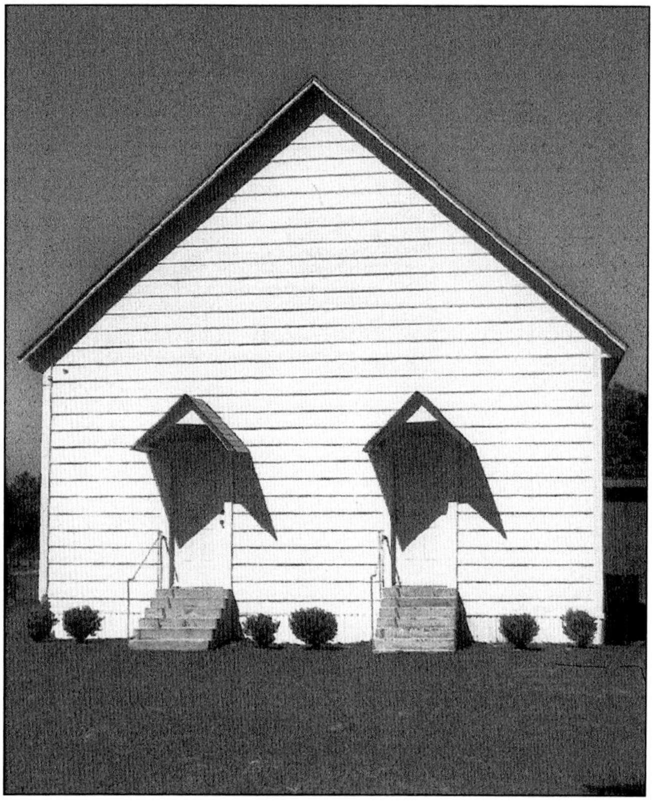

Providence Primitive Baptist Church. Constituted on August 20, 1860, at a large spring under some trees, the congregation first met in a nearby school house. The first members were Samuel Castleberry, Pearson Brown, James Giddens, John Williams, Elizabeth Pearson, and Mary Williams, with elders Henry C. Tucker and Warren Dykes as presbytery.

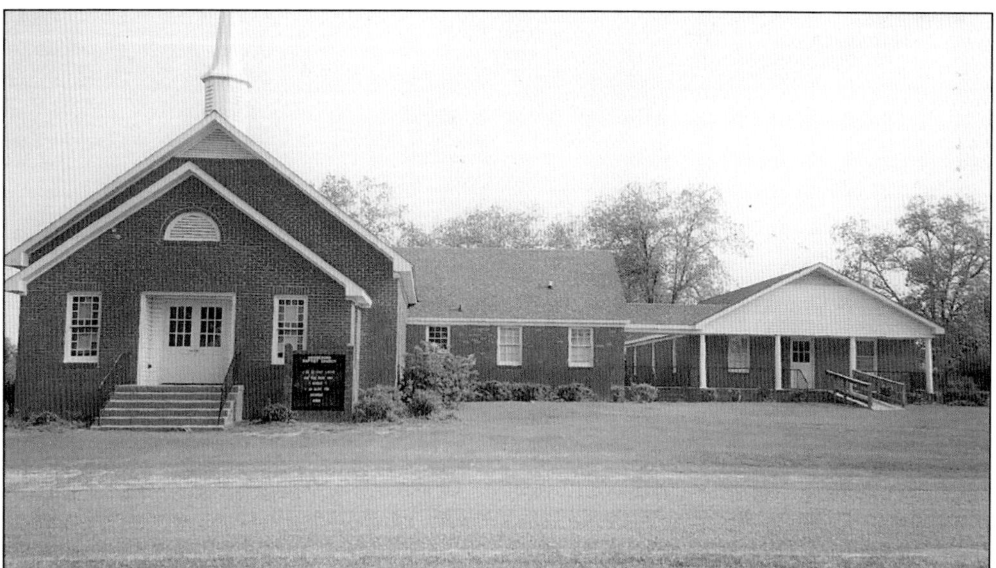

Bridgeboro Baptist Church. Organized in 1932, the land for the building was donated by Mr. W.L. H. Alford and the trees were donated by Mr. J.H. Hillhouse. All labor was volunteer. By 1970, the church was completely remodeled inside and out and a pastorium acquired.

Four

EDUCATION

In the early days, education was provided by the parents. As communities grew families would pool their resources and employ a teacher and provide a building. These were crude wooden structures often with sand floors and big fireplaces or pot bellied stoves. The seats were rough hewn and textbooks few. It was not until the last quarter of the 19th century that education was made public. By the time the first volume of The History of Worth County was published in 1934, there were 26 school districts.

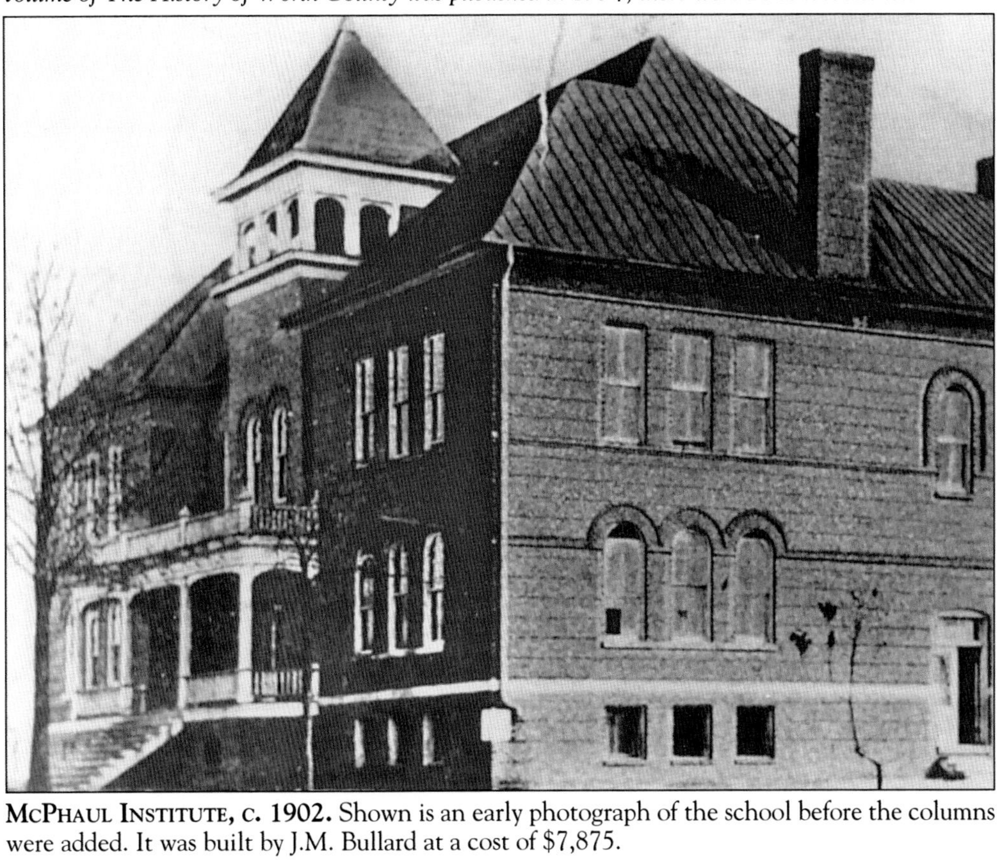

MCPHAUL INSTITUTE, C. 1902. Shown is an early photograph of the school before the columns were added. It was built by J.M. Bullard at a cost of $7,875.

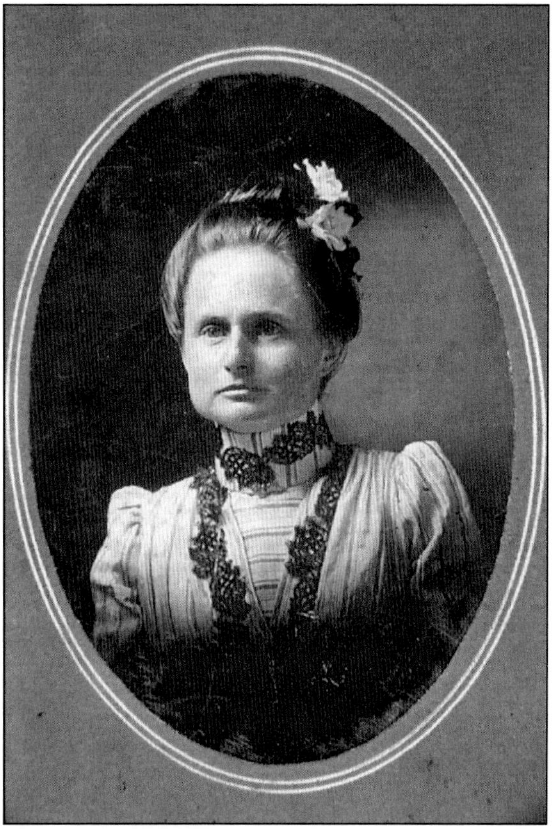

ANNABEL METHVIN PRIEST HICKS (1864–1944). Miss Methvin came to Worth County from Twiggs County in 1887 to teach at Isabella.

TEACHER'S LICENSE OF MISS ANNABEL METHVIN, 1888. Based on a successful examination, a permanent teacher's license was granted. This was signed by W.L. Sikes, Worth County School Commissioner.

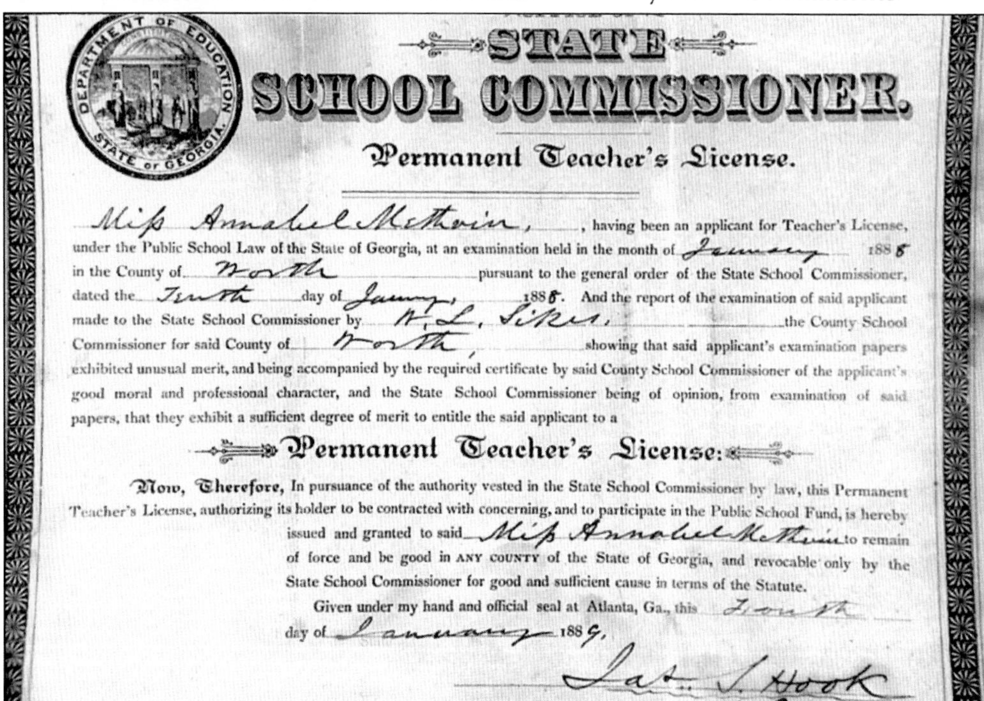

STATE
SCHOOL COMMISSIONER.

Permanent Teacher's License.

Miss Annabel Methvin, having been an applicant for Teacher's License, under the Public School Law of the State of Georgia, at an examination held in the month of January 1888 in the County of North pursuant to the general order of the State School Commissioner, dated the Tenth day of Jany, 1888. And the report of the examination of said applicant made to the State School Commissioner by W. L. Sikes, the County School Commissioner for said County of North, showing that said applicant's examination papers exhibited unusual merit, and being accompanied by the required certificate by said County School Commissioner of the applicant's good moral and professional character, and the State School Commissioner being of opinion, from examination of said papers, that they exhibit a sufficient degree of merit to entitle the said applicant to a

Permanent Teacher's License:

Now, Therefore, In pursuance of the authority vested in the State School Commissioner by law, this Permanent Teacher's License, authorizing its holder to be contracted with concerning, and to participate in the Public School Fund, is hereby issued and granted to said Miss Annabel Methvin to remain of force and be good in ANY COUNTY of the State of Georgia, and revocable only by the State School Commissioner for good and sufficient cause in terms of the Statute.

Given under my hand and official seal at Atlanta, Ga., this Fourth day of January 1889.

Jas. S. Hook
St. Com.

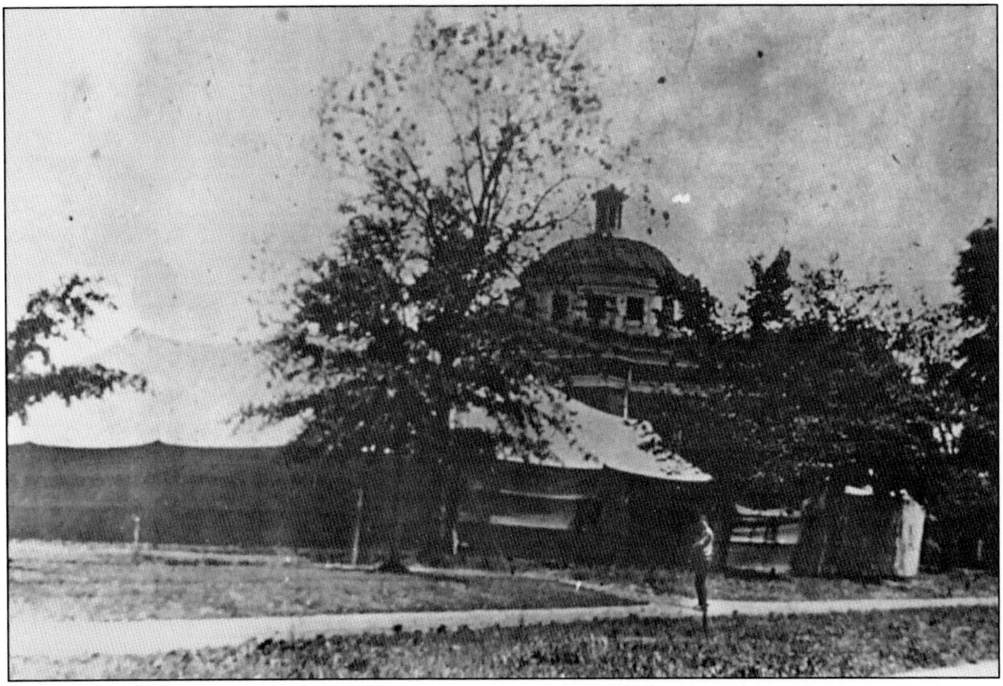

REDPATH CHAUTAUQUA TENT. The annual appearance of this traveling chautauqua was enjoyed by all. It furnished a background of culture for all ages—lectures, plays, music, and story hour for children—all had a place on the program. Pinson Memorial Methodist Church is in the background.

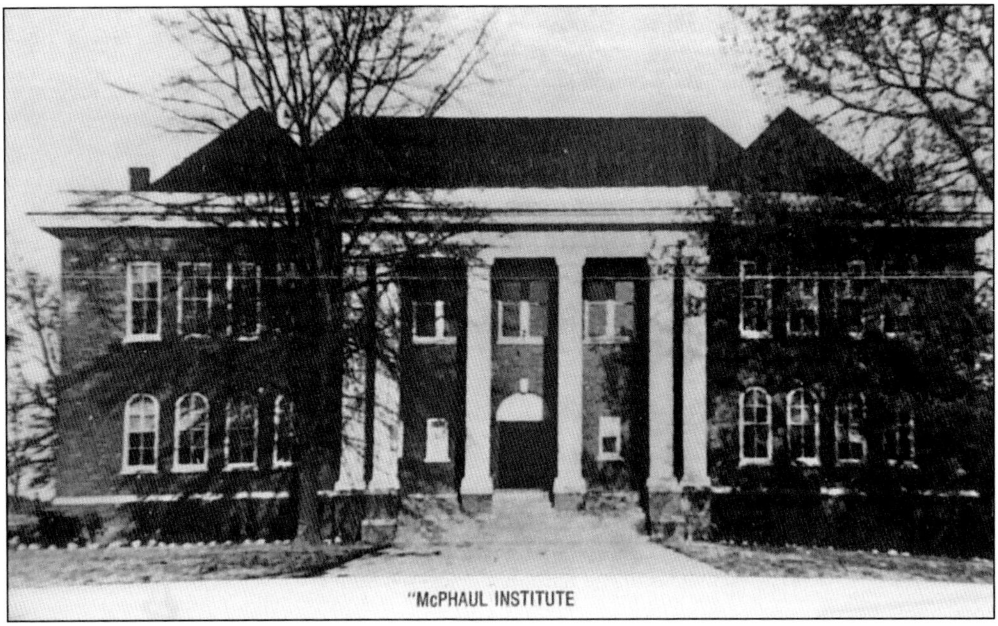

McPHAUL INSTITUTE. The land was donated by Mrs. Mamie McPhaul Jeffords in memory of her first husband, W.H. McPhaul. It provided a place for educating all ages until it was burned in 1972.

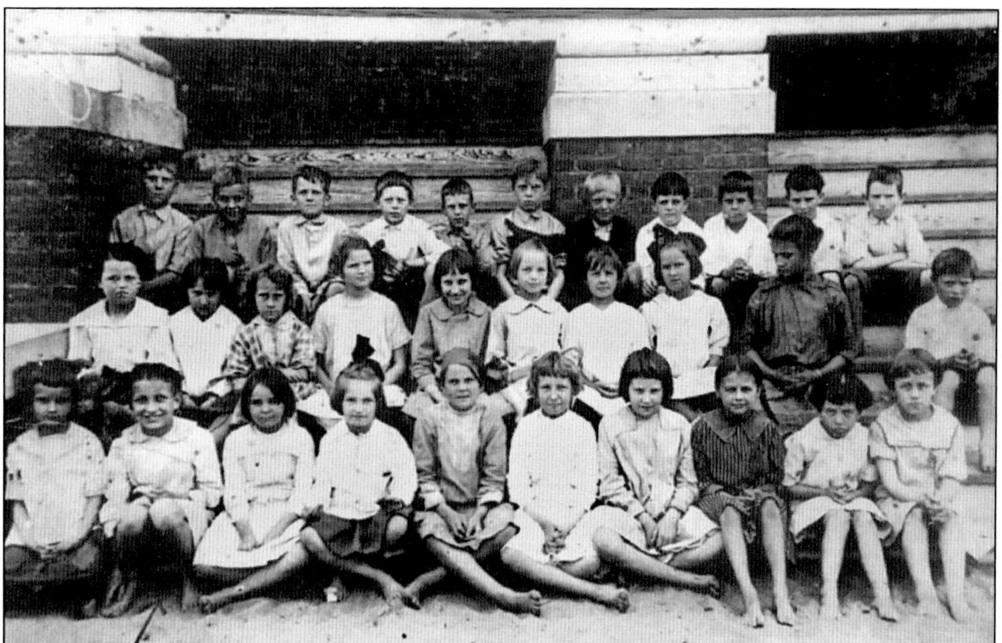

First Grade Class, McPhaul Institute, 1911–1912.

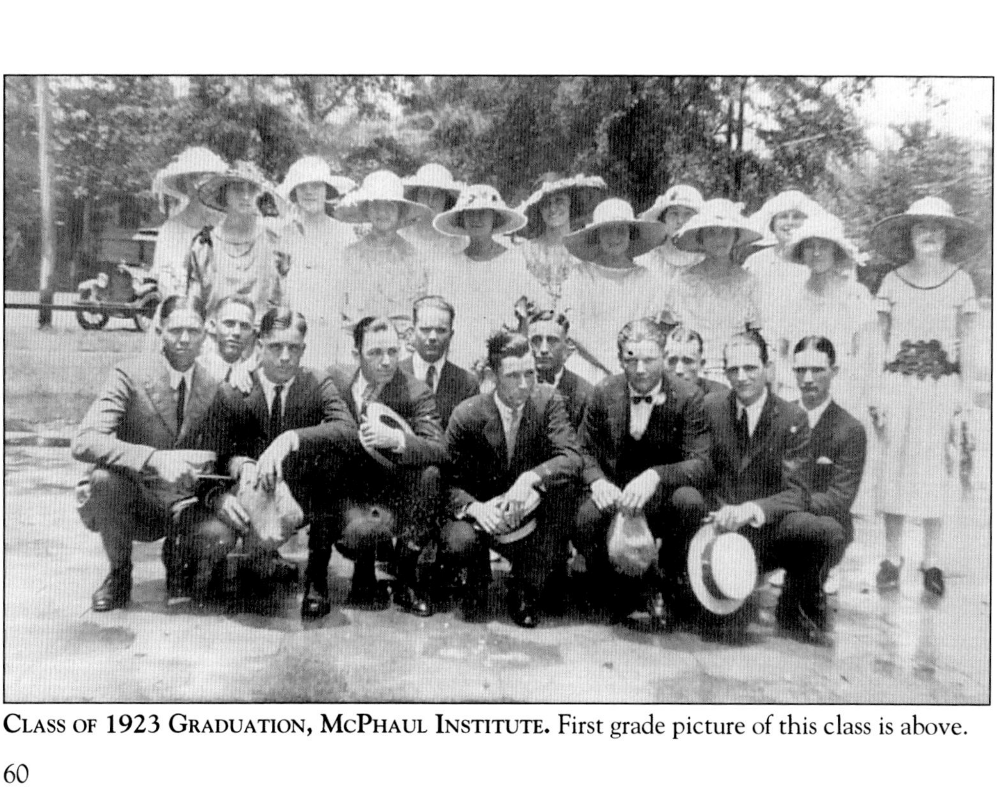

Class of 1923 Graduation, McPhaul Institute. First grade picture of this class is above.

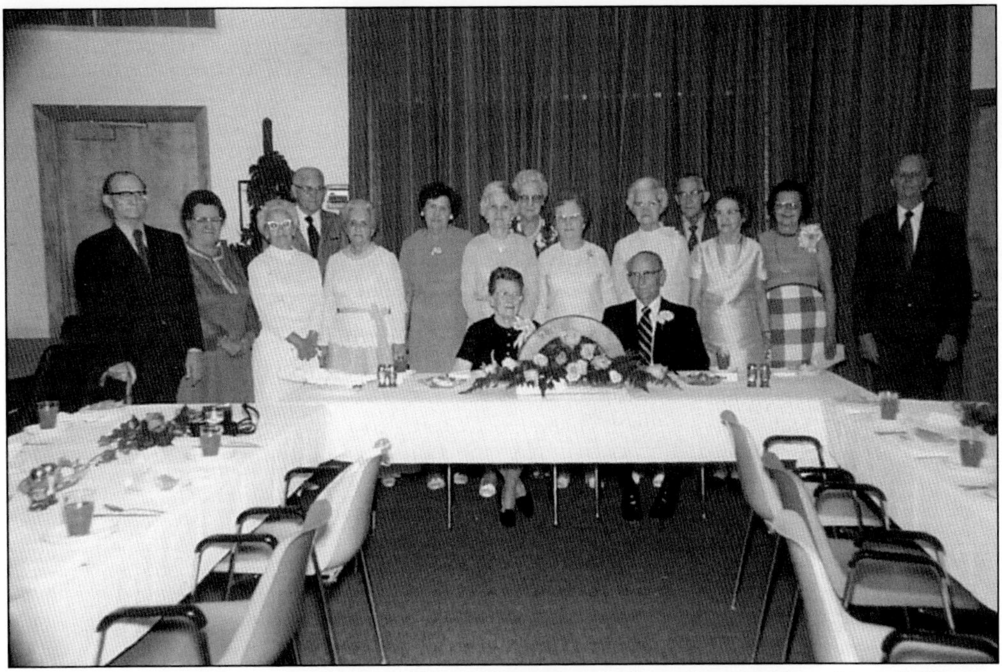

50TH REUNION OF CLASS OF 1923 MCPHAUL INSTITUTE. Seated are teachers Lizzie J. Deariso and George I. Martin. Among those standing are Wynt Warren, Fred Park, Bessie Nelms McCord, Lois Gammage, Velma Nelms, Bessie Mae Deariso Keown, Opal Wingate.

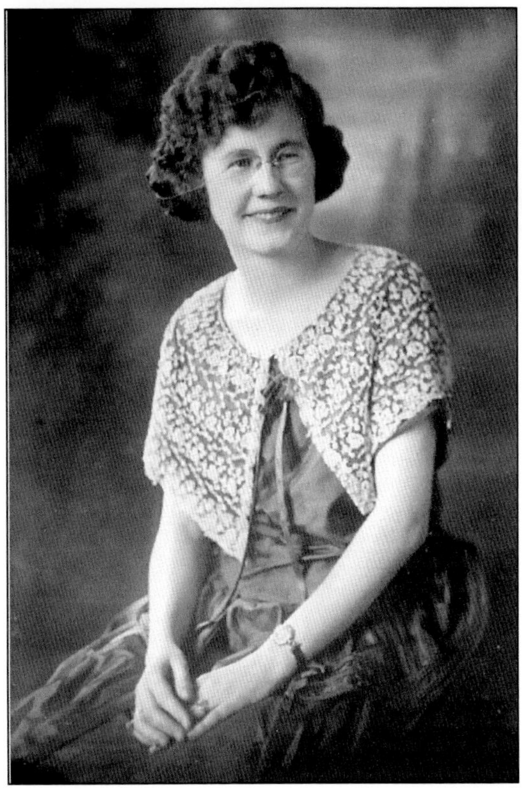

LIZZIE J. DEARISO, TEACHER AND COUNTY SCHOOL SUPERINTENDENT. Deariso Primary School was named after Miss Lizzie J. and the building was incorporated into the Worth County High School.

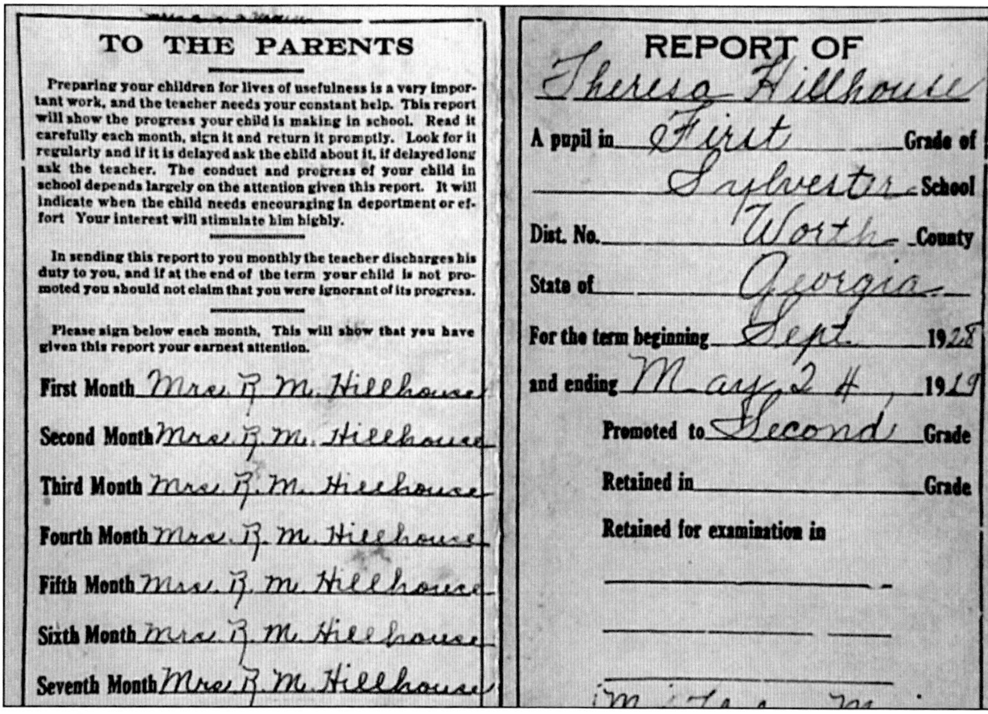

TO THE PARENTS

Preparing your children for lives of usefulness is a very important work, and the teacher needs your constant help. This report will show the progress your child is making in school. Read it carefully each month, sign it and return it promptly. Look for it regularly and if it is delayed ask the child about it, if delayed long ask the teacher. The conduct and progress of your child in school depends largely on the attention given this report. It will indicate when the child needs encouraging in deportment or effort. Your interest will stimulate him highly.

In sending this report to you monthly the teacher discharges his duty to you, and if at the end of the term your child is not promoted you should not claim that you were ignorant of its progress.

Please sign below each month. This will show that you have given this report your earnest attention.

First Month Mrs. R. M. Hillhouse
Second Month Mrs. R. M. Hillhouse
Third Month Mrs. R. M. Hillhouse
Fourth Month Mrs. R. M. Hillhouse
Fifth Month Mrs. R. M. Hillhouse
Sixth Month Mrs. R. M. Hillhouse
Seventh Month Mrs. R. M. Hillhouse

REPORT OF
Theresa Hillhouse
A pupil in First Grade of
Sylvester School
Dist. No. Worth County
State of Georgia
For the term beginning Sept. 1928
and ending May 24, 1929
Promoted to Second Grade
Retained in Grade
Retained for examination in

First Grade Report Card of Theresa Hillhouse, 1928–1929. Mrs. Thelma Majors was the teacher.

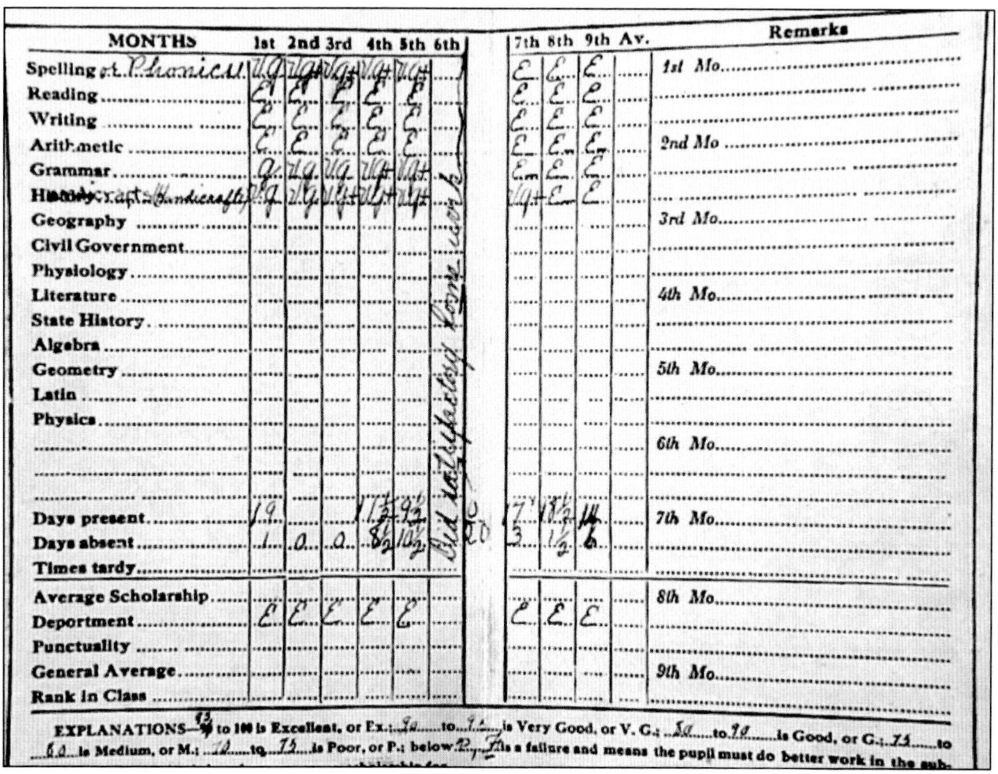

MONTHS	1st	2nd	3rd	4th	5th	6th	7th	8th	9th	Av.
Spelling or Phonics	VG	VG	VG	VG+	VG+		E	E	E	
Reading	E	E	E	E	E		E	E	E	
Writing	E	E	E	E	E		E	E	E	
Arithmetic	E	E	E	E	E		E	E	E	
Grammar	G	VG	VG	VG+	VG+		E	E	E	
Handicraft	VG	VG	VG+	VG+	VG+		VG+	E	E	
Geography										
Civil Government										
Physiology										
Literature										
State History										
Algebra										
Geometry										
Latin										
Physics										
Days present	19			17½	9½	20	17	18½	14	
Days absent	1	0	0	8½	10½		3	1½	6	
Times tardy										
Average Scholarship										
Deportment	E	E	E	E	E		E	E	E	
Punctuality										
General Average										
Rank in Class										

Remarks: 1st Mo. 2nd Mo. 3rd Mo. 4th Mo. 5th Mo. 6th Mo. 7th Mo. 8th Mo. 9th Mo.

Did satisfactory home work

EXPLANATIONS—93 to 100 is Excellent, or Ex.; 90 to 93 is Very Good, or V. G.; 80 to 90 is Good, or G.; 75 to 80 is Medium, or M.; 70 to 75 is Poor, or P.; below 70 is a failure and means the pupil must do better work in the sub-

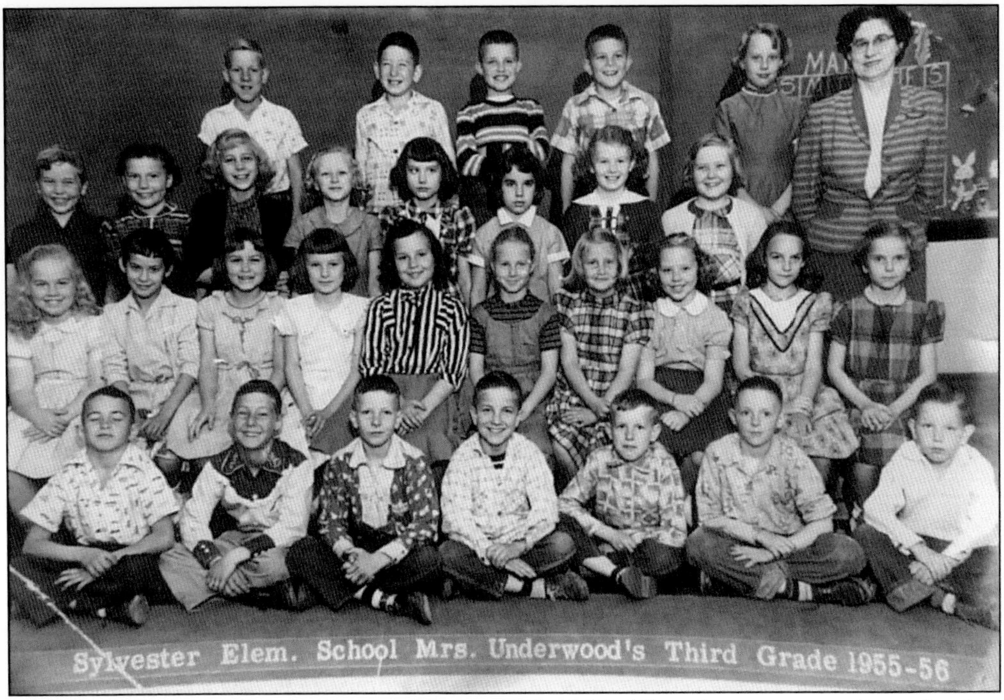

Mrs. Underwood's Third Grade Class, 1955–1956. This class was attending school at McPhaul Institute.

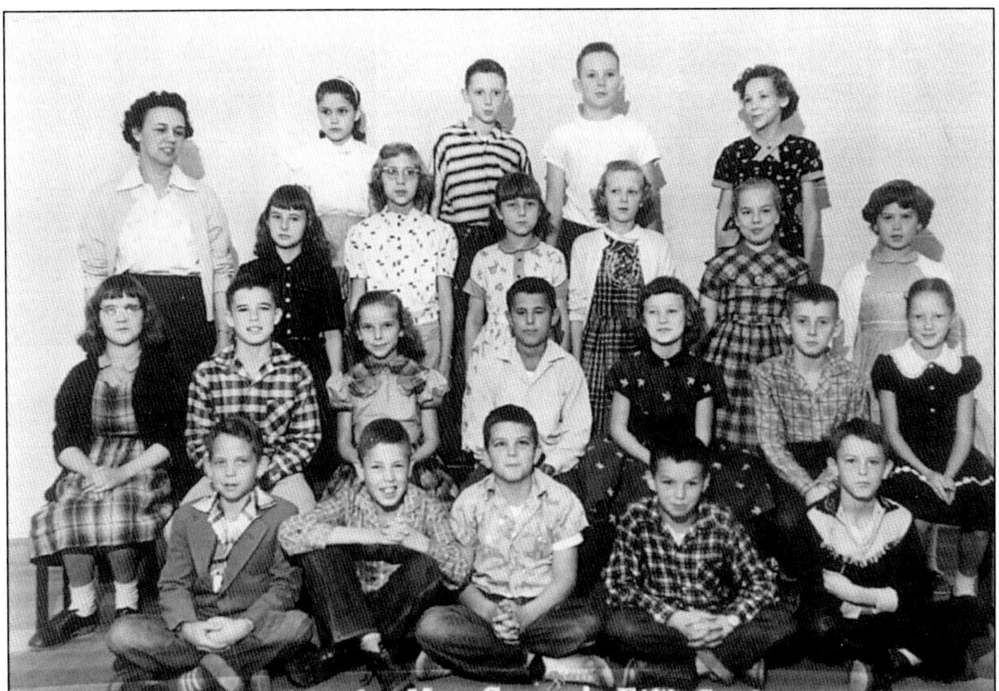

Mrs. Cooper's Fifth Grade Class, 1957–1958. This was the first year this class attended school in the new Sylvester Elementary School.

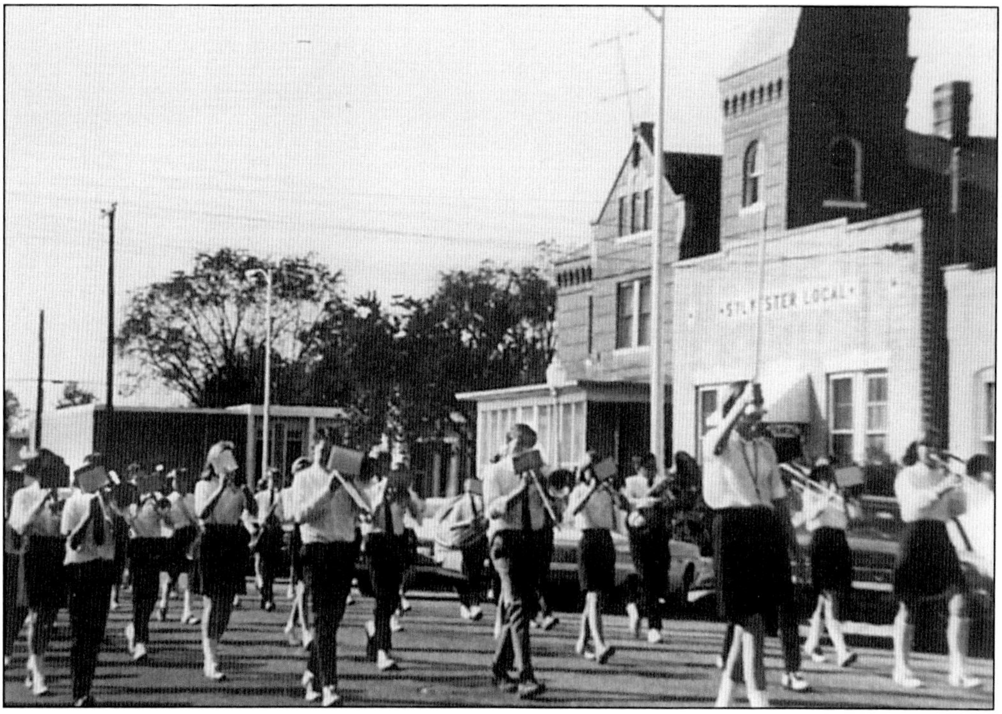

Worth County Junior High Band on Parade, c. 1970. Lila Gammage is leading the band with baton held high.

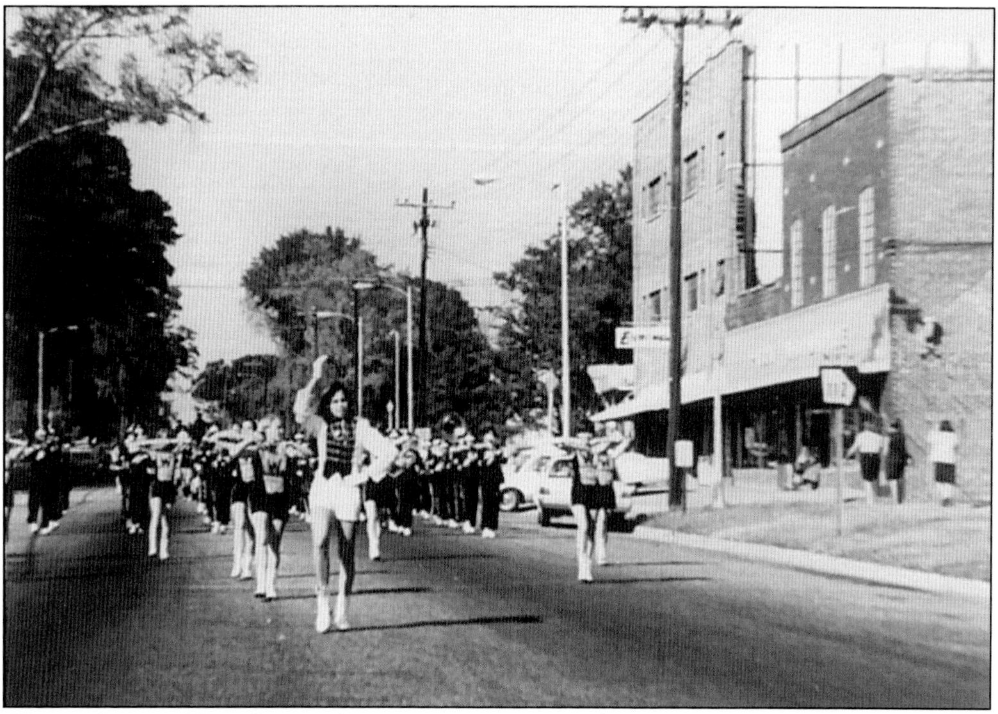

Worth County High School Band on Parade. Marching south on Isabella Street, the senior band struts its stuff.

Students at the Old Vickers Still School. Located in the northeastern part of the county, this school had 4 teachers and 143 students in 1934.

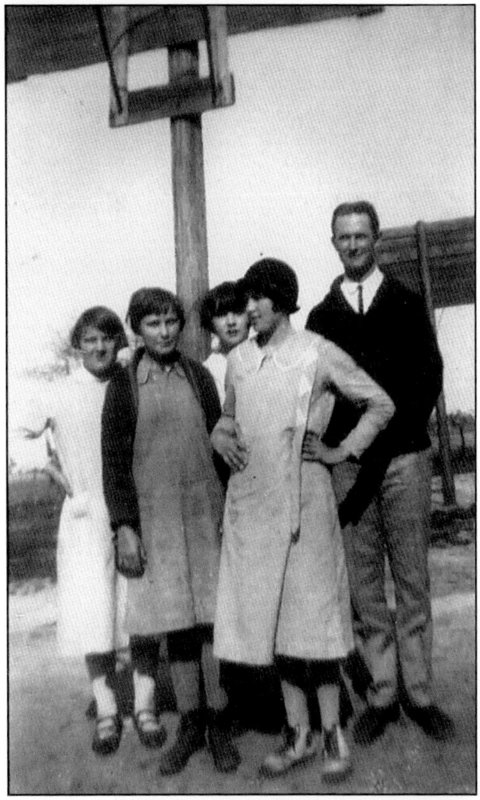

Warwick School. Built in 1923, it originally housed both elementary and high school grades.

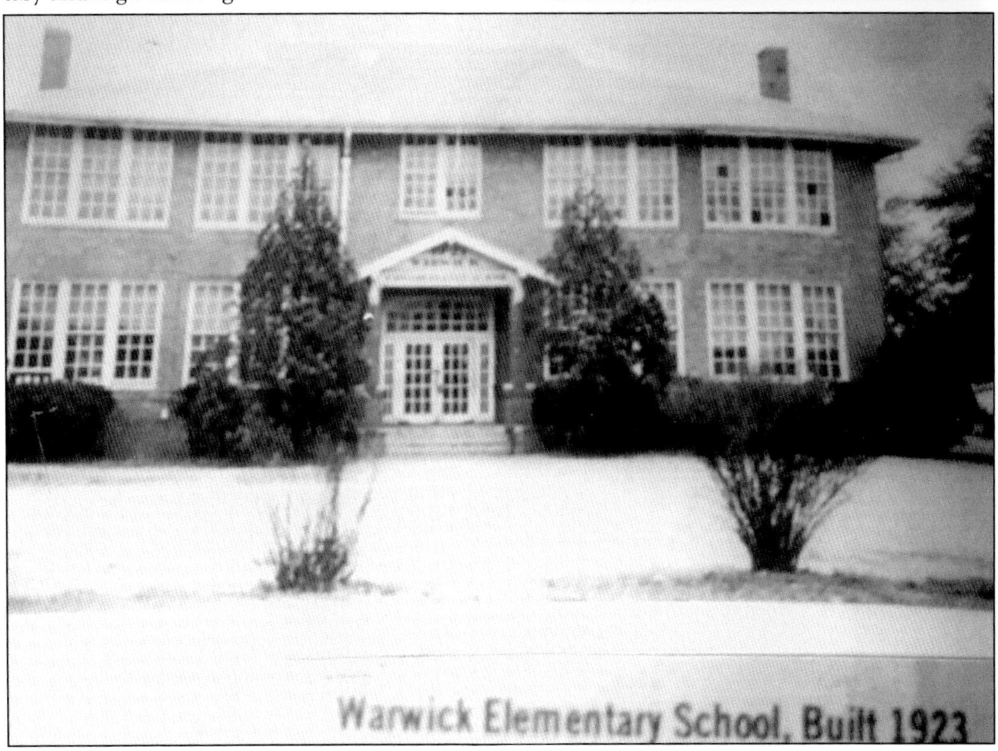

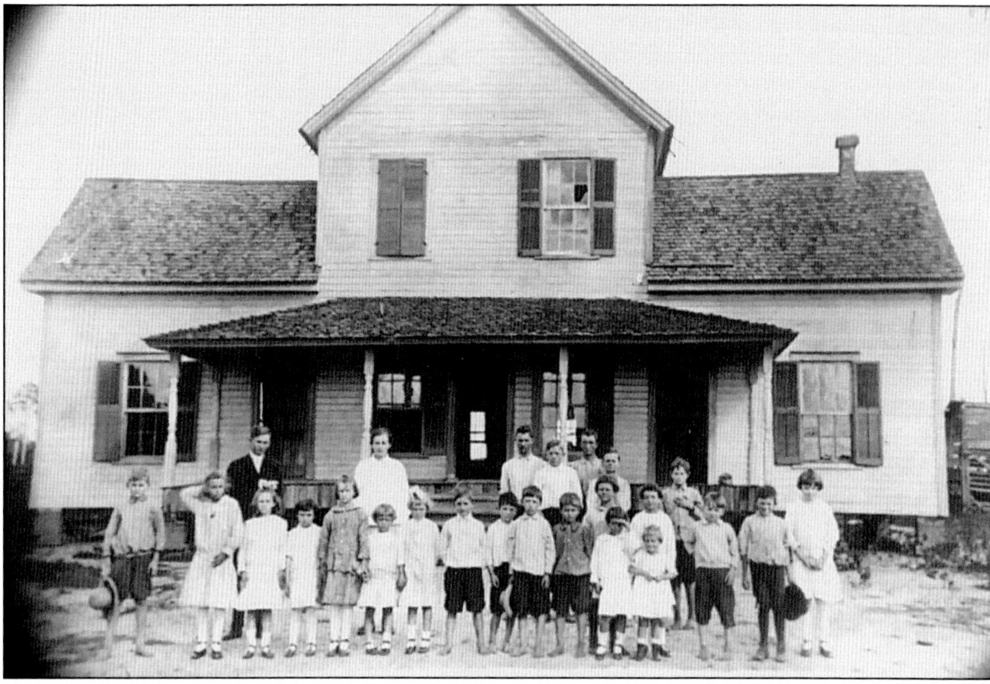

Red Rock School, c. 1915. The first school was in a wood-frame building.

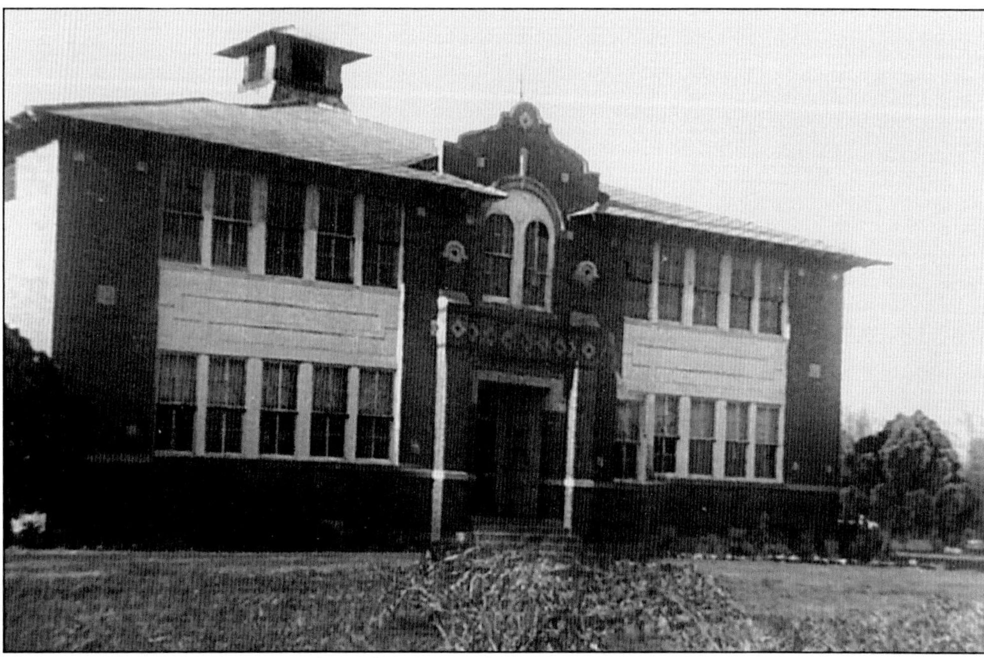

Second Red Rock School. This school is no longer active. In 1934, there were 4 teachers and 129 students.

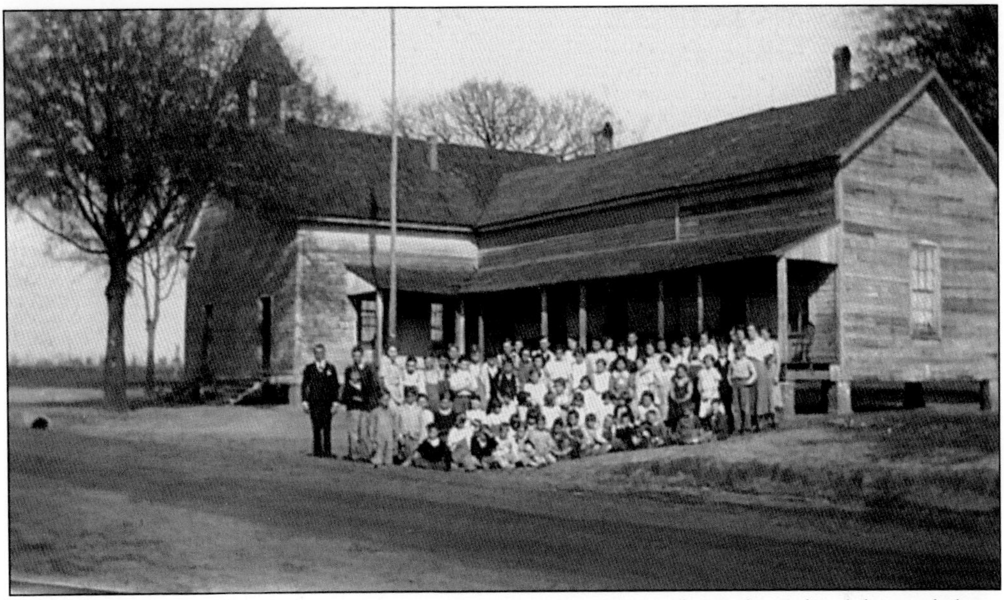

Doles School. Another example of a wooden schoolhouse was the Doles School, located about 12 miles north of Sylvester. In 1934, it had 3 teachers and 91 students.

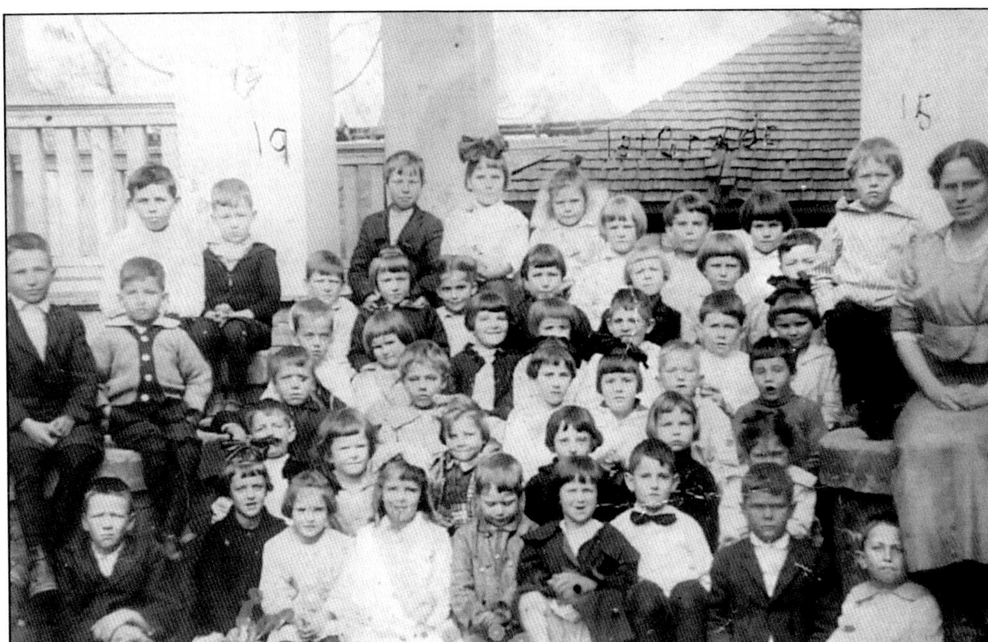

First Grade Warwick School, 1915. This was the previous school built prior to 1923 when the two-story brick building was erected.

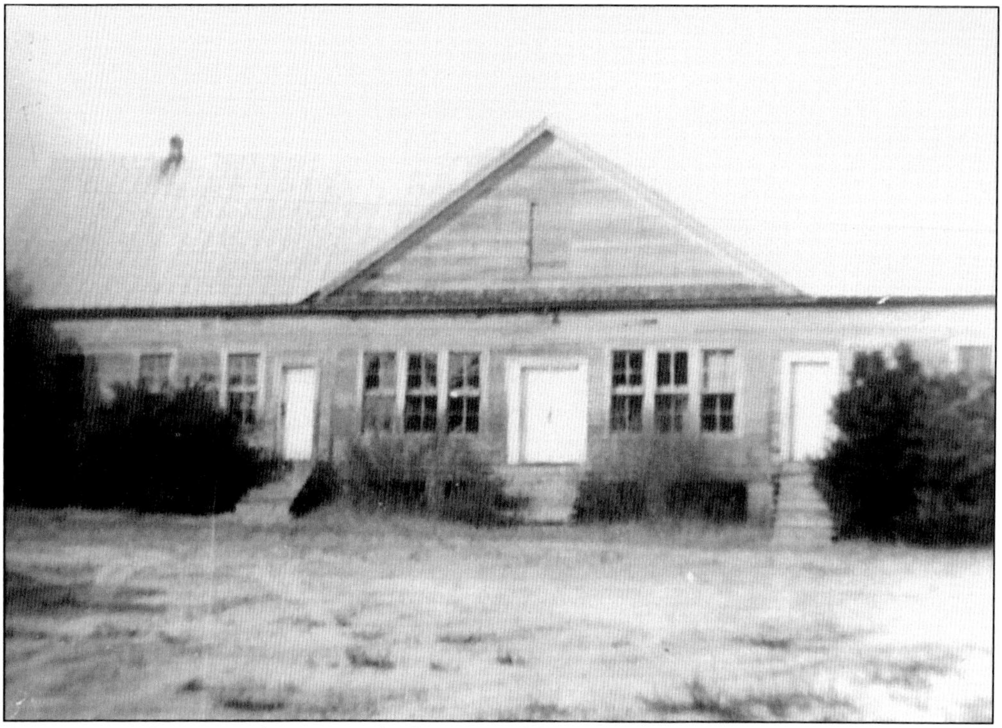

OLD MINTON SCHOOL. This is now the location of the Minton Community Center.

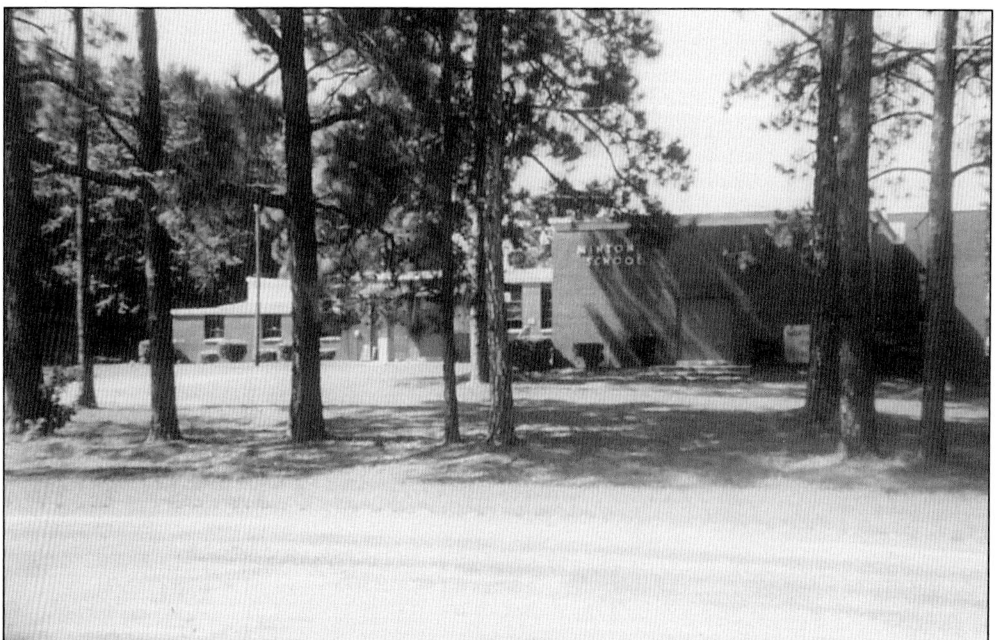

WORTH COUNTY HEAD START, FORMERLY MINTON SCHOOL. This is a community school that found another life after all elementary schools in the county were consolidated.

Five

FARMING

Worth County's sandy loam is excellent for many different crops. Agriculture and its related businesses provide much of the county's income. Peanuts, grains, cotton, corn, tobacco, and melons are the main crops and the county is blessed with large areas of timber better known as the Southern Pines.

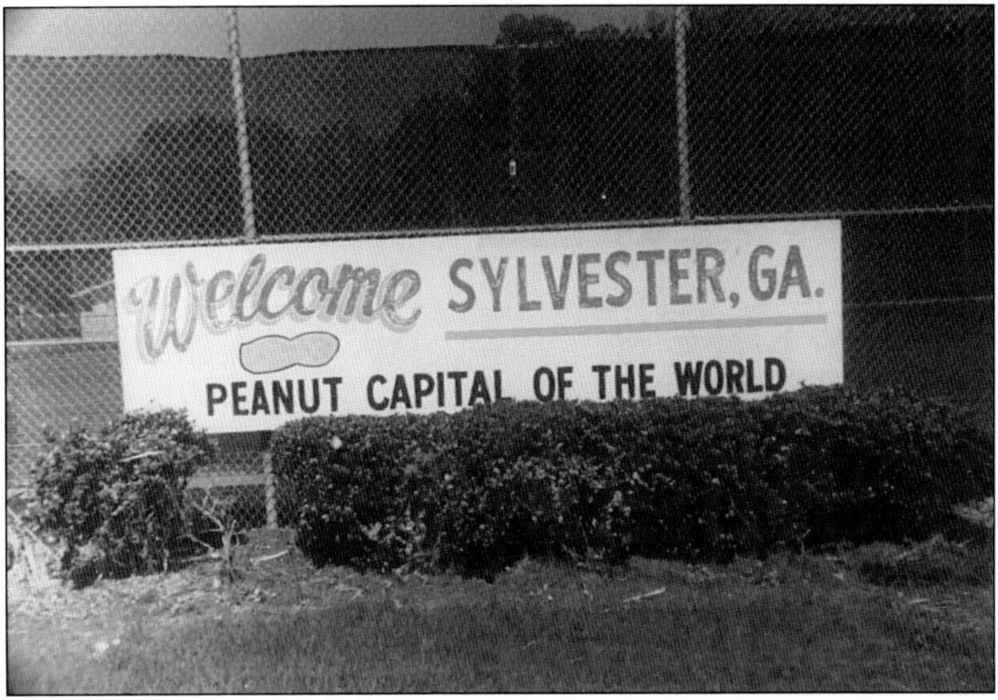

WELCOME SIGN ON U.S. HIGHWAY 82. Sylvester is the peanut capital of the world.

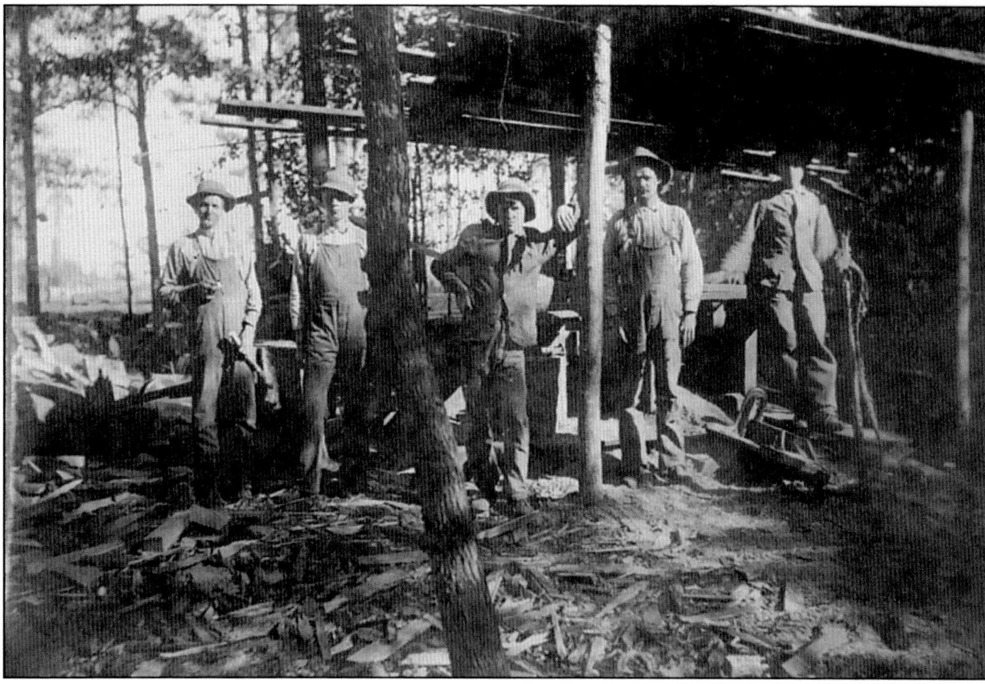

WHIDDON SAWMILL. This was one of the many sawmills in the county.

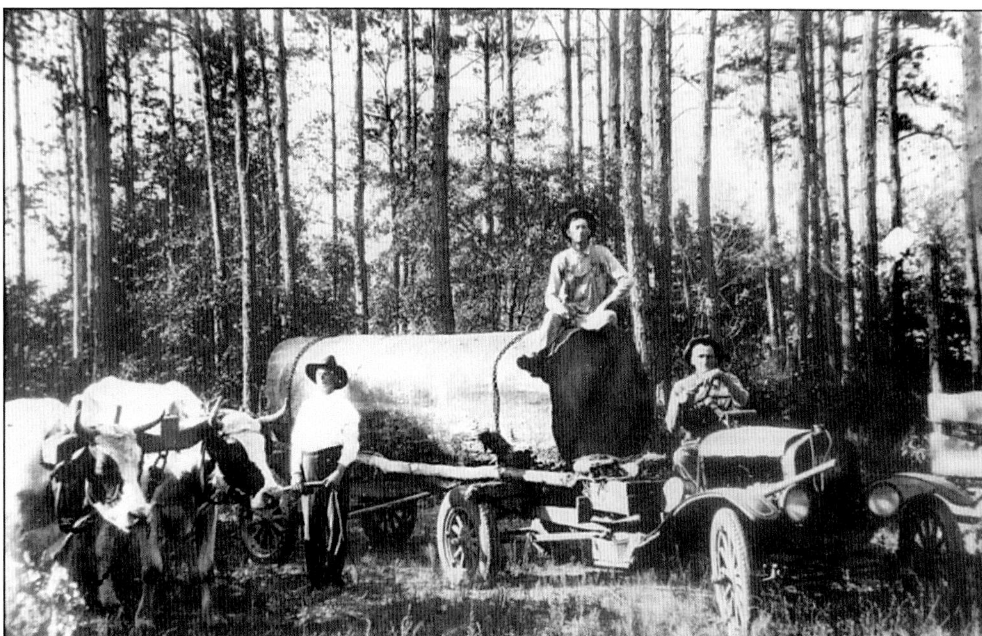

WHIDDON OXEN HAULING LOGS TO SAWMILL. Note the huge log being hauled. Oxen were used to move the logs from the forest to a place where they could be loaded.

1887 TAX RECEIPT. This receipt was issued to Mrs. Henrietta Caroline Methvin for land lot 427 in the 7th District containing 490 acres. The tax for the year 1887 was $2.47.

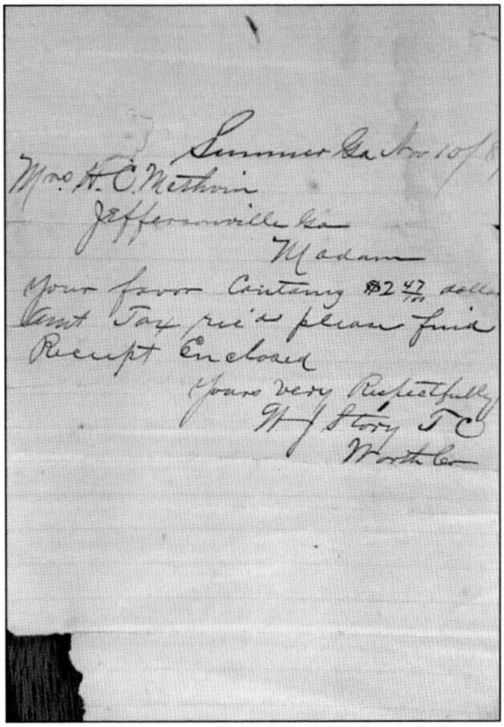

Sumner Ga Nov 10/8

Mrs H. C. Methvin
Jeffersonville Ga

Madam

Your favor Containg $2 47/100 doll[ars]
amt Tax rec'd please find
Receipt Enclosed

Yours very Respectfully
W J Story T C
Worth Co

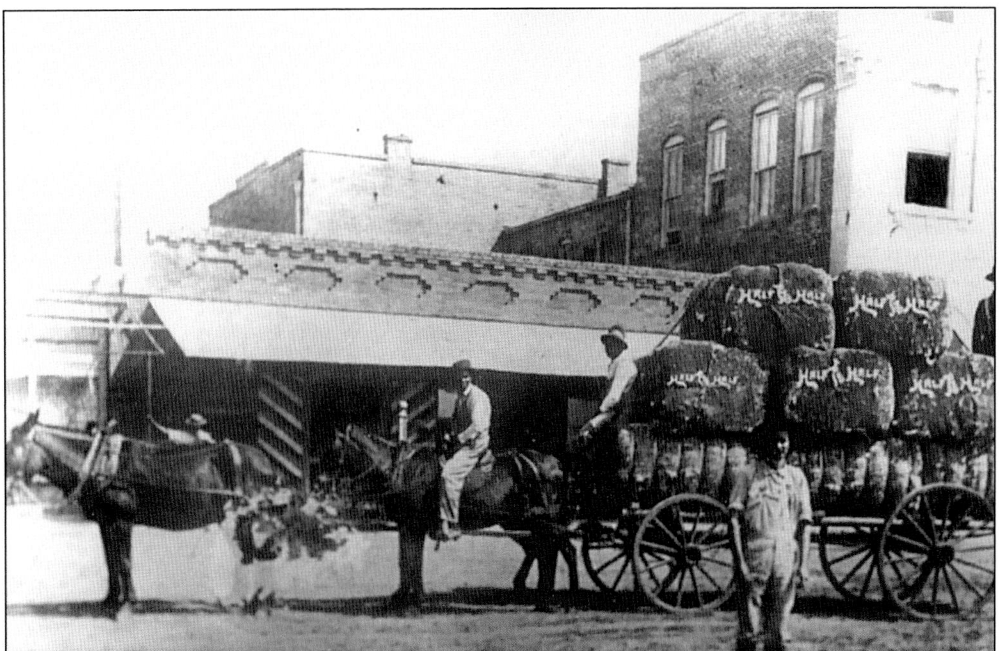

LOAD OF COTTON, c. 1914. Pictured on Front Street is a wagon load of Half & Half cotton. W.C. Cannon is pictured in the center front and on the far right is Otto Shipp; the other men are unidentified. Mr. Cannon was a seed dealer. At one time Sylvester had six cotton gins and at least five cotton warehouses.

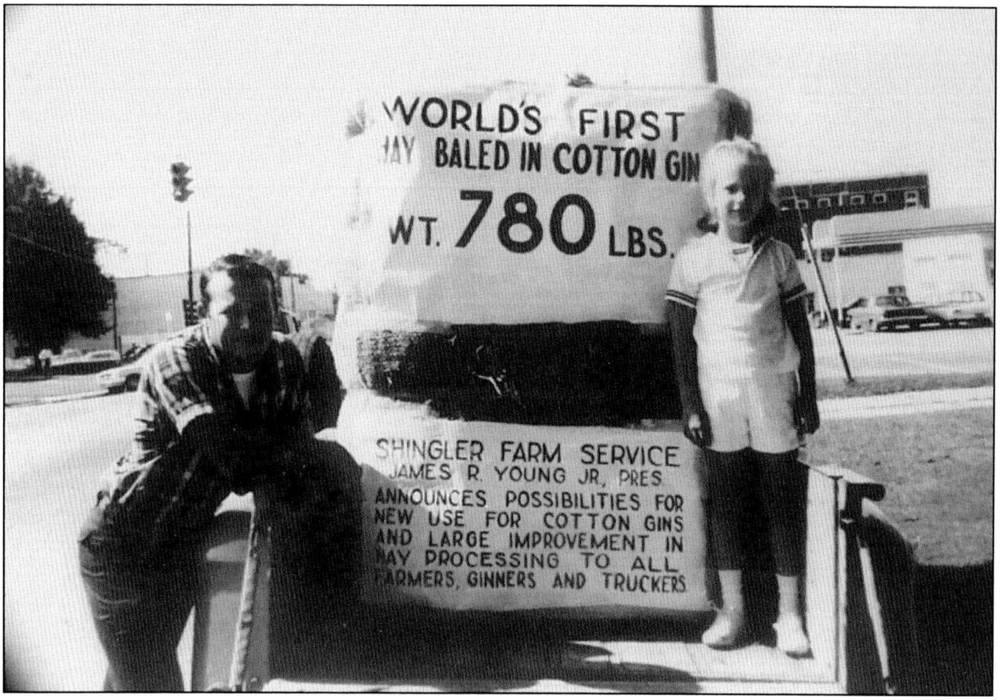

SHINGLER FARM SERVICE, 1965. Pictured is the first hay baled in a cotton gin. In front are James and Marsha Young.

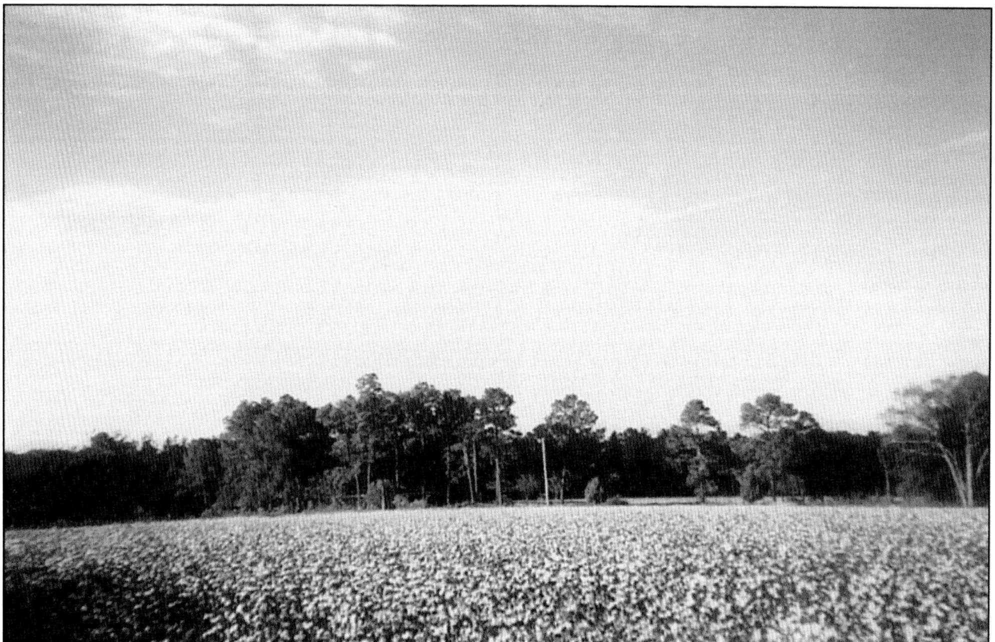

GEORGIA SNOW (COTTON FIELD), 2002. Although it is rarely cold enough for real snow, every year sees fields of white during cotton season.

COTTON PICKING TIME, 2002. This is the modern way to pick cotton.

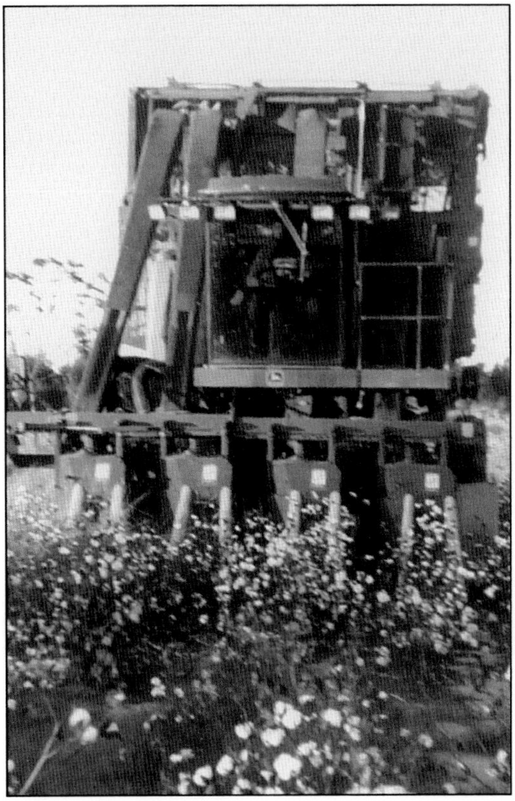

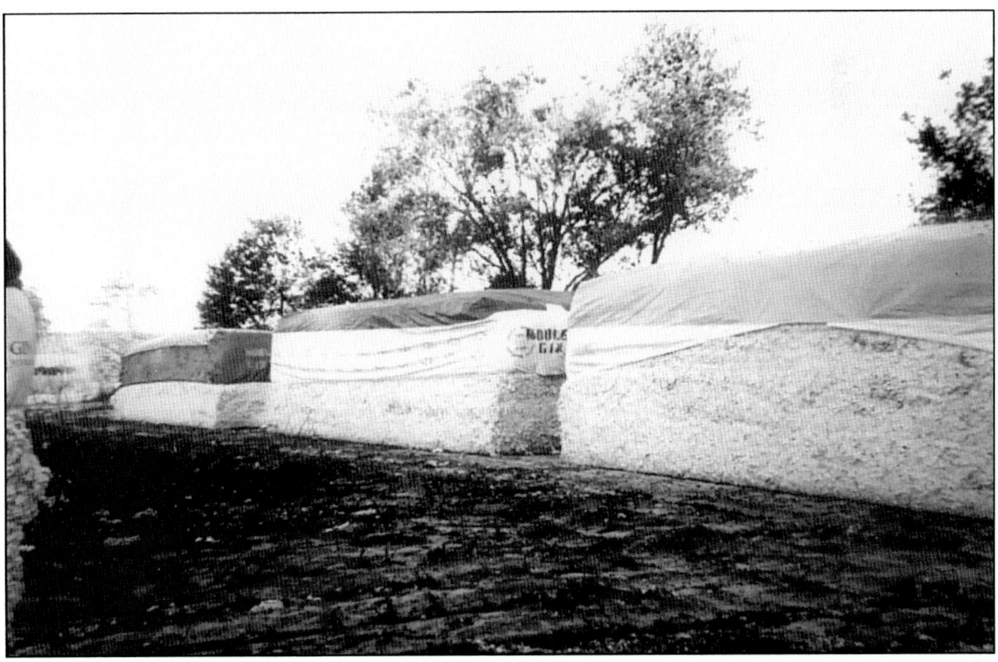

COTTON MODULES, 2002. Each module may contain 12 to 15 bales of cotton when processed.

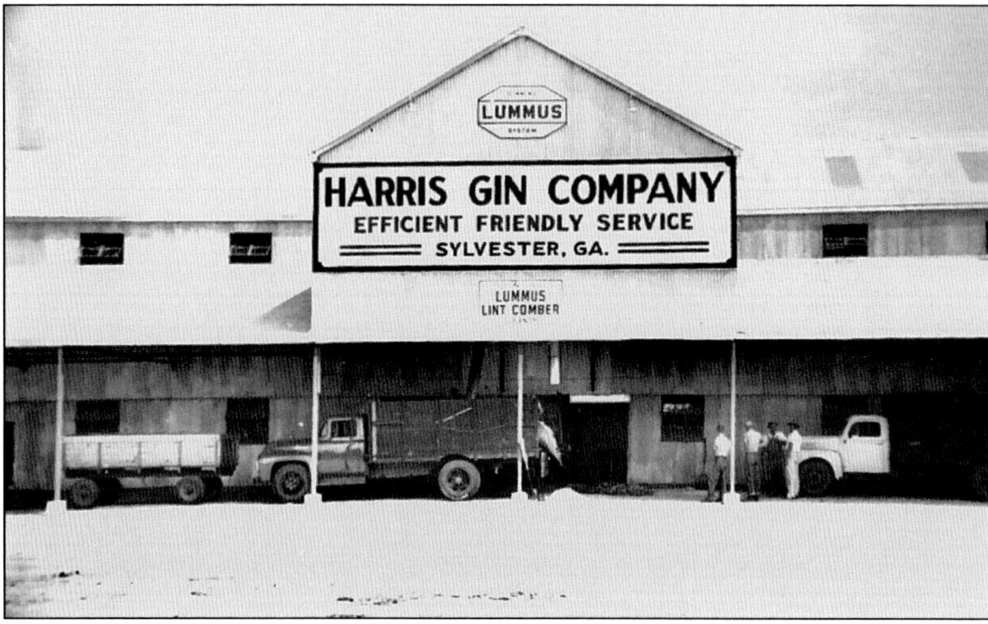

HARRIS GIN COMPANY. Taking cotton to be ginned is the final step in growing cotton. The seeds are separated from the lint and the lint is packed into bales.

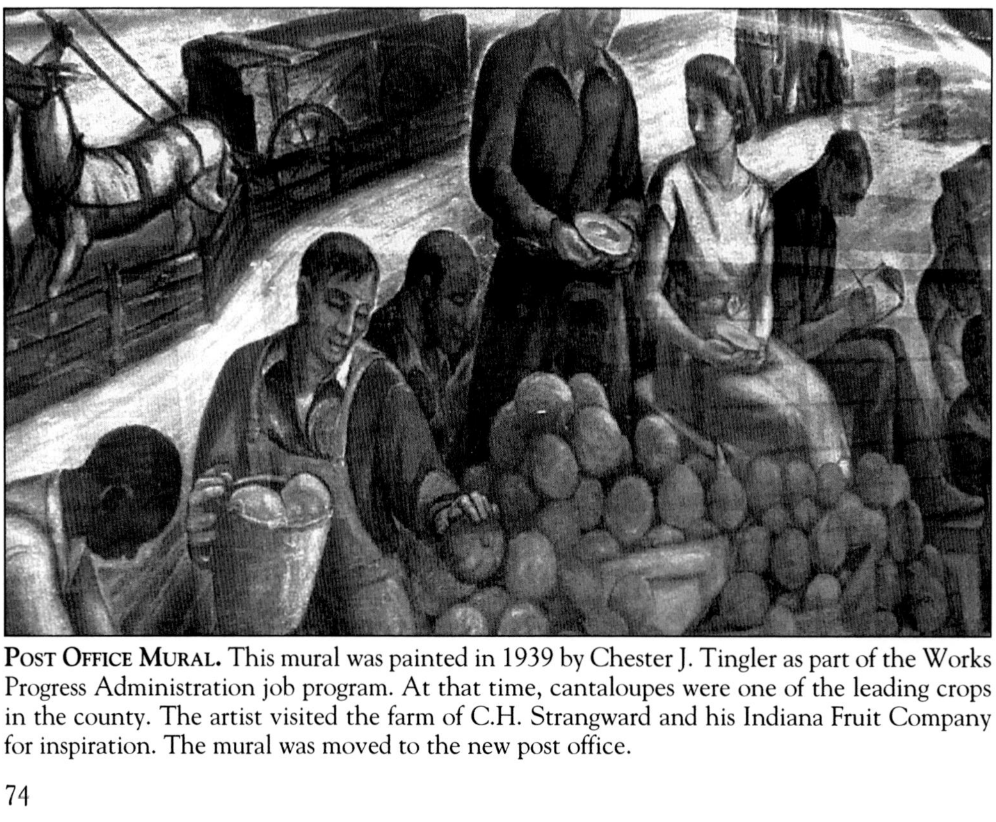

POST OFFICE MURAL. This mural was painted in 1939 by Chester J. Tingler as part of the Works Progress Administration job program. At that time, cantaloupes were one of the leading crops in the county. The artist visited the farm of C.H. Strangward and his Indiana Fruit Company for inspiration. The mural was moved to the new post office.

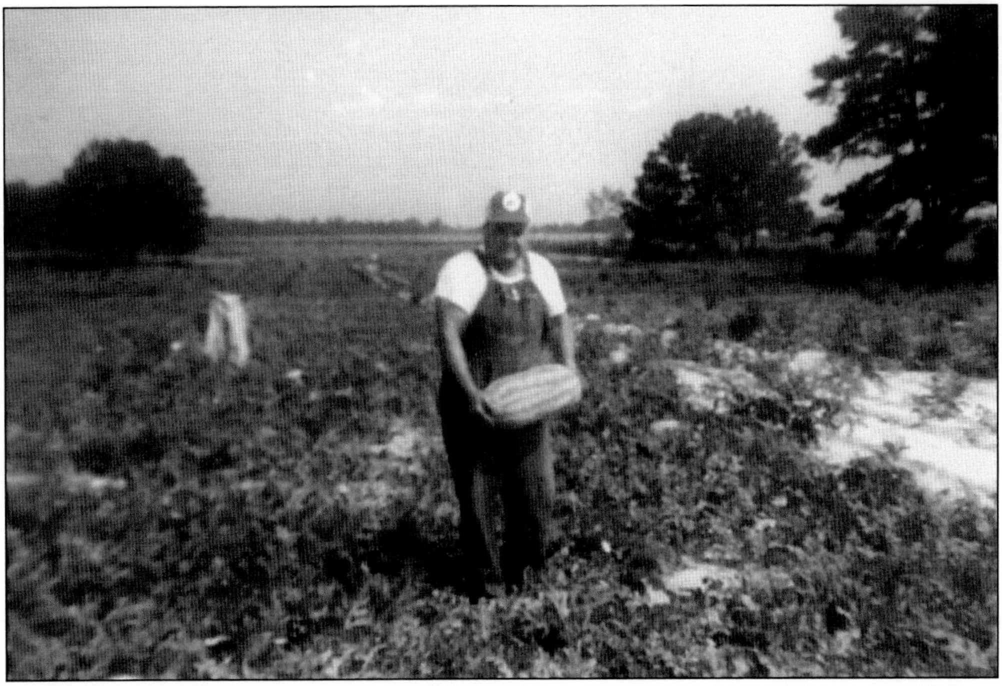

Herman Gill in Watermelon Patch. Watermelons are harvested in mid-June to mid-July.

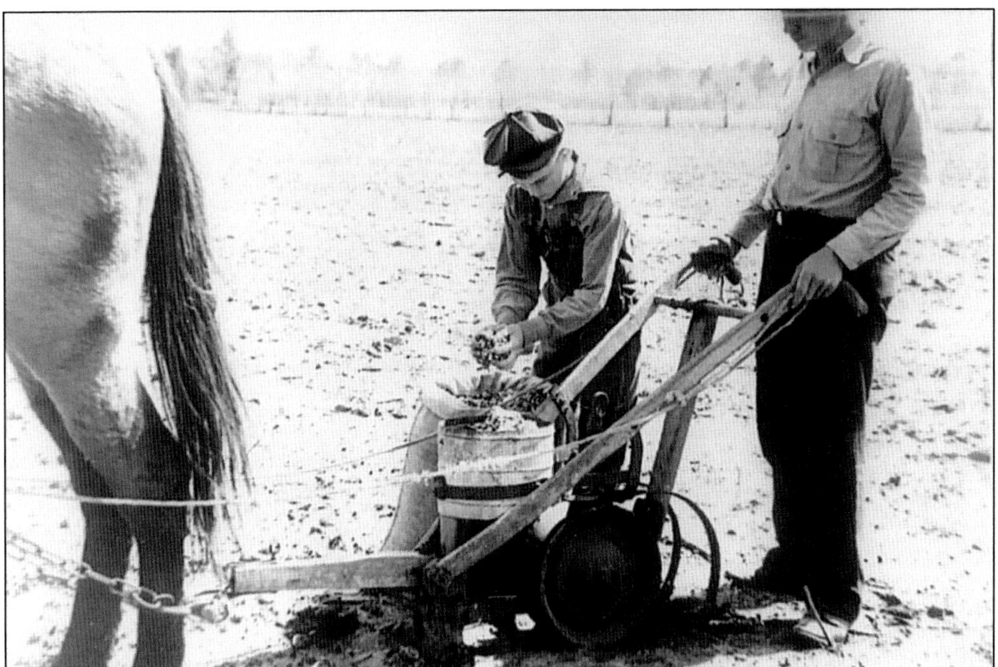

Planting Peanuts the Old Fashioned Way. Peanut seed is placed in the hopper of the mule-drawn planter.

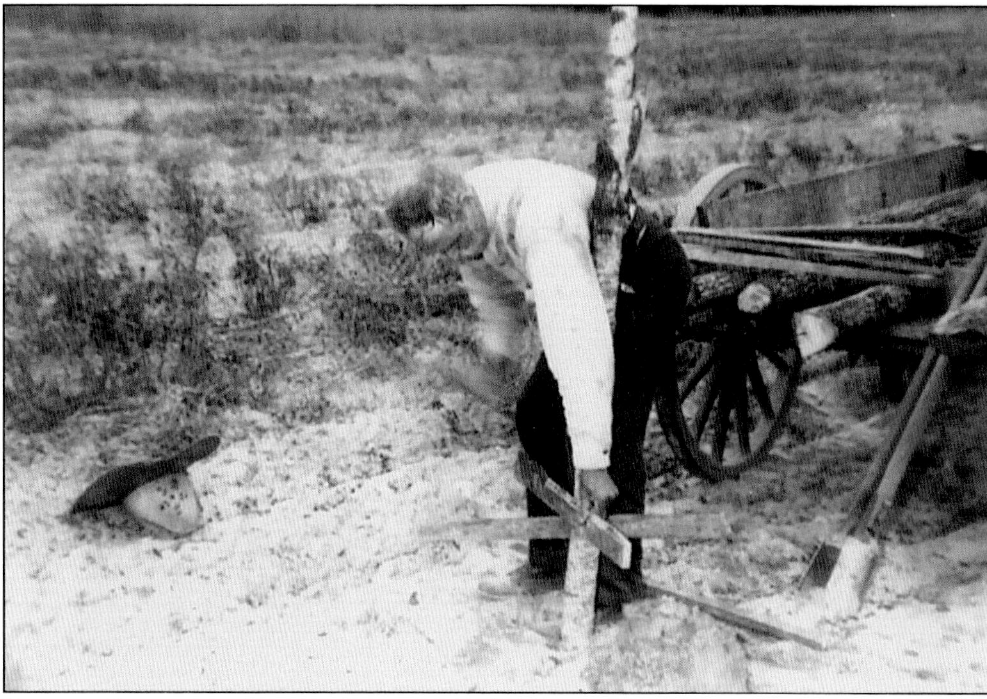

Putting Cleats on a Peanut Stack Pole. Cleats were put on the pole to keep the peanuts off the ground while they air-dried.

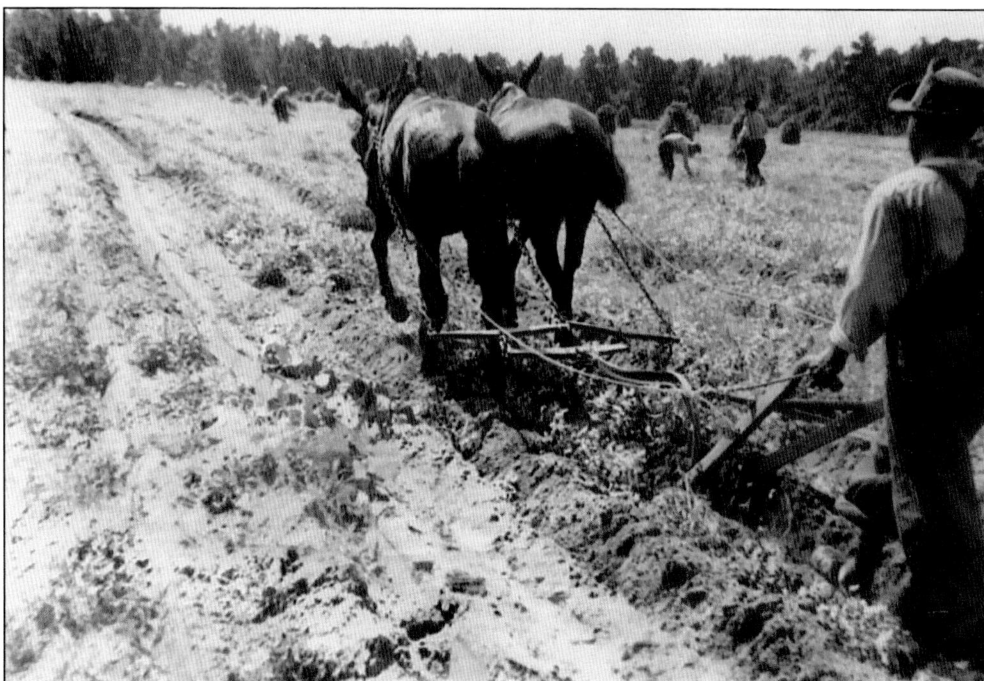

Plowing Up Peanuts that are Ready to Harvest. A mule-drawn plow puts the peanuts in rows.

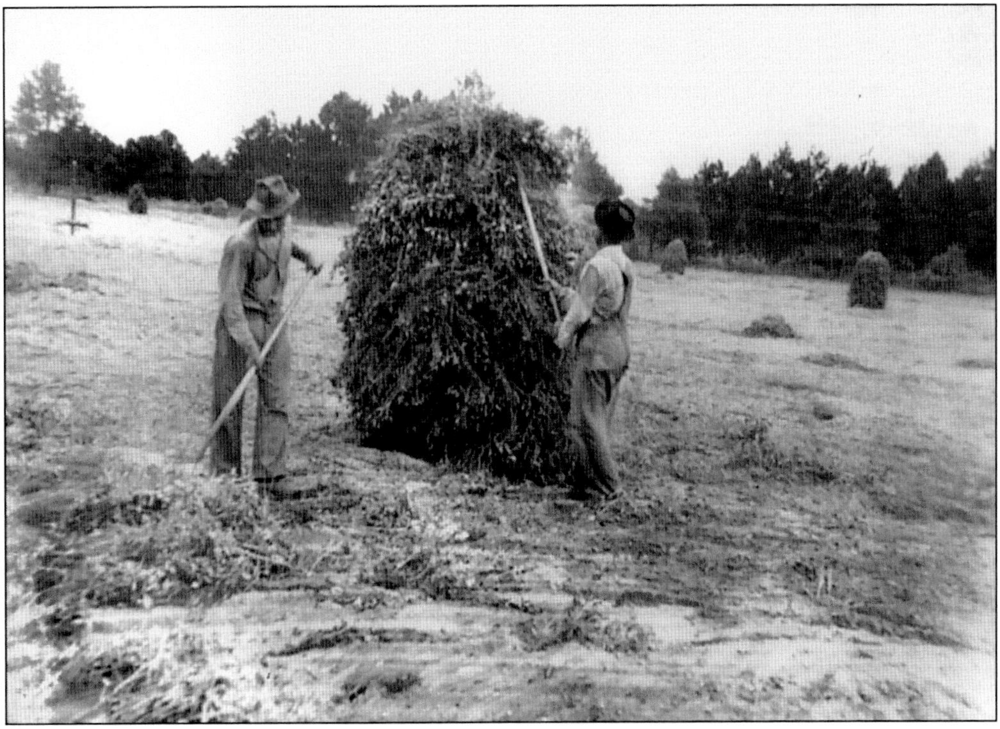

STACKING PEANUTS BY HAND. Plowed peanuts are gathered and stacked on poles to dry.

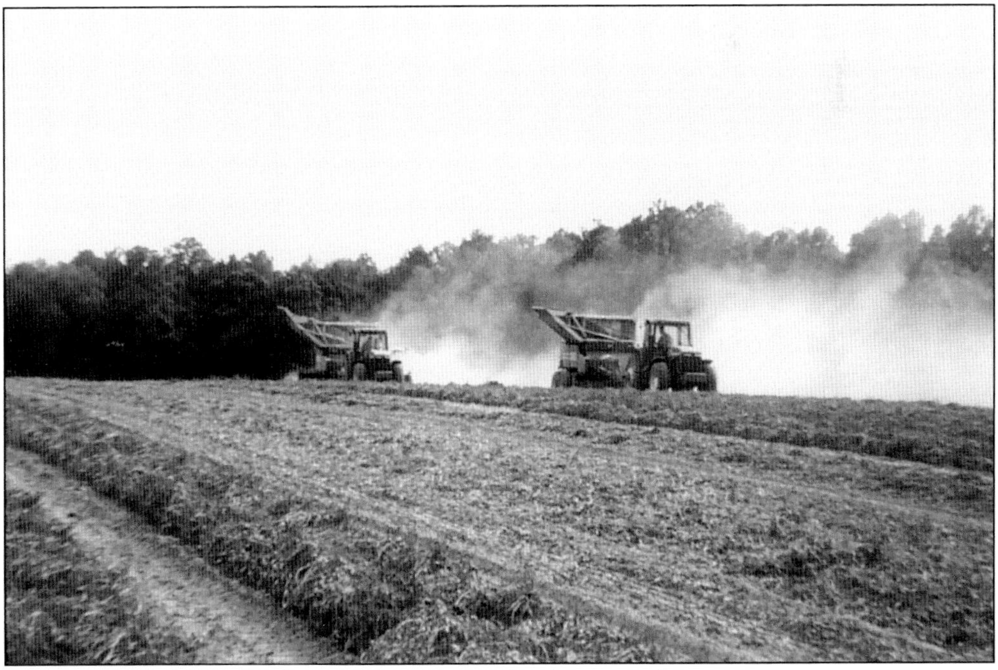

COMBINING PEANUTS. Modern machinery is used today to combine peanuts.

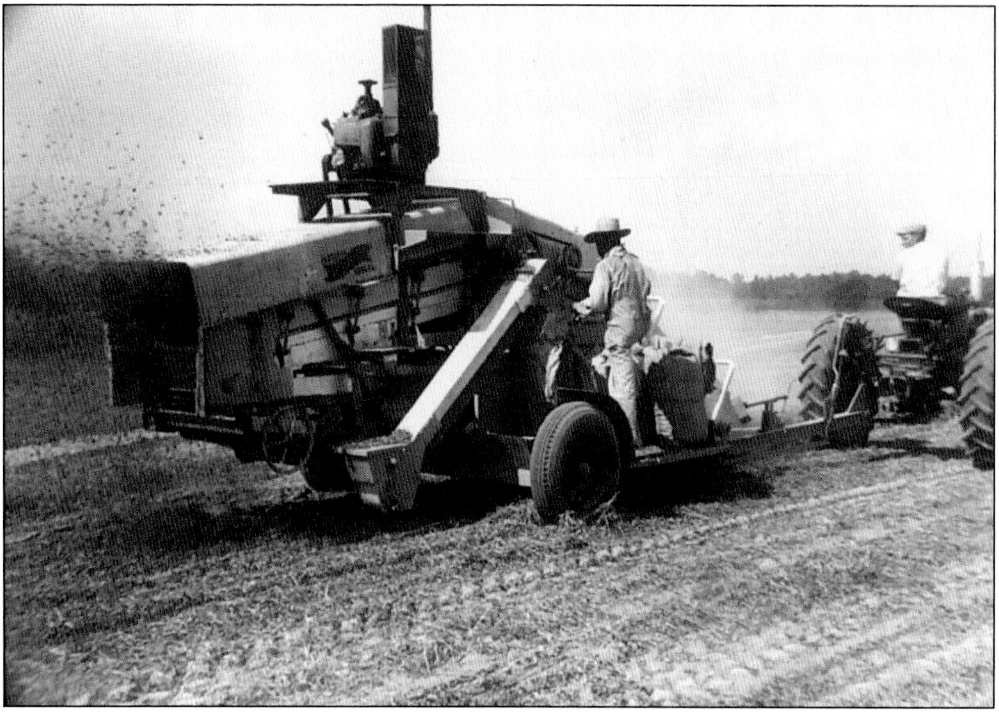

THRESHING PEANUTS. Threshers separate the peanuts from the vines.

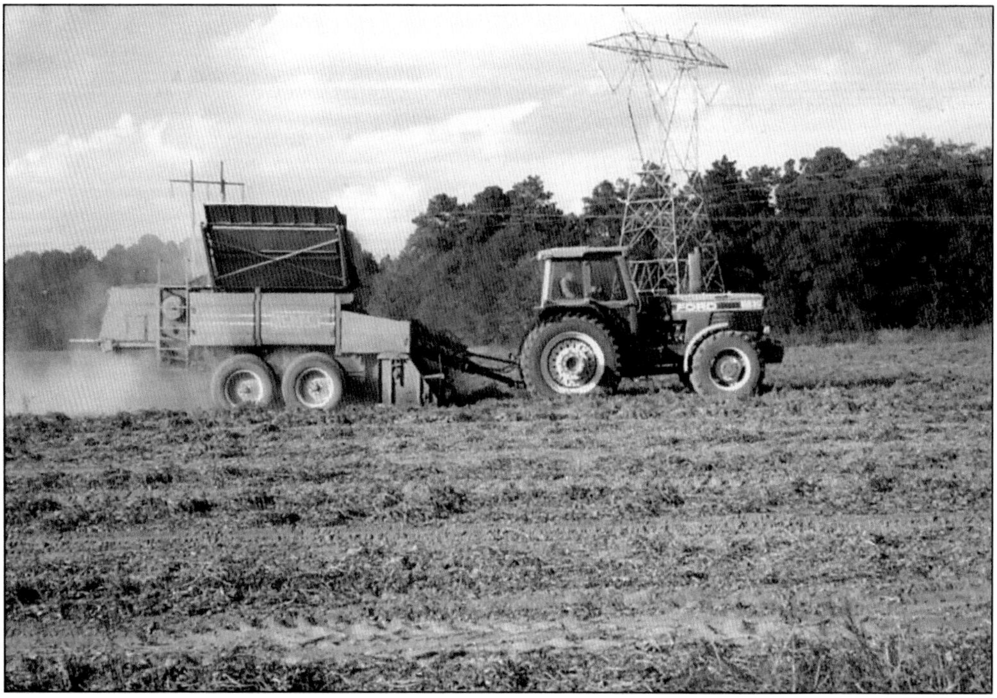

PEANUT HARVEST, 1998. This is a more modern harvesting machine than the one above.

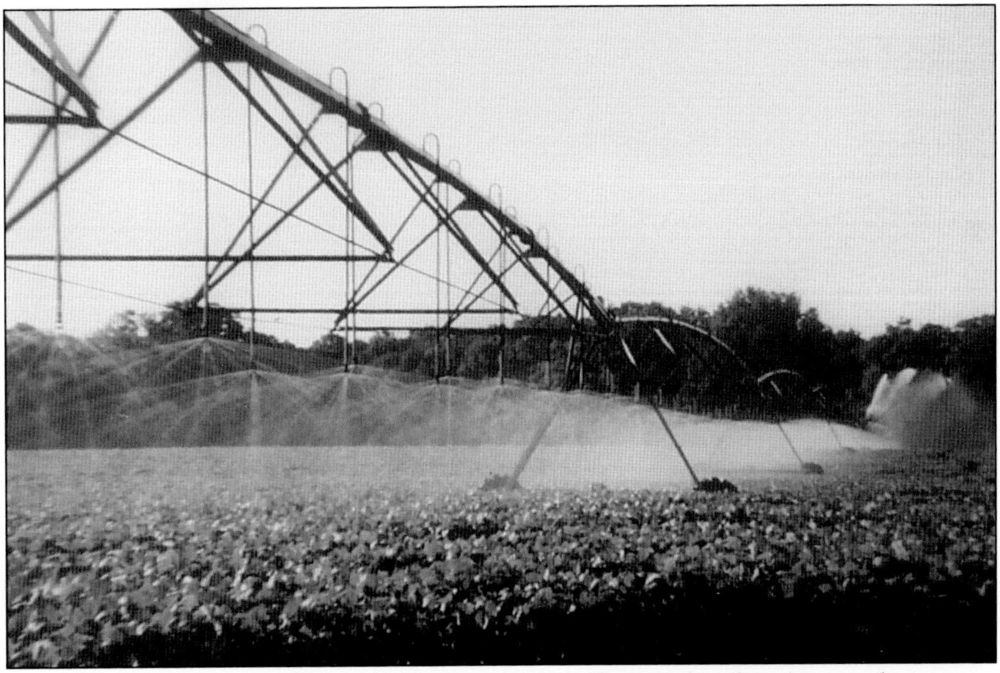

IRRIGATING SOYBEANS. Modern irrigation equipment is illustrated in this photograph.

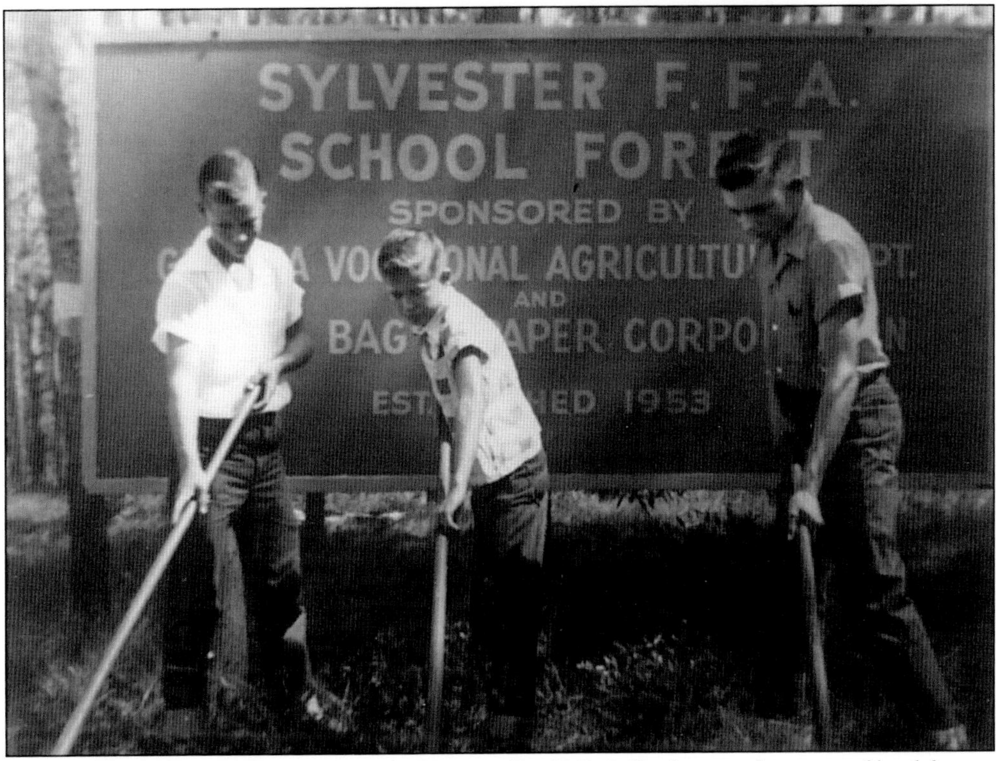

FUTURE FARMERS OF AMERICA SCHOOL FOREST. Dr. T.C. Jeffords gave this tract of land for use by the Future Farmers of America.

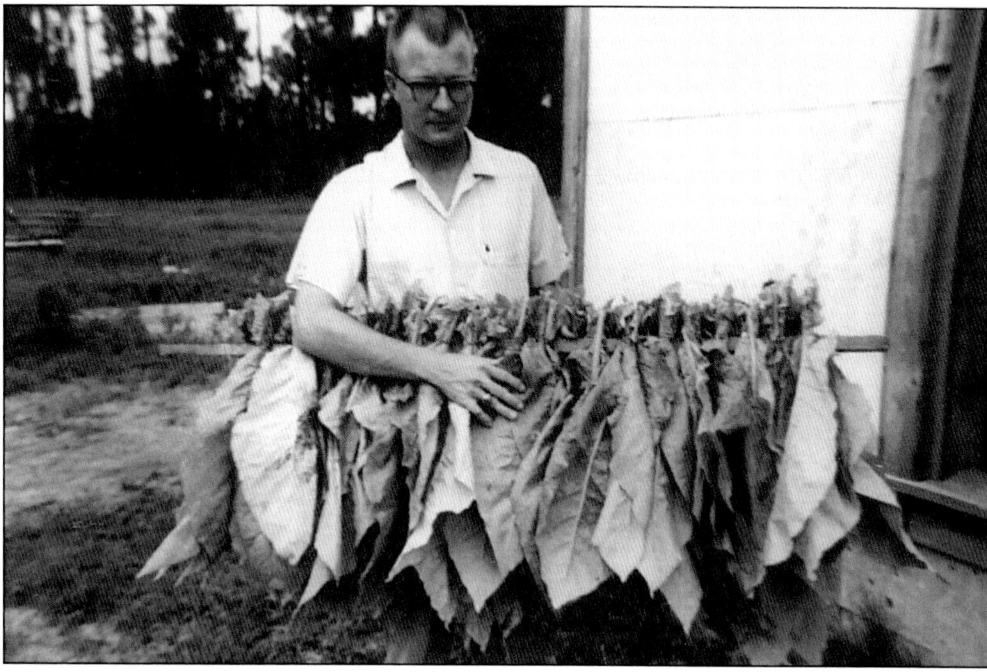

JOEL GUNNELS, COUNTY AGENT, EXAMINING TOBACCO. Gunnels was county agent from 1960 to 1965.

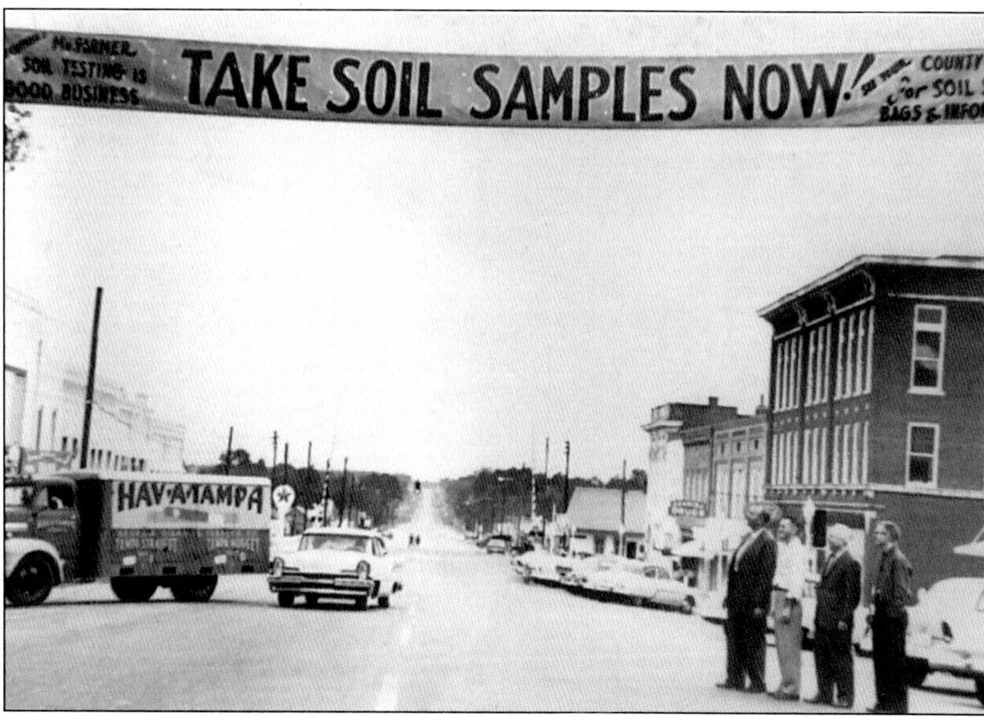

TAKE SOIL SAMPLES NOW! This was good advice then and now also.

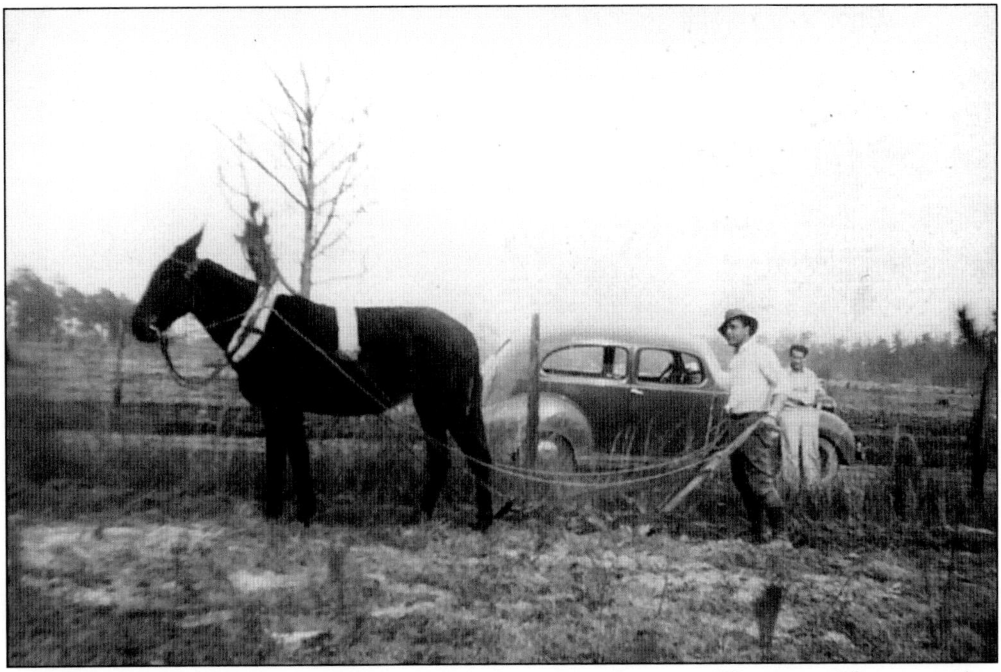

Plowing the Old-Fashioned Way at the Champion Farm at Warwick. This is another example of the "hay burning" engine.

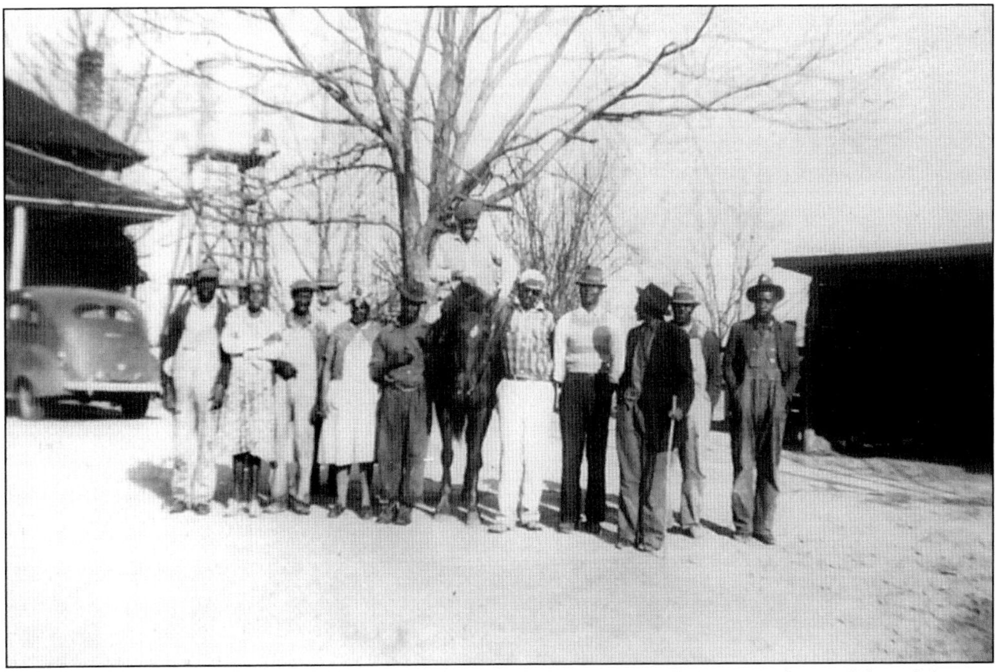

J.C. Champion's Farm Hands. In earlier times, farming required many mules and farm laborers to plant and harvest crops.

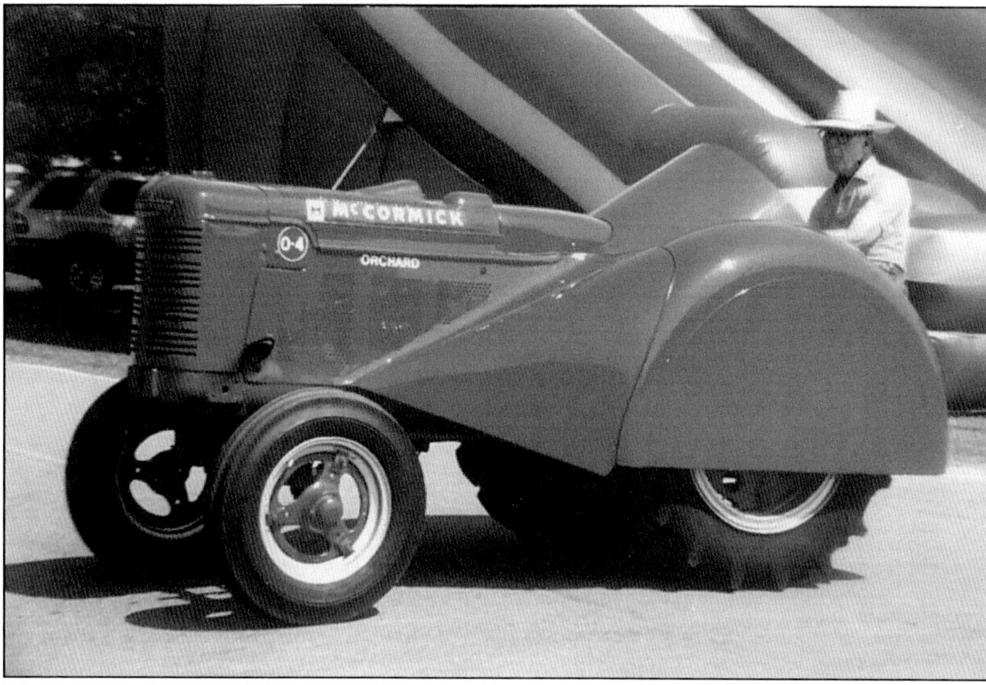

McCormick Orchard Tractor. This specially adapted tractor is used in orchards.

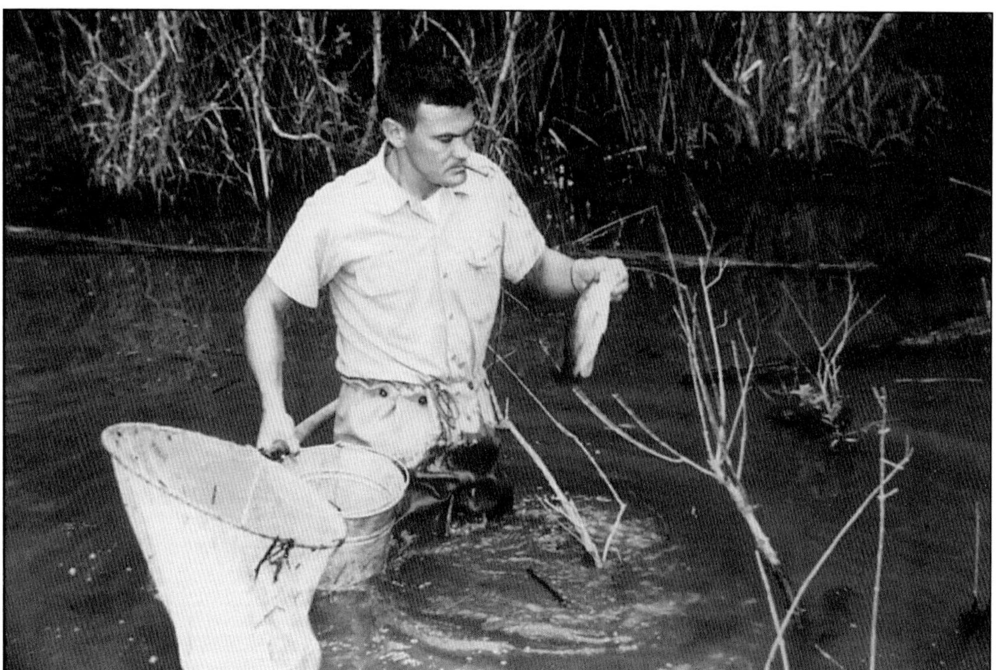

Biologist Checking Fish At Lake Blackshear. Lake Blackshear was created with backwater by damming the Flint River.

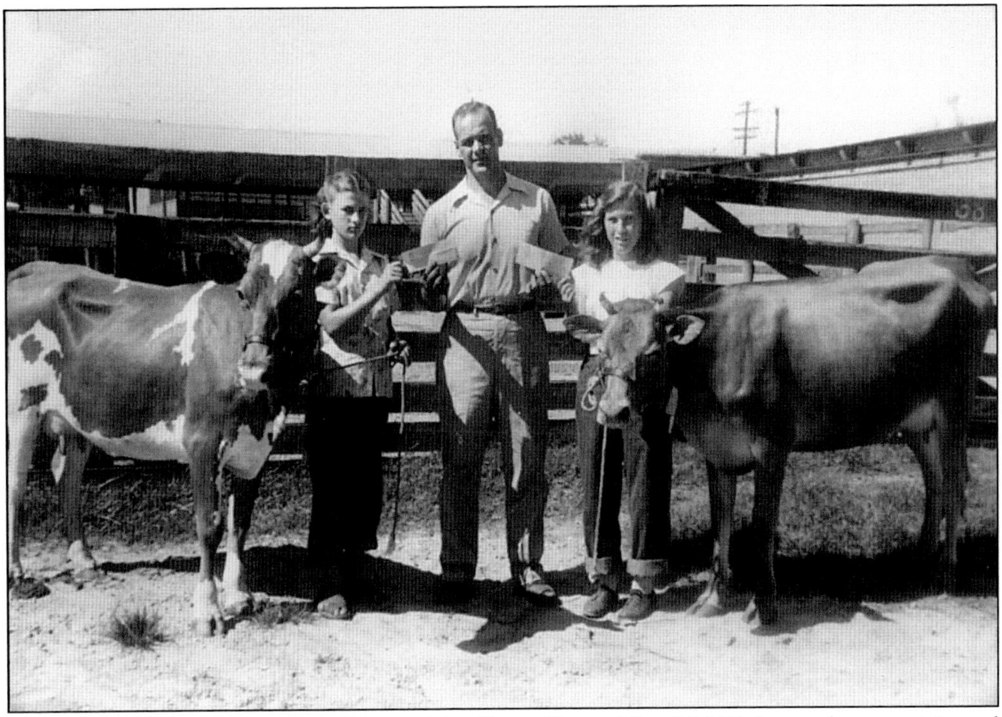

HARMON JEFFORDS PRESENTING CHECKS FOR PRIZE COWS. The 4-H Club members participated in various animal husbandry activities.

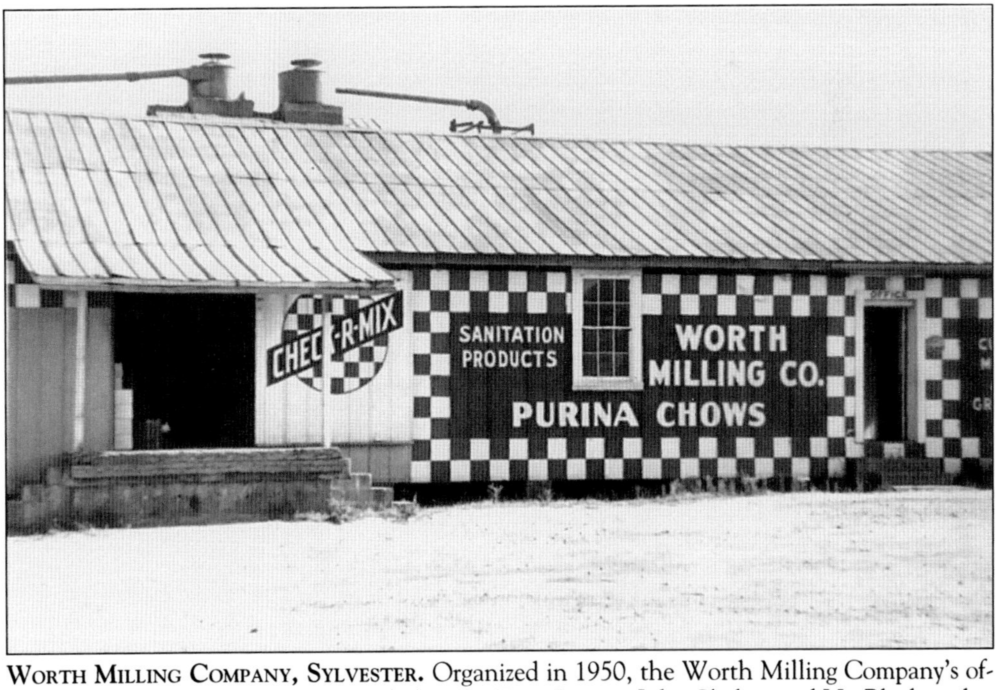

WORTH MILLING COMPANY, SYLVESTER. Organized in 1950, the Worth Milling Company's officers were Harmon Jeffords, James Sledge, Dr. Tom Sutton, John Sledge, and J.L. Blackstock.

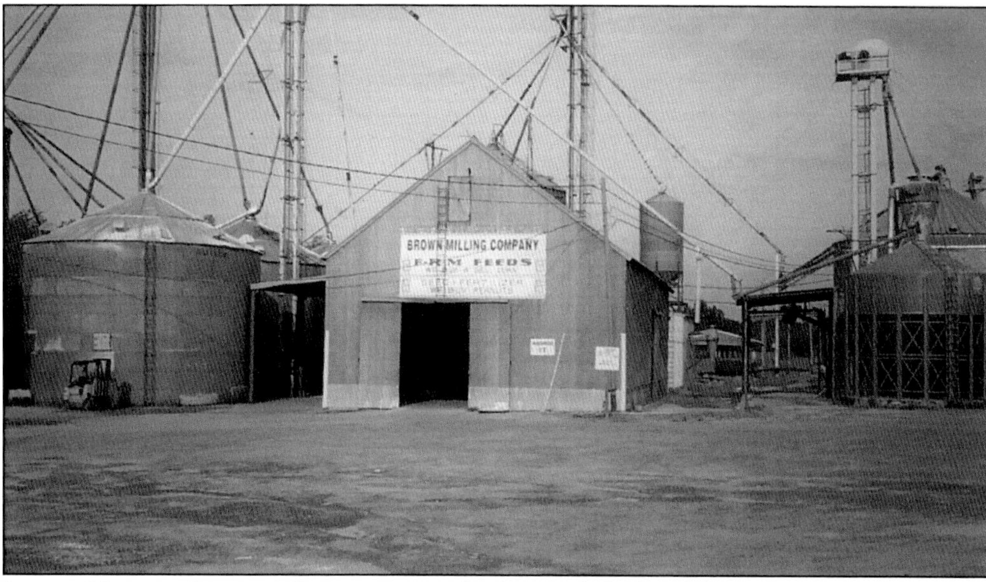

BROWN MILLING COMPANY, BRIDGEBORO. This livestock feed and farm supply business was organized in 1963 with F.D., F.A., and J.M. Brown as officers.

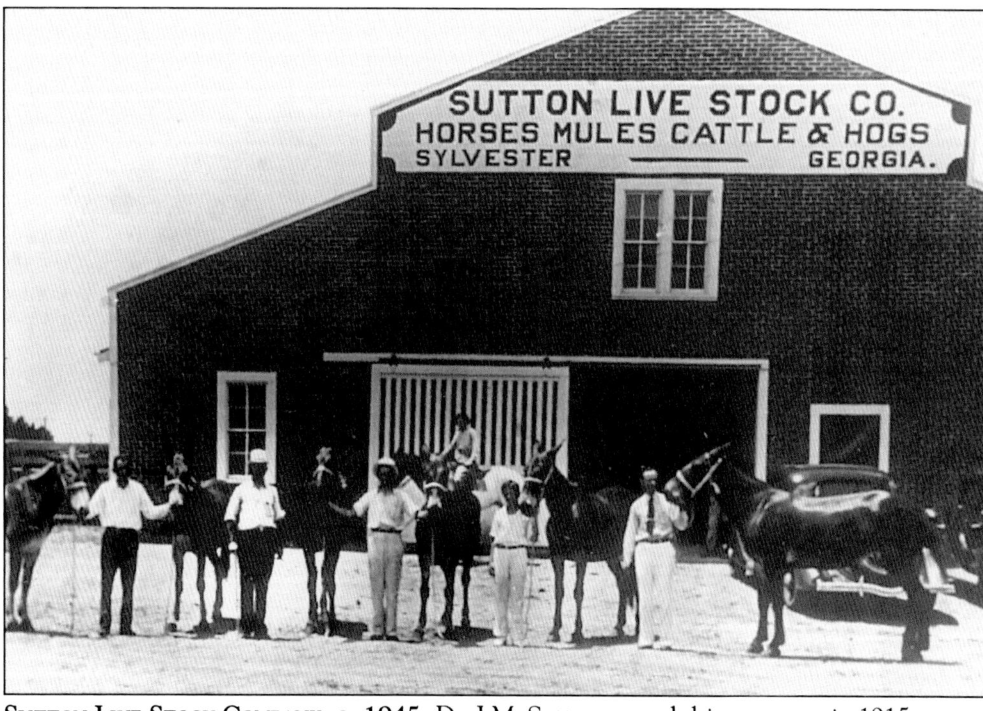

SUTTON LIVE STOCK COMPANY, C. 1945. Dr. J.M. Sutton started this company in 1915.

Six

PEOPLE

The backbone of any county is its citizens. It took sturdy pioneer stock to make a home and earn a living in those early days. Life was hard. This is reflected in some of the photographs in this chapter. As conveniences made life easier, it is reflected in the faces and dress of the adults and children.

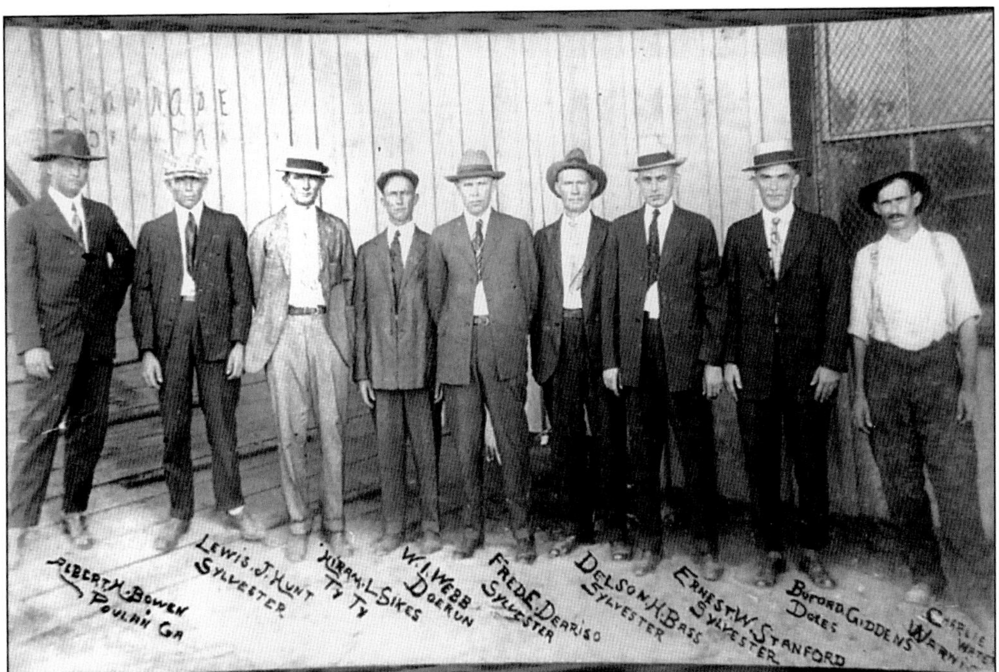

YOUNG MEN LEAVING FOR WORLD WAR I. This photograph shows a group of young men from around the county as they prepare to leave for World War I. They were the first group to go.

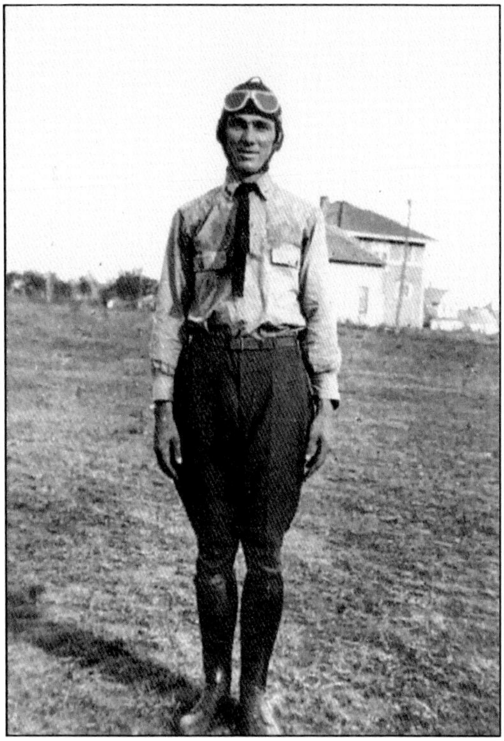

John Grover Hillhouse (1888–1918), in World War I Uniform. John Hillhouse died as a result of injuries from an aviation accident.

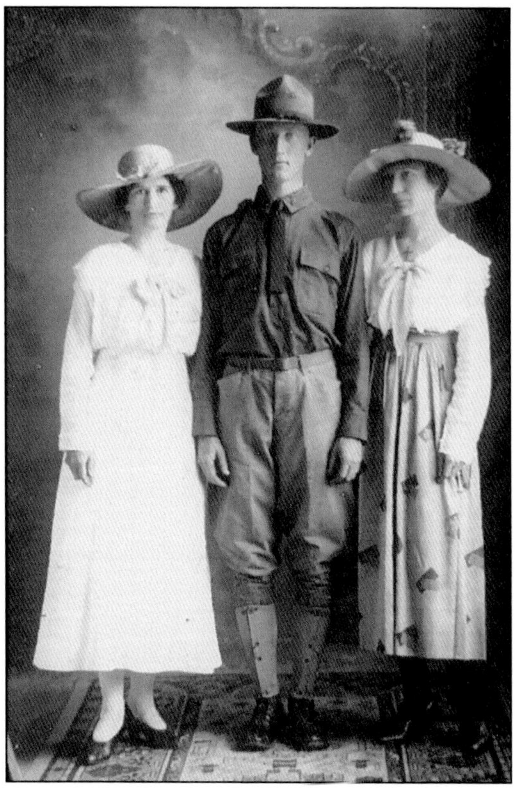

Lundy Family, c. 1918. Members of the family, pictured from left to right, are Mary Elizabeth Lundy Fleming, Basil Lundy, and Nettie Lundy Bullard.

BENNIE C. MOREE, BENDORFF, GERMANY, 1919. Bennie is shown overseas in his military uniform.

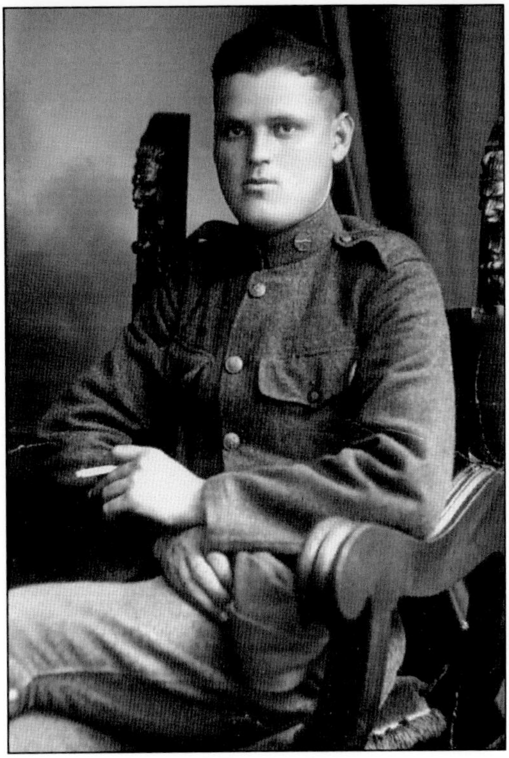

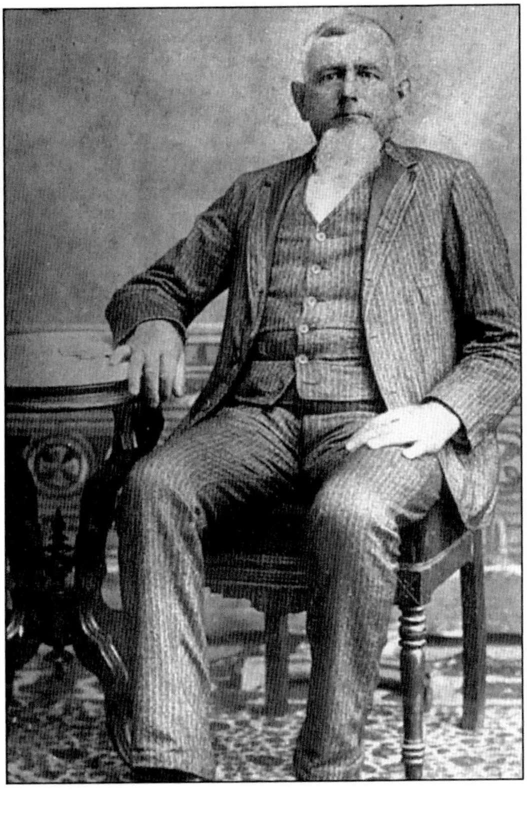

THOMAS JEFFERSON HARRIS (SEPTEMBER 30, 1830–DECEMBER 28, 1899). A pioneer citizen of Worth County, Thomas Harris is buried in the old Smoak Cemetery just over the line in Crisp County.

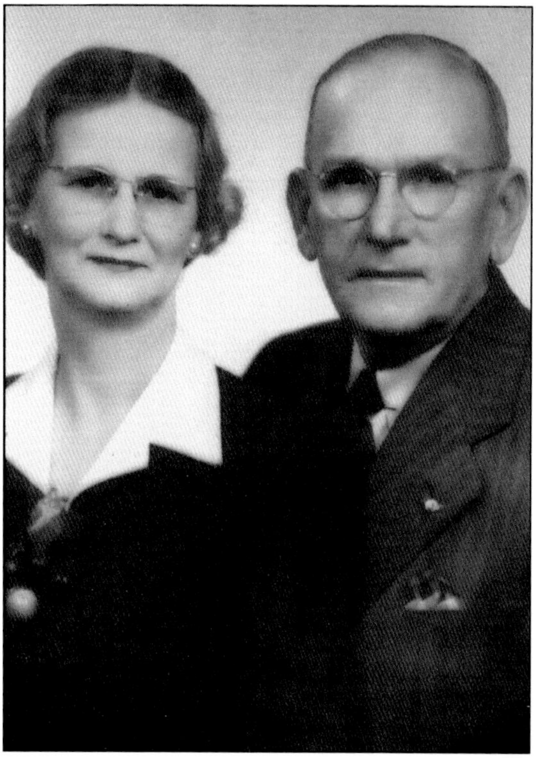

Dr. and Mrs. Gordon S. Sumner. Dr. Sumner (1883–1953) was the son of Joseph L. and Sarah Josephine Thornhill Sumner. Mrs. Sumner (1892–1967) was the former Mattie Lou Chapman.

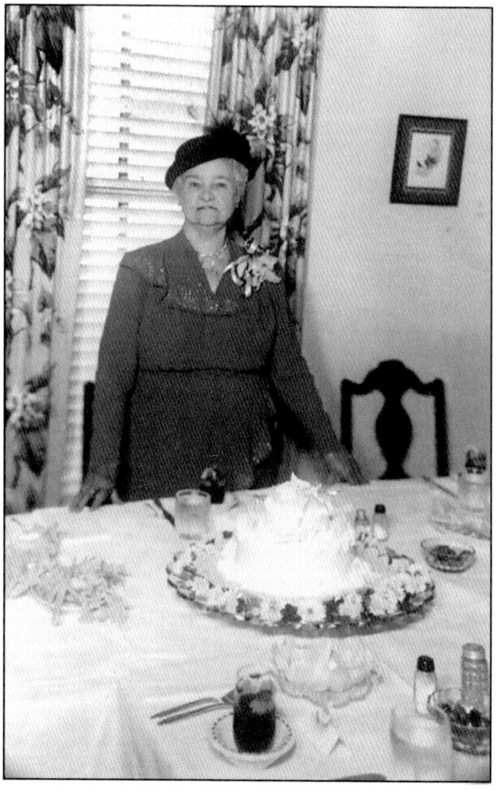

Lillie Martin Grubbs. Mrs. Grubbs was the wife of Clifford Grubbs, newspaper editor and owner, and she was author of *The History of Worth County, Georgia, 1854–1934*.

ROSALIE MANGHAM TIPTON (1885–1973). She is shown with her home canned blueberries.

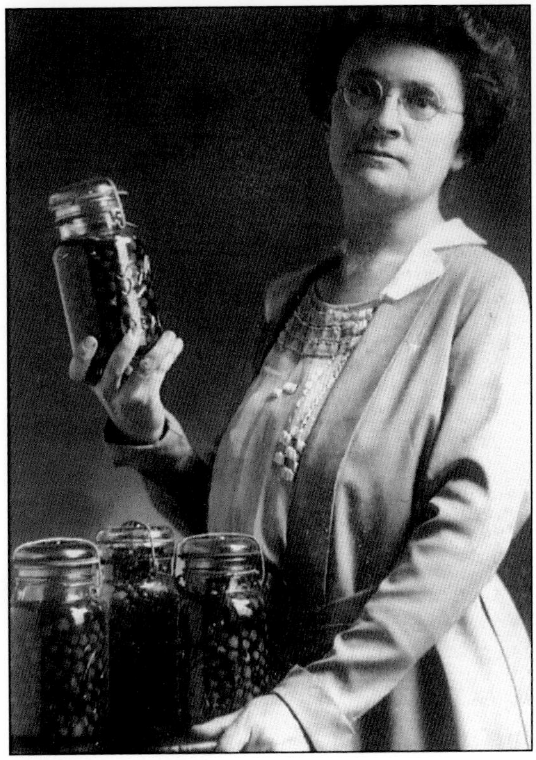

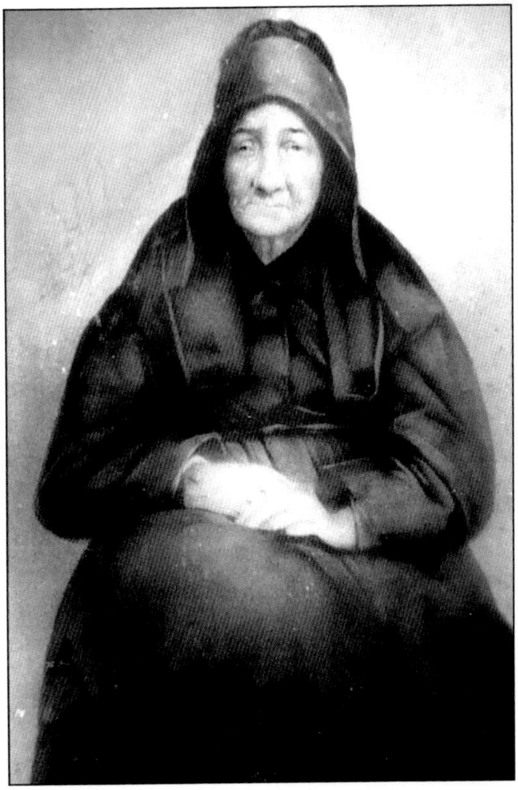

MAHALA SMITH SUMNER (1799–1882). She immigrated to this area from Emanuel County (*c.* 1830) with her husband, Joseph Sumner. White's *History of Georgia* lists this family as one of the earliest of Irwin County from which Worth County was carved.

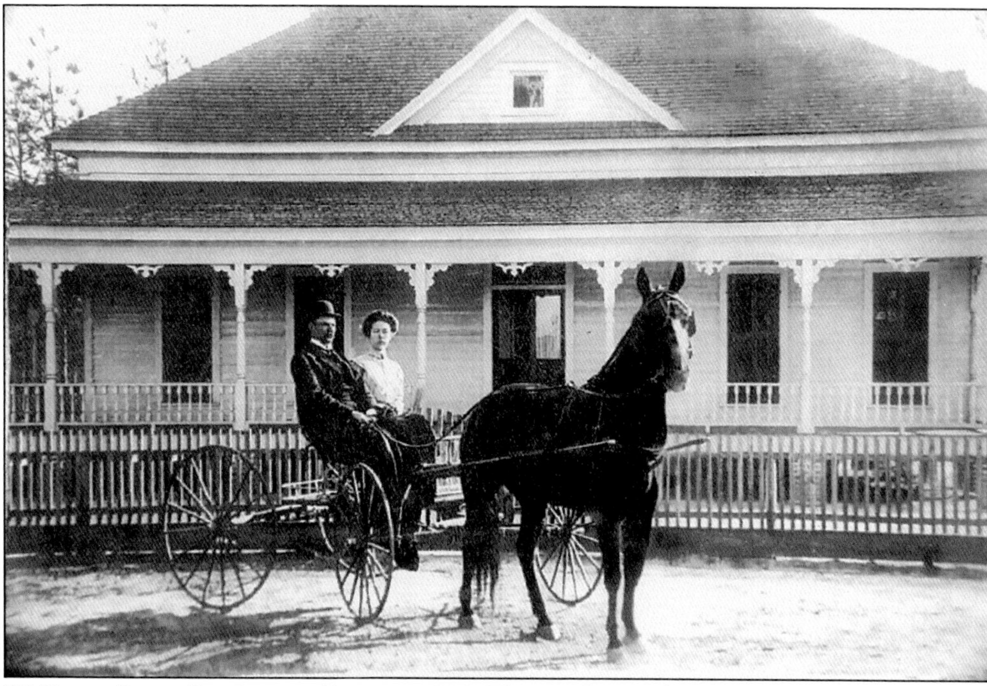

W.G. and Berta Lee Jenkins Ford, c. 1909. The couple is in front of their home at 906 North Isabella Street, which was a wedding gift from G.G. Ford.

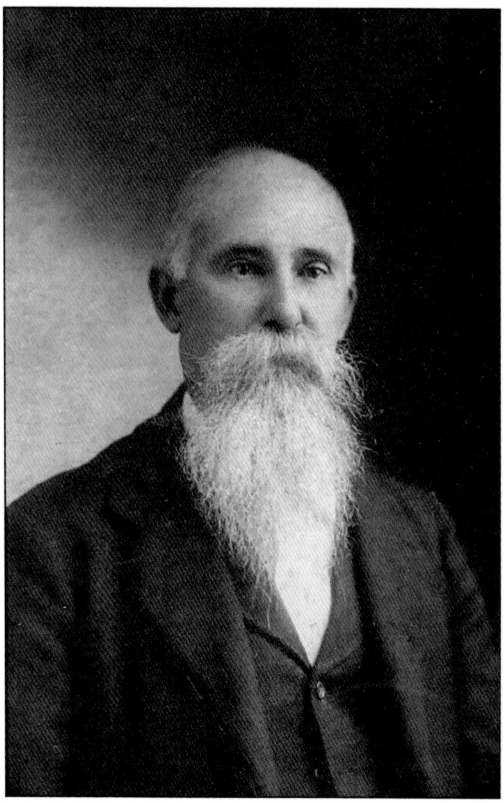

Gary Green Ford II (January 14, 1843–August 5, 1916). G.G. Ford was a Confederate States of America veteran, farmer, state senator, and president of Sylvester Banking Company.

JOE (1850–1931) AND EVA LILLA MOREE (1859–1950) SHIVER. The Shivers were residents of the Red Rock community.

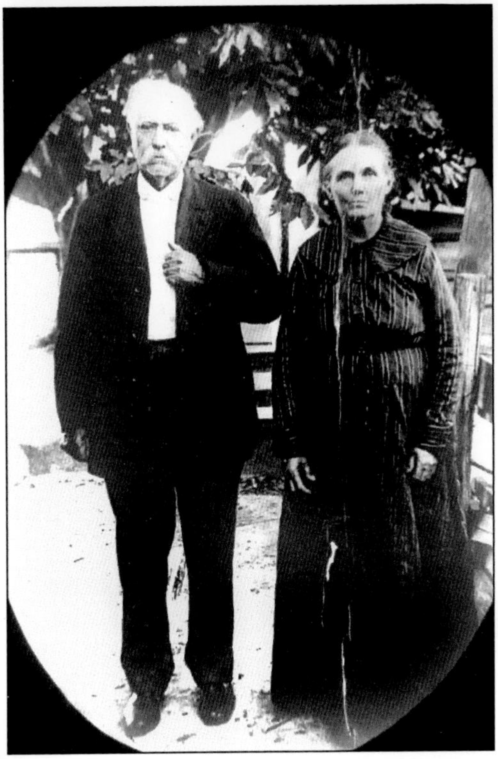

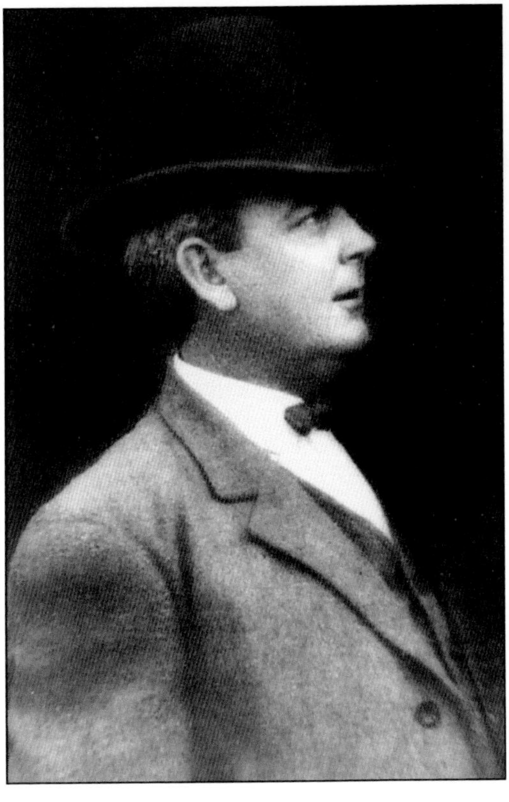

HENRY HAMPTON ROUSE (1875–1928), MERCHANT AND FARMER. He was the son of Capt. James Monroe Rouse (1830–1892), who had 14 children by three wives.

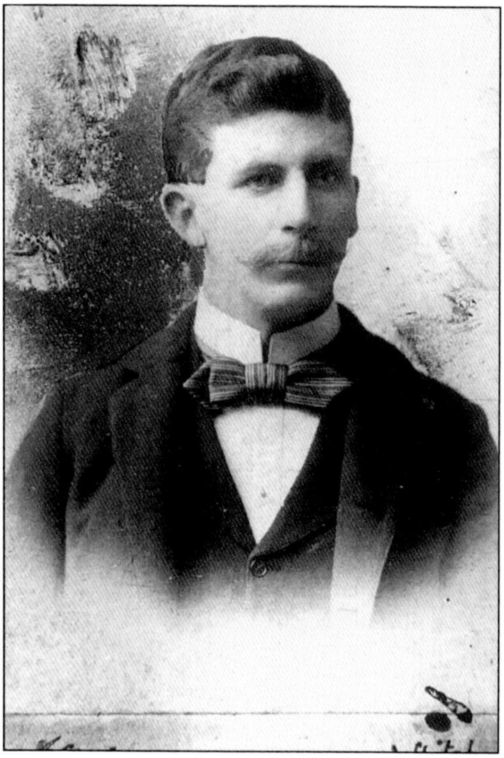

JOHN MILTON BULLARD (1868–1936), BUILDER AND BUSINESSMAN. Among the many building projects John Bullard handled was the construction of the McPhaul Institute.

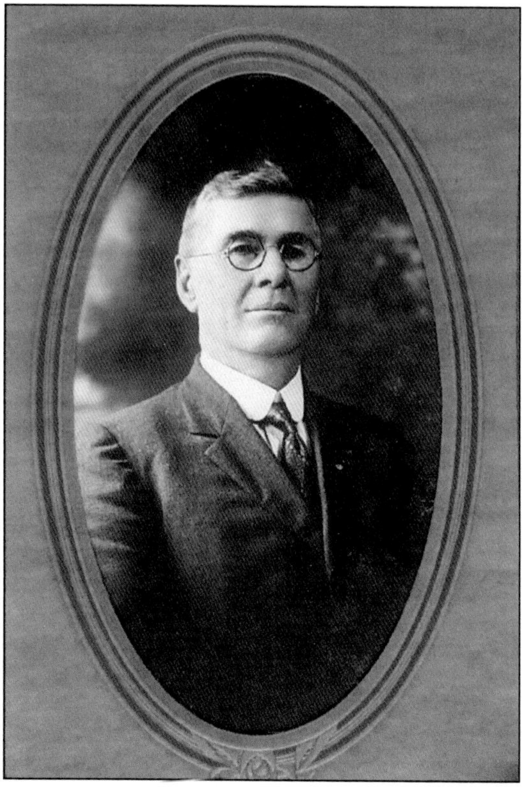

CHARLES WESLEY HILLHOUSE (1861–1930). He came to Sylvester in 1891, and as a building contractor was responsible for the construction of many homes and businesses. He also served in the State Legislature and as mayor of Sylvester.

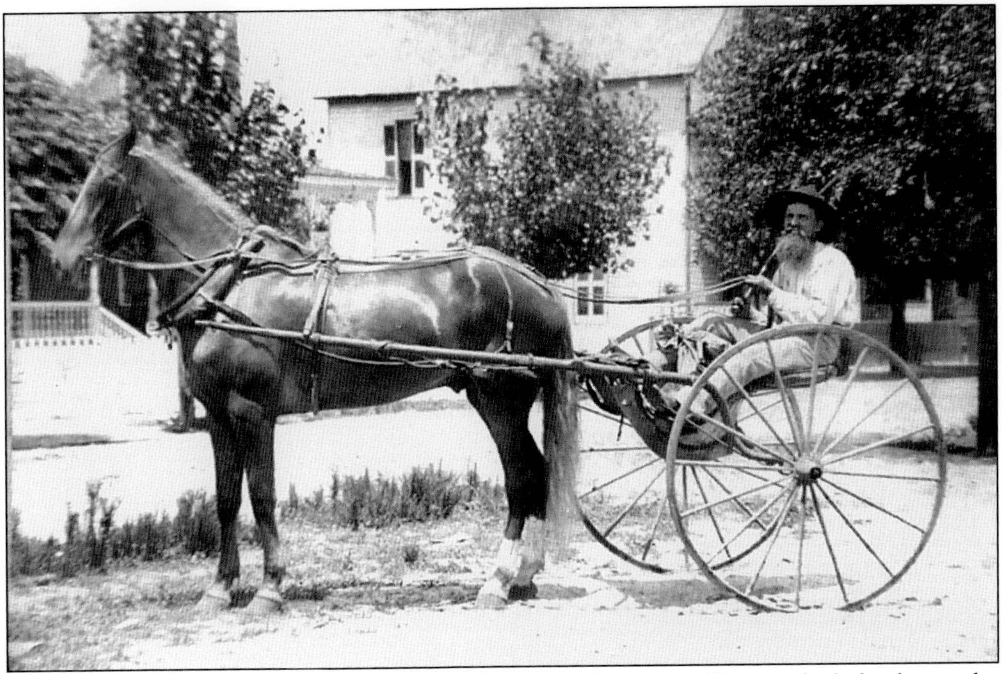

Joel Culpepper (1851–1935), Rural Mail Carrier. As a lover of history, he helped trace the path of the Thigpen Trail across the county.

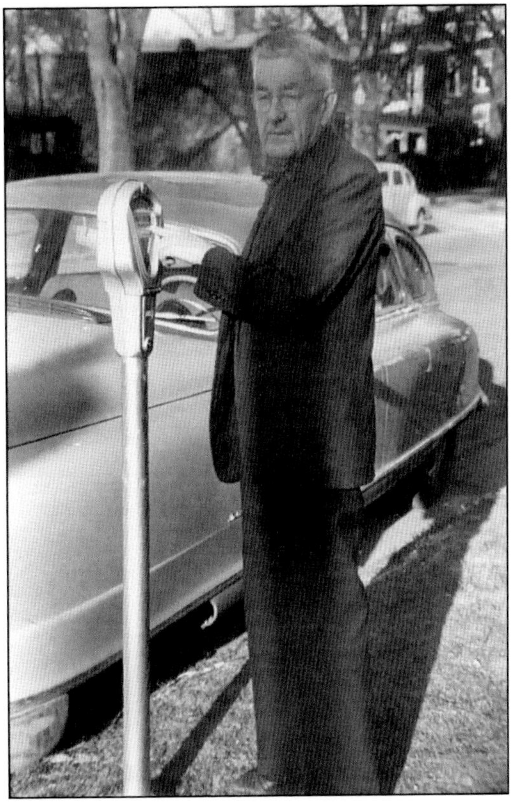

R. Britt Pollard, b. 1874. Pollard served for many years as the city clerk of Sylvester and the clerk of the county commissioners. He is shown with the newly installed parking meters.

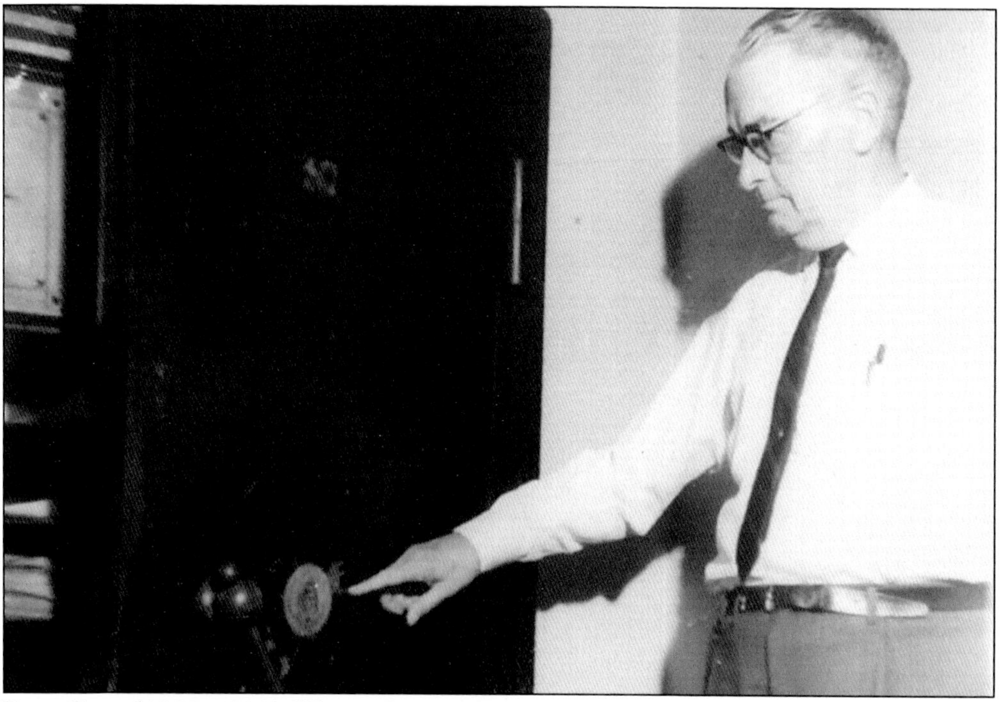

RUSH CAMP (1907–1974), WORTH COUNTY TAX COMMISSIONER. Camp is pictured pointing to scars left on the safe in his office by "would be thieves."

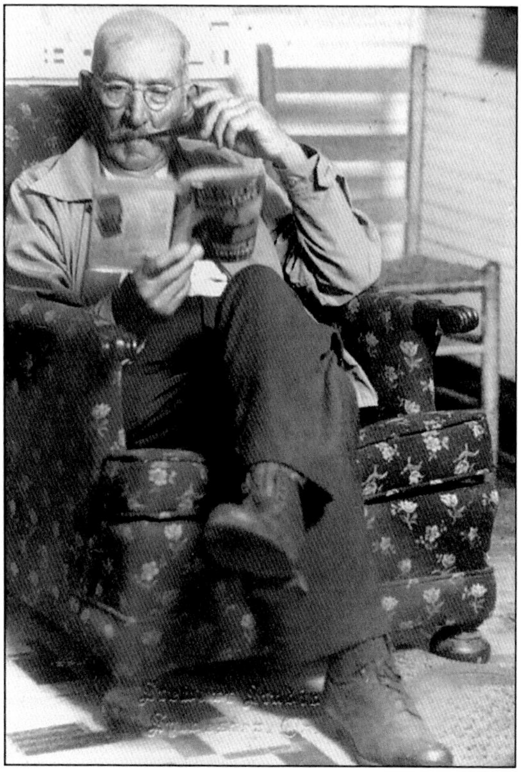

GEORGE F. SUMNER (1869–1953). The oldest son of Joseph L. and Josephine T. Sumner, he farmed a large acreage. Sumner was a Royal Arch Mason and Methodist known for his jolly laugh.

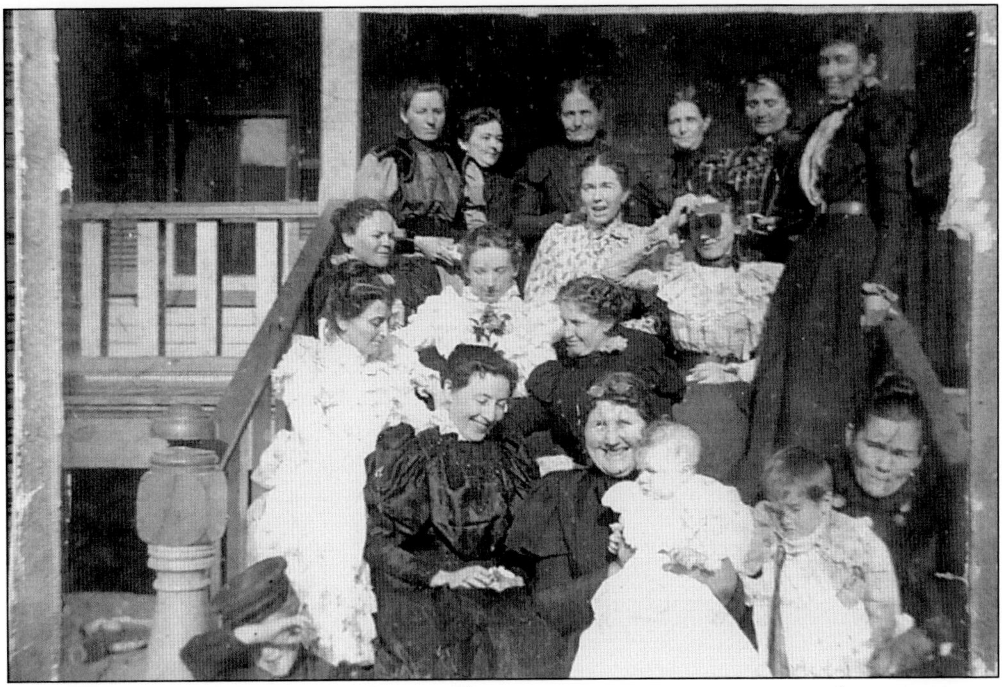

MRS. HEINSOHN'S GAY NINETIES PARTY. Theme parties were a great source of entertainment in earlier times.

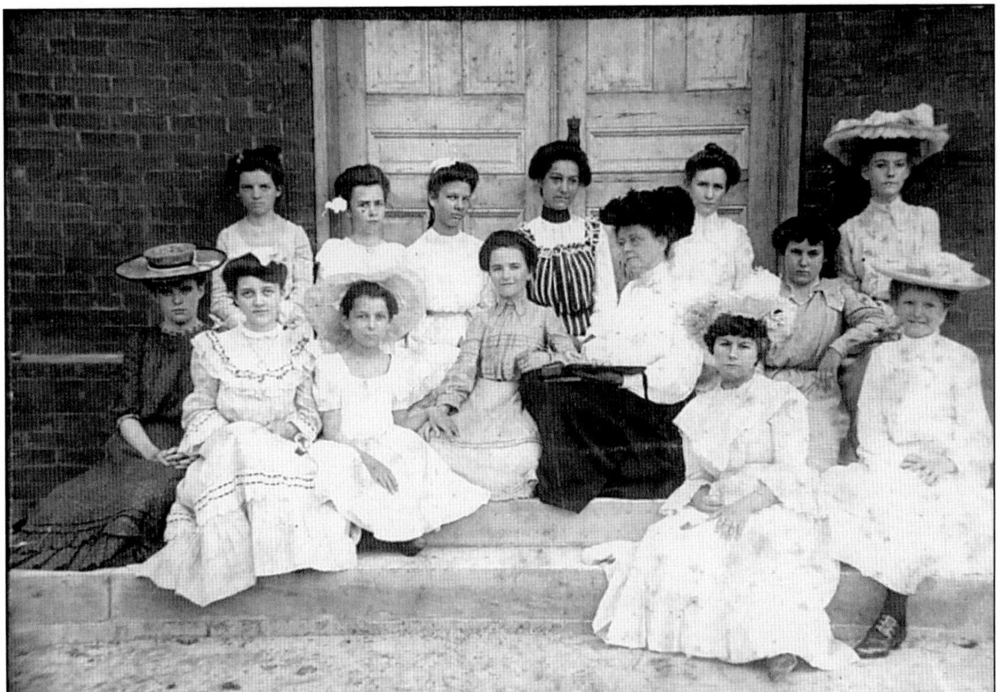

GAY NINETIES PARTY. A Sunday school social, perhaps?

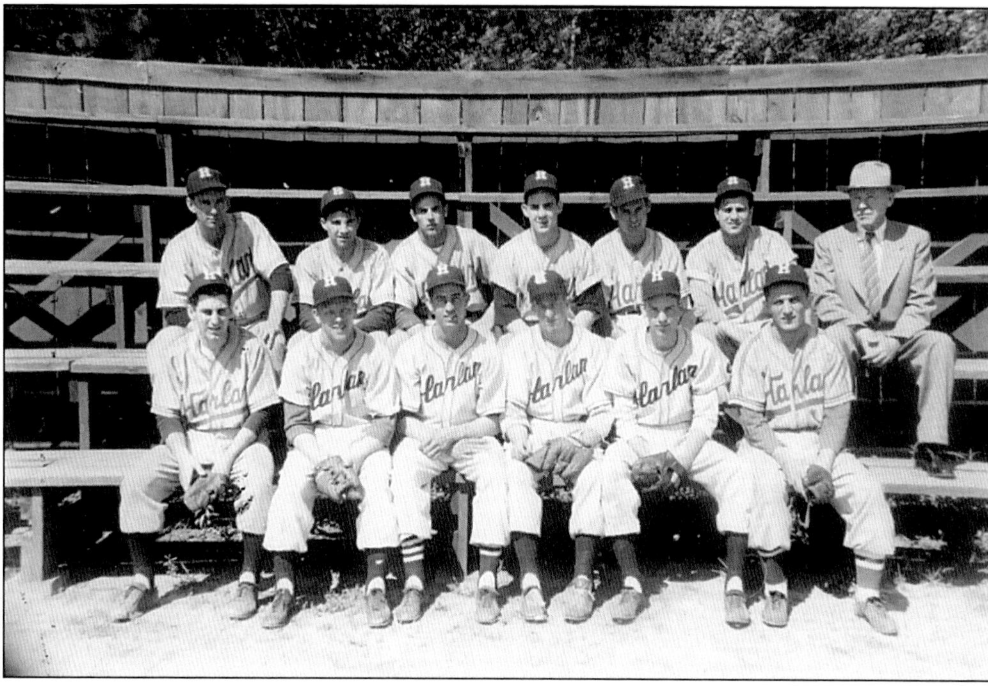

HARLAN BALL TEAM AND FRED DEARISO, MANAGER. Fred Deariso played baseball throughout his school and college years. He continued this love by sharing his talents and enthusiasm with young men of the county.

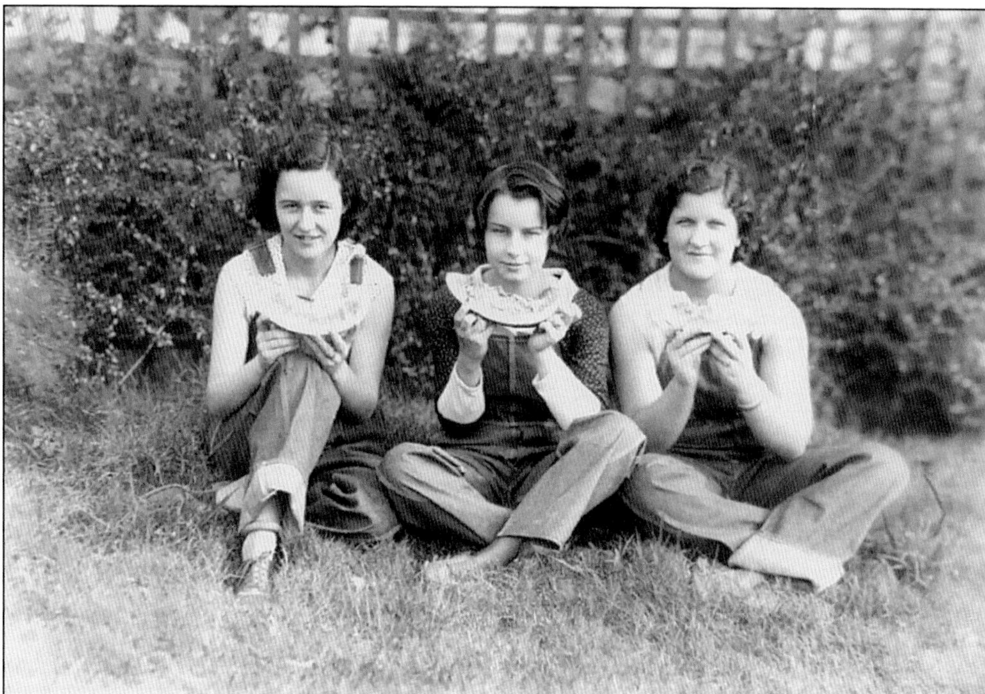

WATERMELON TIME, C. 1932. Pictured from left to right are Runelle Lundy, Inez Christopher, and Vivian Geeslin.

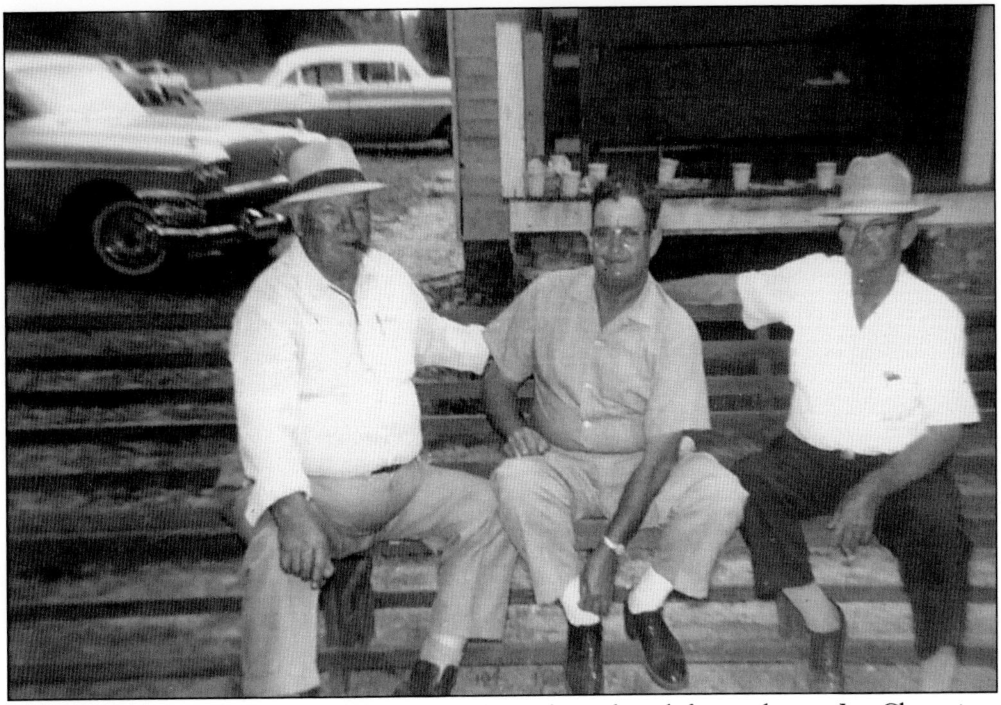

Catching Up on the News at Oakfield. Shown here, from left to right, are Jim Champion, Clyde Champion and Sam James.

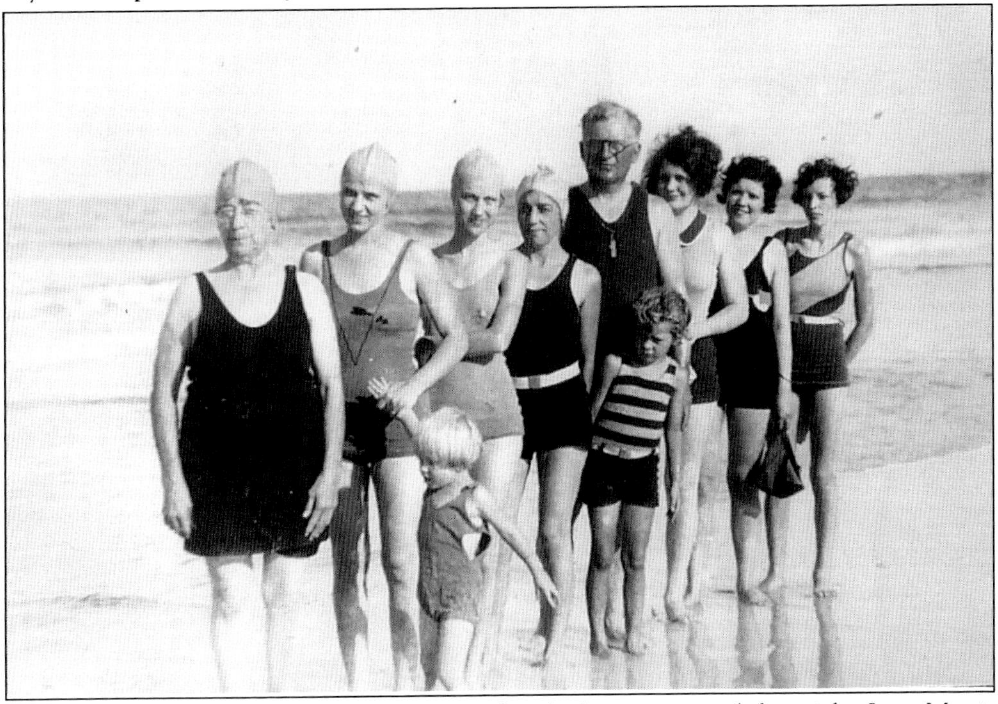

A Day at Jacksonville Beach, c. 1930. In their bathing suits are, left to right, Lena Morris King, Martha Mathis Turley, Patty Turley, unidentified, Mildred King Methvin, Glenda Methvin, S.R. Methvin, M.D., Nell Davidson Pugh, Esma Dorsey, and unidentified.

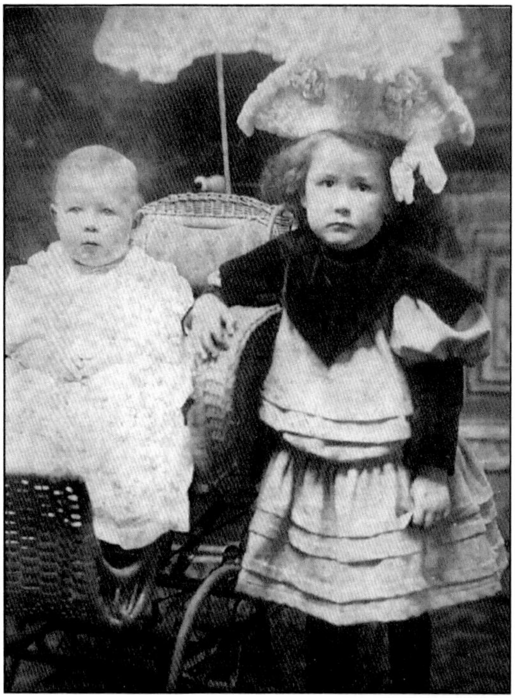

Rouse Children, c. 1906. Pleas Rouse (b. 1905) and his sister Gladys Inez (1901–1950) who later married Simon Elmer Harris.

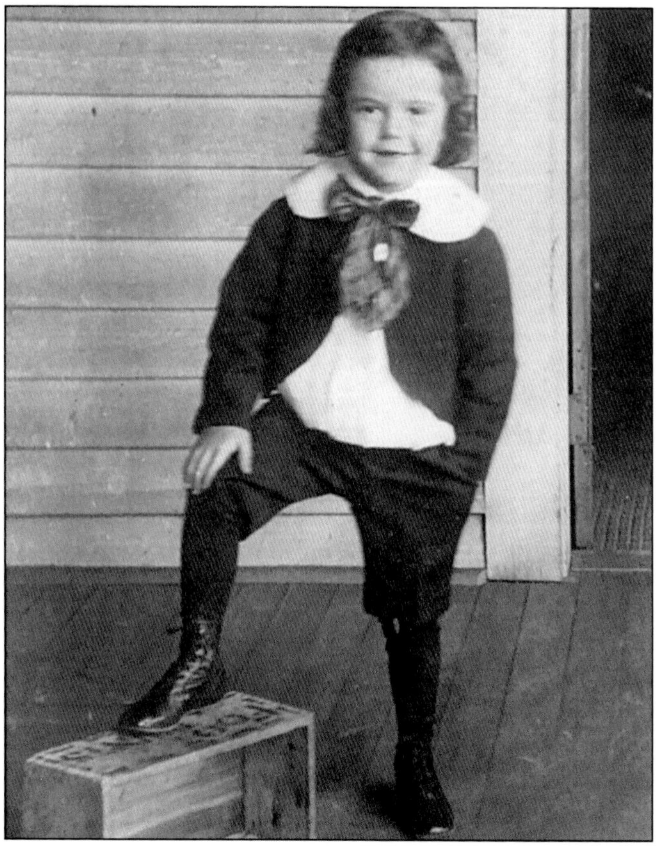

Weldon Gates Ford (1914–1977). He was the son of Dr. William Green and Berta Lee Jenkins Ford.

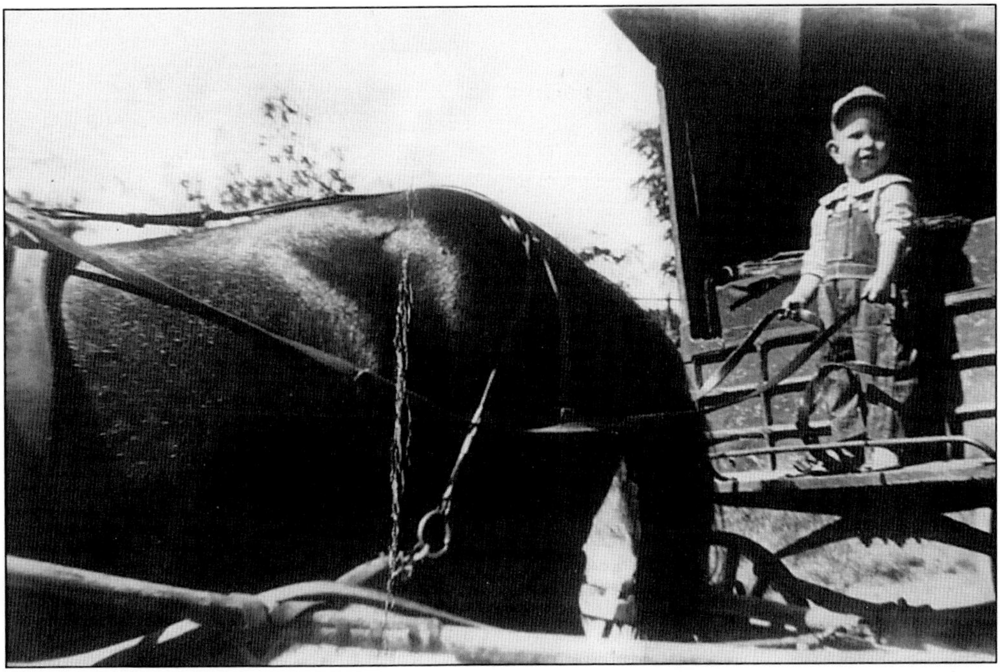

GIDDY UP BUCK! Shown is Charles Reynolds who was helping his Dad, Cortez, at the railway freight depot, *c.* 1933.

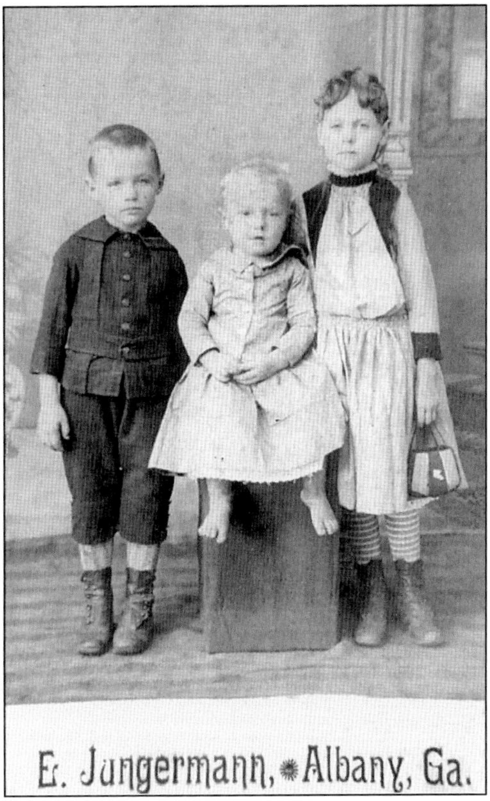

HILLHOUSE CHILDREN. Pictured, left to right, are Henry Bryon (b. 1885), John Grover (b.1888), and Eudora (b.1883), the children of Charles W. and Mary Ellen Hancock Hillhouse.

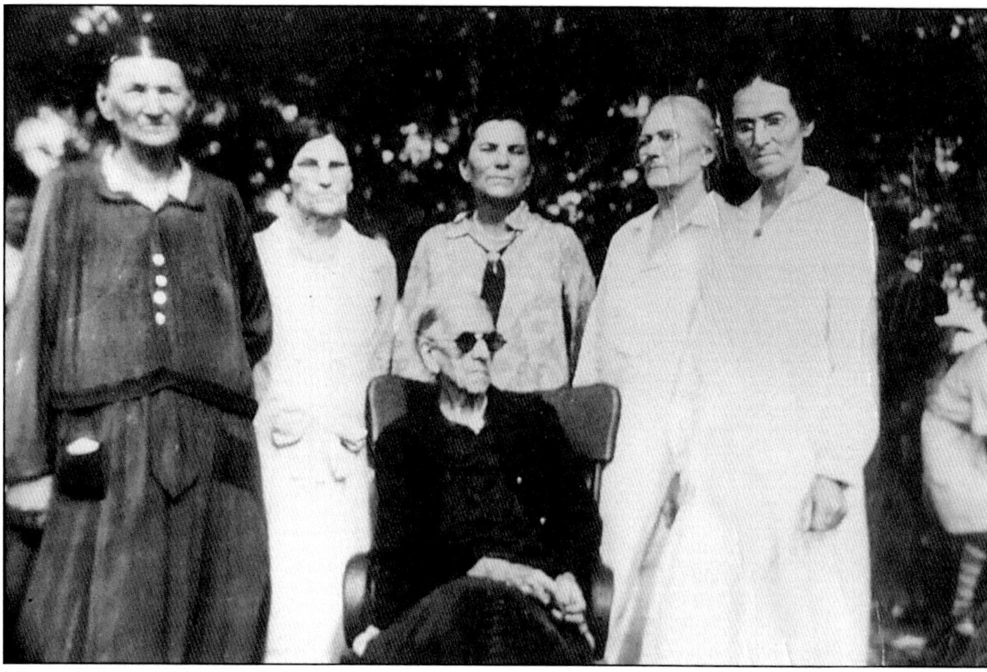

MRS. SUMNER AND HER GIRLS. Shown are Mrs. Sarah Josephine Thornhill Sumner (1845–1931) and five of her six daughters. Her daughters were Vida Lee Simmons, Mary Elizabeth Spring Glover, Sarah Lucy Conoly, Tempy McLeod Short, Emma Susan Houston, and Talitha Estelle Mims.

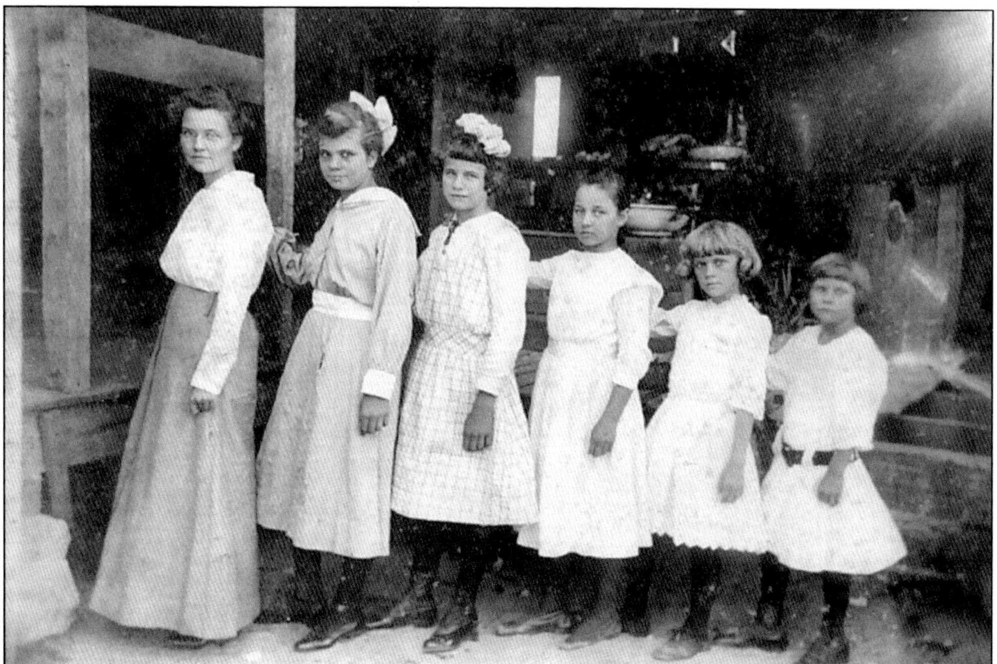

KEMP SISTERS AND FRIEND. Pictured, left to right, are Ocie, Annie, Lois, Alma Jackson, Eunice, and Frances.

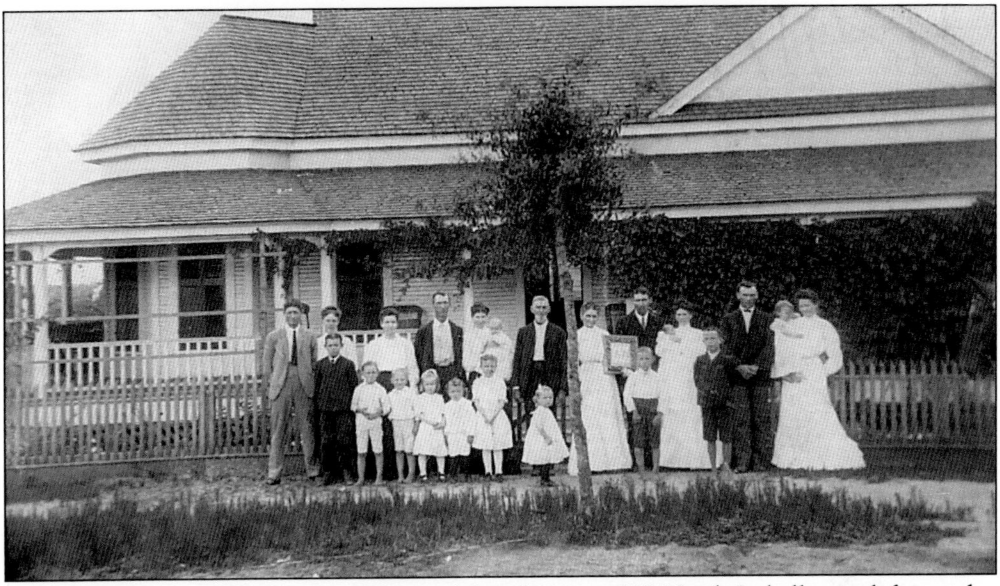

HART FAMILY, C. 1906. Shown in front of their home at 508 North Isabella are, left to right, (front row) Cecil Jennings, Willie Frank Gammage, Emil Gammage, Nettie Mae Hart Jennings, Bud Jennings, Eva Louise Jennings, Ella Mae Gammage, Edwin Jennings, and Emmett Jennings; (back row) George Hart, Mattie Bell Hart, Nettie Hart Jennings, D.L. Gammage, Mary Hart Gammage holding Lois, Daniel Franklin Hart, Amoretta Floretta Milner Hart, Herbert Hart, Nora Kinard Hart holding Herbert Jr., Millard Lee, and Ammie Hart Lee holding Amoret.

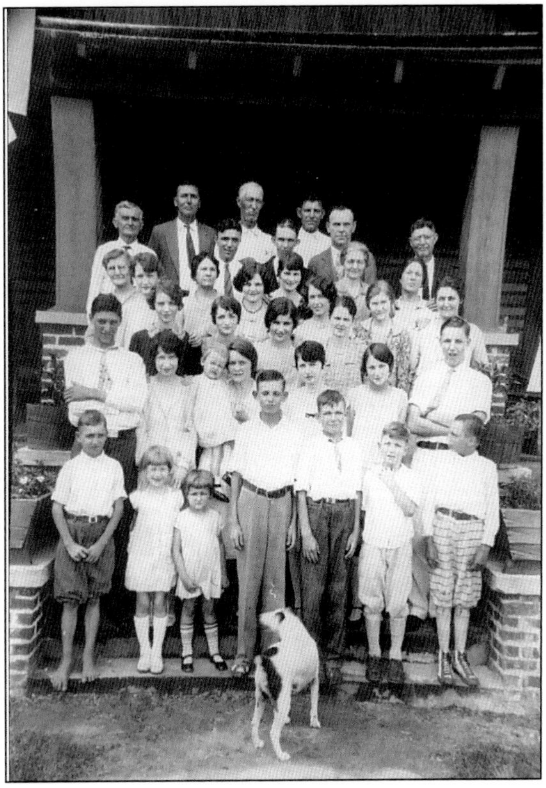

HART FAMILY REUNION, C. 1927. Shown in front of the George Hart home on US Hwy 82 are, left to right, (first row) Harold Gammage, Martha Pope, Myrtle Jennings, D. L.Gammage, Jr., Olin Gammage, Milton Pope, Byron Hart; (second row) Dan Hart, Sarah Gammage, Louise Jennings, Myrtle Fleming Jennings, Mattie Bell Gammage, Ada Belle Hart, John D. Pope; (third row) Mildred Lee, Vernon Gammage, Eula Mae Pope, Mabel Lee, Mary Hart Gammage, Lois Hart Pope; (fourth row) Nettie Hart Jennings, Lois Gammage, Nora Kinard Hart, Amoret Lee, Ella Mae Gammage Folsom, Carrie Hart, Ammie Hart Lee, Mattie Bell Hart; (fifth row) Tim Jennings, Herbert Hart, Sr., Tim Jennings, Jr., D. L. Gammage, Sr., A. J. Folsom, Cecil Jennings, Millard Lee, and George Hart. Also pictured is the dog Foch who was named after WWI General Foch.

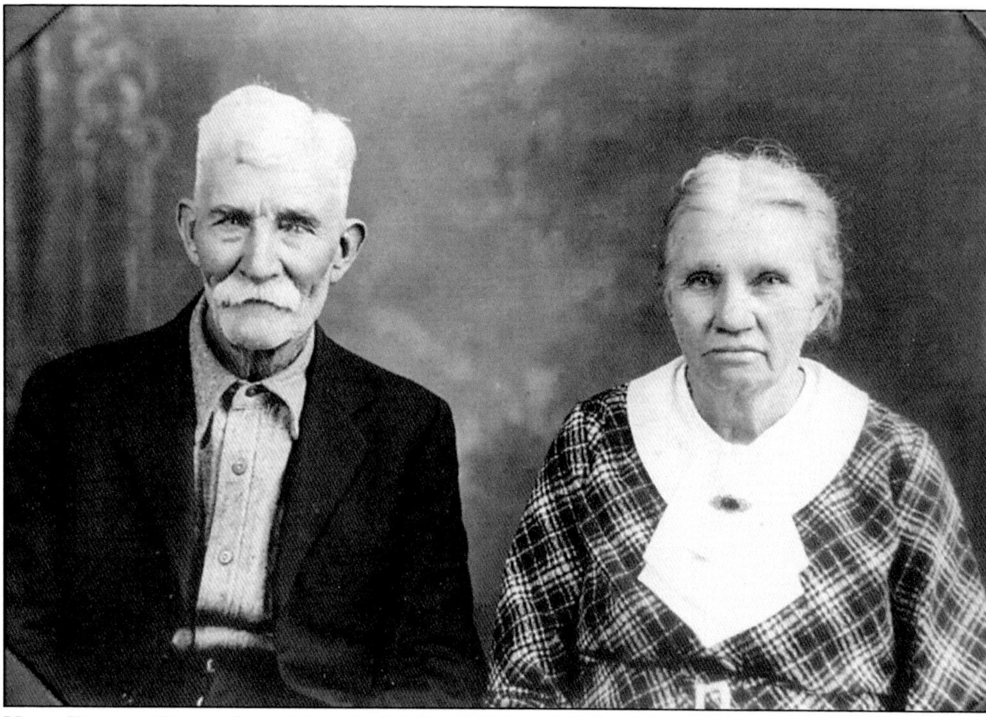

Kemp Family. Pictured are John H. (1860–1951) and Sallie Joiner (1869–1950) Kemp.

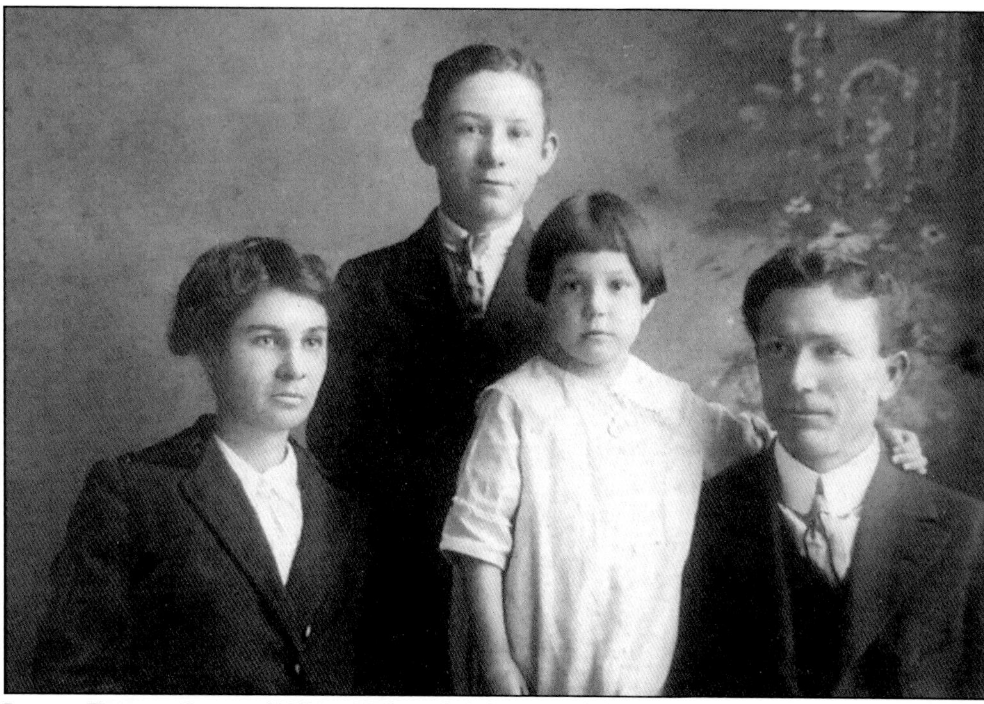

Lundy Family. George (1874–1926) and Ada Kinard (1878–1930) Lundy are shown with their children.

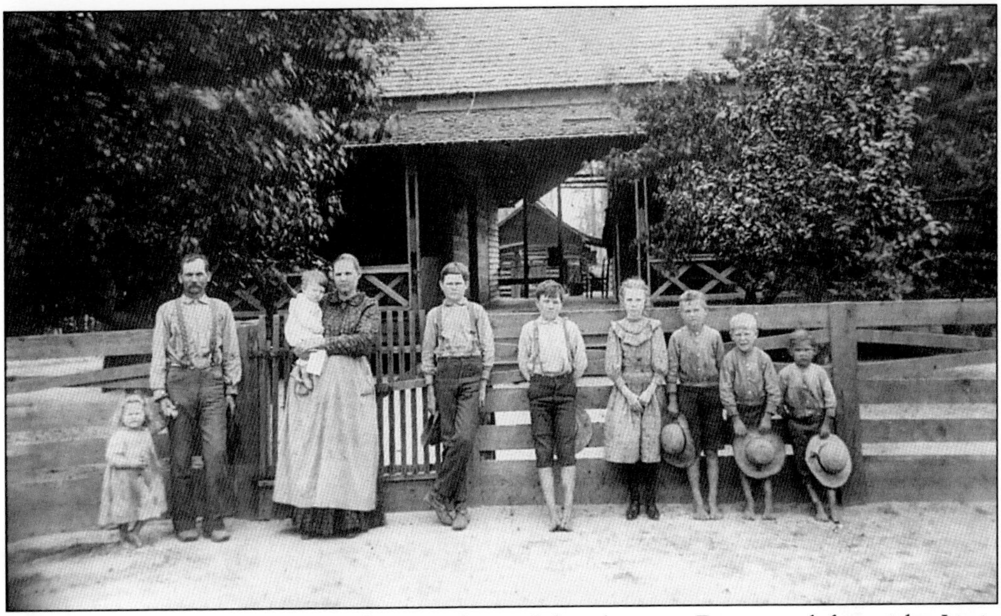

R.L. Deariso Family, c. 1900. Shown in front of their home at Egypt are, left to right, Lizzie J., R.L., Mollie holding John, Oscar, Carl, Vera, Leonard, Fred, and Edwin.

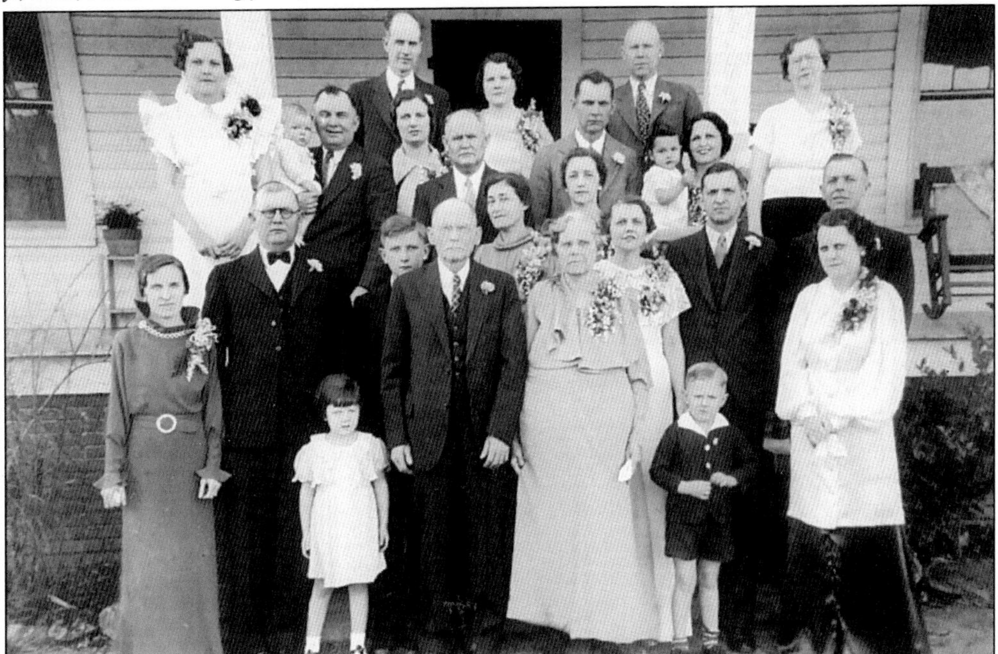

R.L. and Mollie Ford Deariso's Golden Wedding Anniversary, January 8, 1935. Pictured, left to right, are (first row) Vesta, John & Nell Deariso, R.L. and Mollie, Tom Keown, Mildred Geeslin Deariso; (second row) Robert L. (Little Bud) Deariso, Leta Simpson Deariso, Bessie Mae Deariso Keown, T. W. Keown, Otis Deariso; (third row) Adelaide Deariso, Carl Deariso holding Martha Jane, Clara Wingate Deariso, Oscar Deariso, and Irene Nance Deariso; (fourth row) Freeman and Hazel Deariso Groover, Edwin, Caroline and Mamie Gissendanner Deariso, Fred Deariso, and Lizzie J. Deariso.

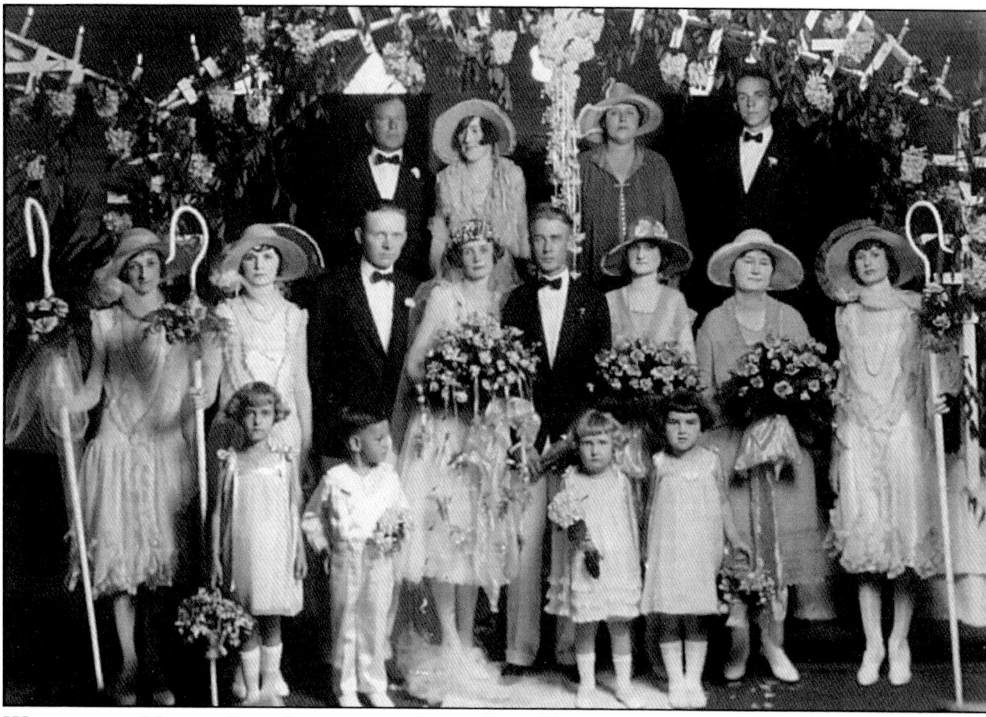

Wedding of Henry Cain Rouse and Eddie Lou Kelly, c. 1905. Also in the wedding party were Mary Rouse Posey, Lester Rogers, Gladys Rouse, and Edith Heyward.

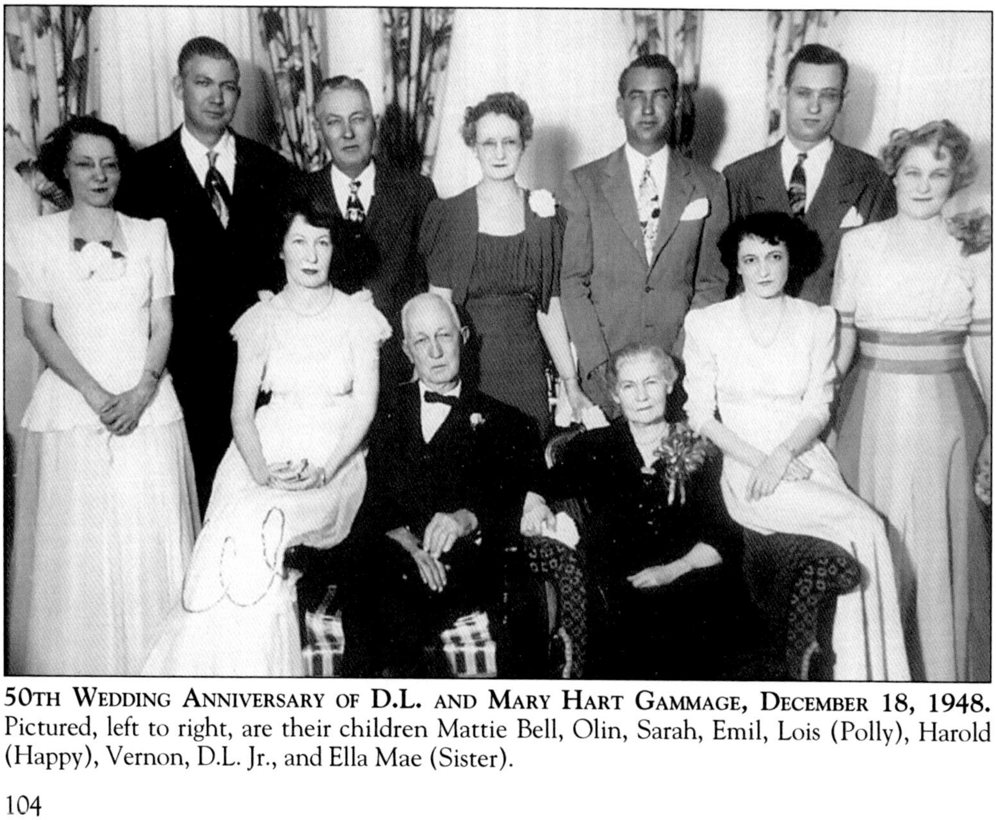

50th Wedding Anniversary of D.L. and Mary Hart Gammage, December 18, 1948. Pictured, left to right, are their children Mattie Bell, Olin, Sarah, Emil, Lois (Polly), Harold (Happy), Vernon, D.L. Jr., and Ella Mae (Sister).

WALTER (1879–1938) AND CLAUD RIDLEY (1882–1959) LUNDY.

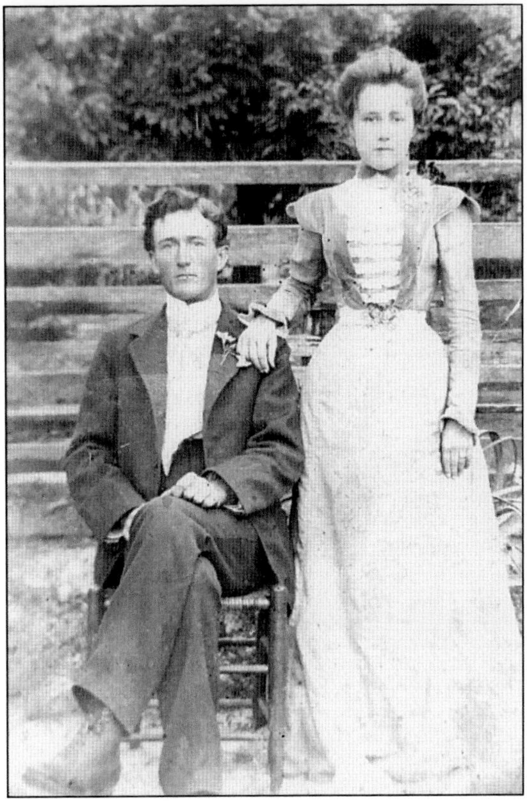

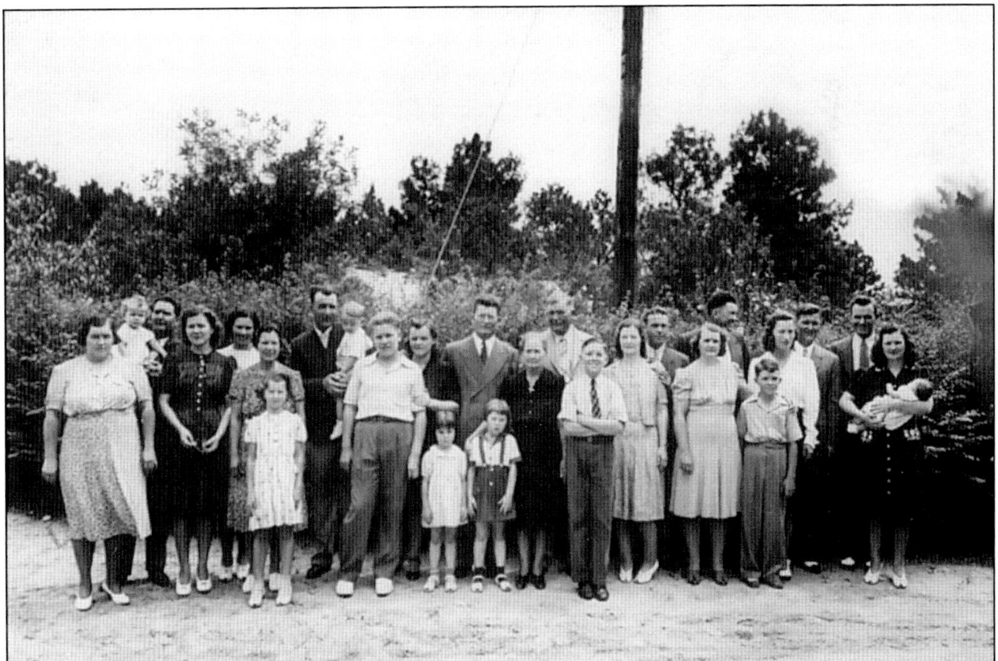

J.C. (JIM) CHAMPION FAMILY OF WARWICK, MID-1940S.

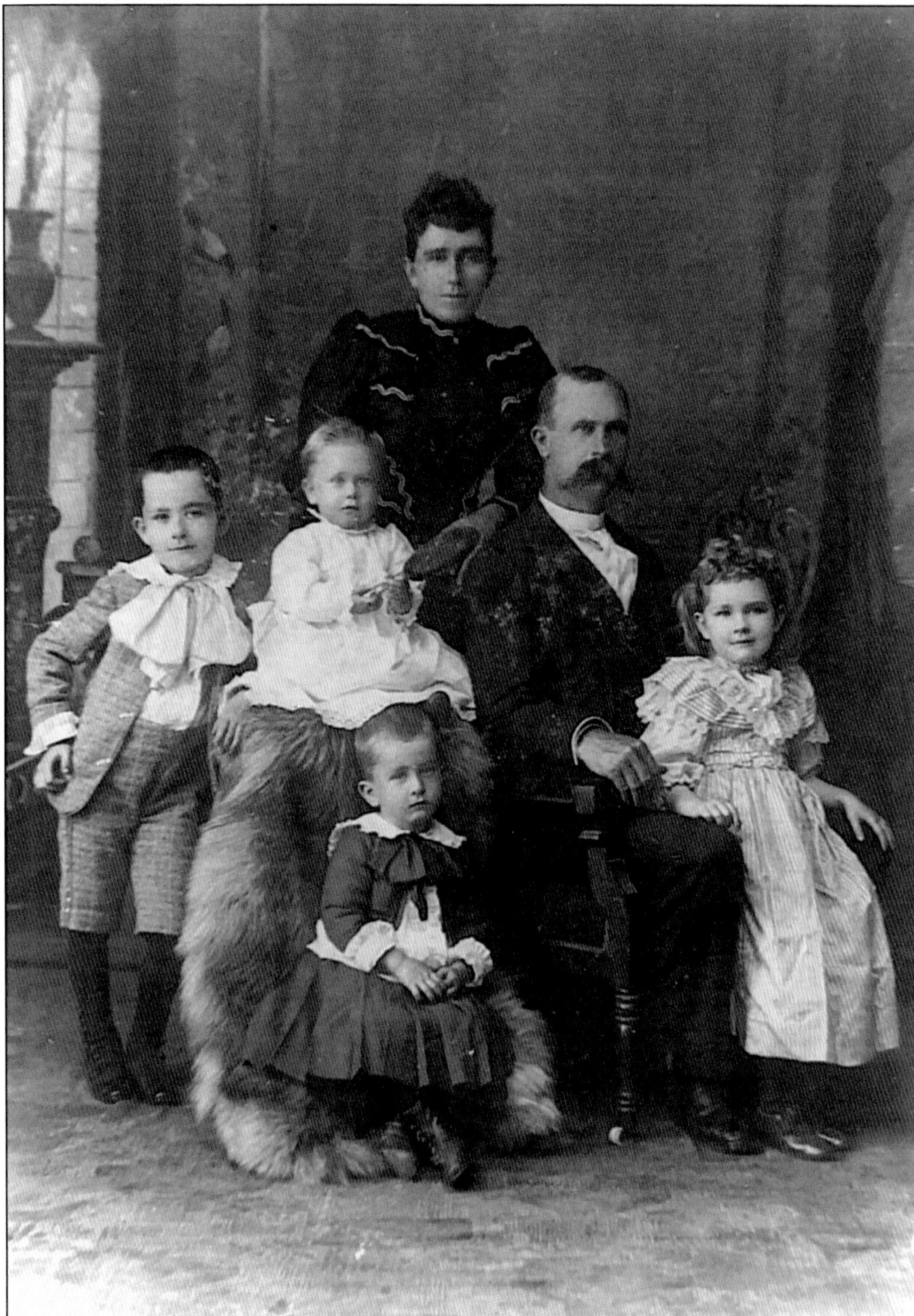

William Jackson (1855–1895) and Rowena Hanes (1861–1959) Ford Family, April 17, 1894. Children shown are, left to right, Brooks (age 7), E. J. (age 1), Willie (age 3) and Eileen (age 5).

Seven

HOMES

Many early homes were built of rough hewn lumber or logs. The local sawmills furnished the lumber. Large porches and open windows provided the cross ventilation needed in the hot months and open fireplaces gave warmth in the winter. Homes were roofed with tin or wooden shingles. Few were constructed with brick and mortar. Fire was an ever present threat. By the turn of the century, more creature comforts and embellishments were added as evidenced by some of the homes on Isabella Street.

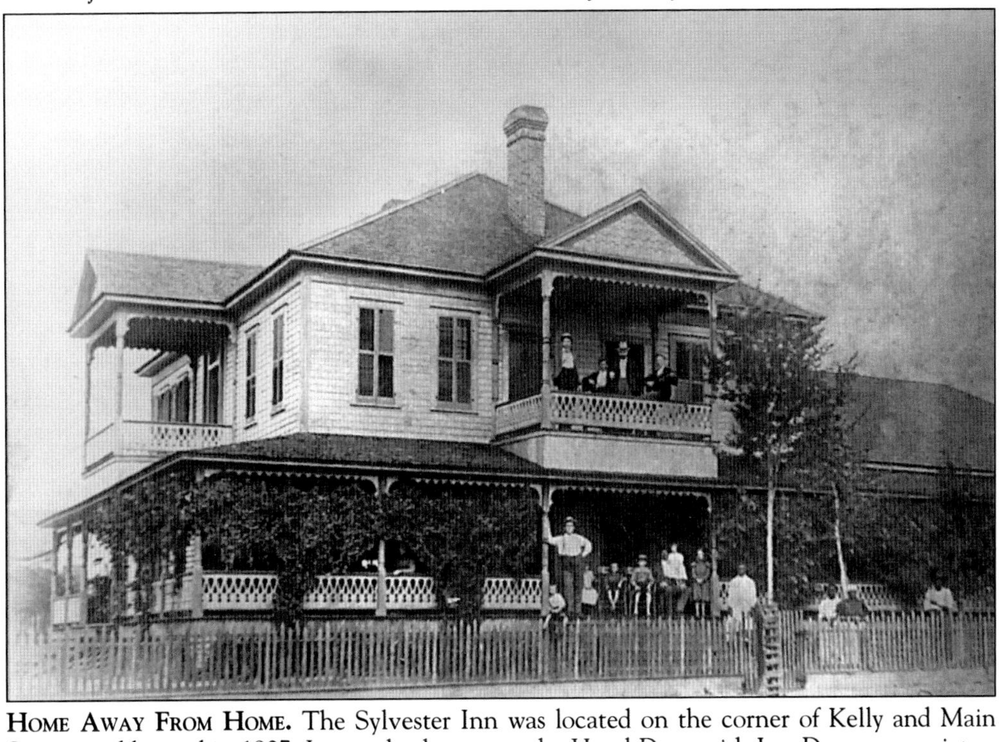

HOME AWAY FROM HOME. The Sylvester Inn was located on the corner of Kelly and Main Streets and burned in 1907. It was also known as the Hotel Dees, with Lee Dees as proprietor. The rate was $2 per day and the newspaper ad proclaimed "Special Attention Given to Commercial Travelers. If you are Pleased Tell Others, And If You Are Not Tell Us."

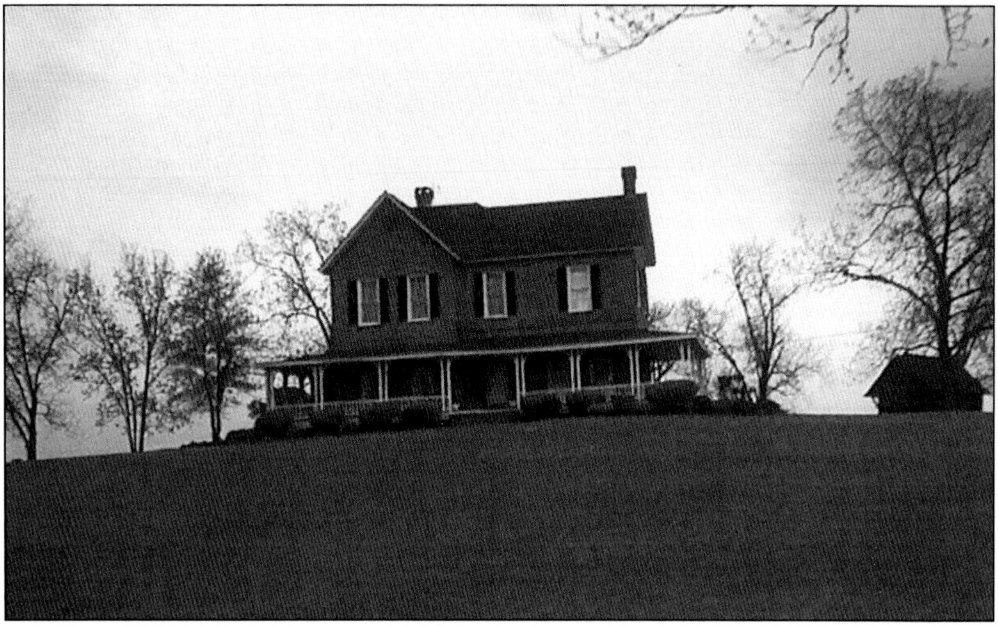

The "Pope" Home. Built before 1900 by Judge David H. Pope for his son, Henry W., it was the first brick structure in Worth County. The land was purchased for $1 an acre. The trees were cut down and shipped to Albany where they were exchanged for the brick that was used in building the house.

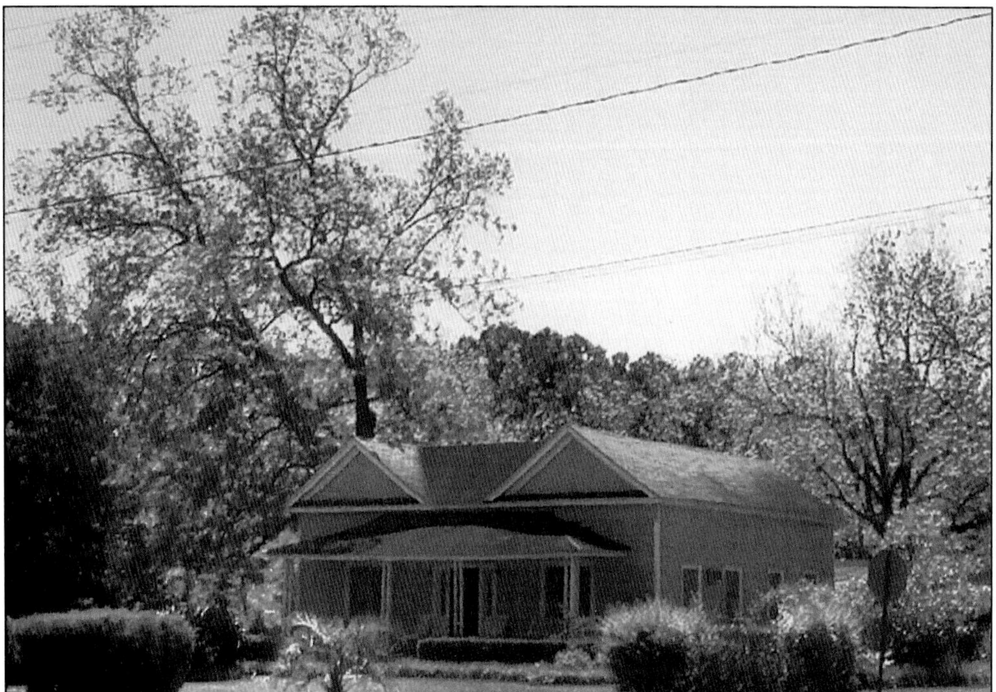

Oldest House in Sylvester. Now located at 310 East Kelly Street, its first location was where the courthouse is now. It was built by William H. McPhaul and later was home to J.S. and Kate Westberry. When the courthouse was built in 1904, it was moved to its present site.

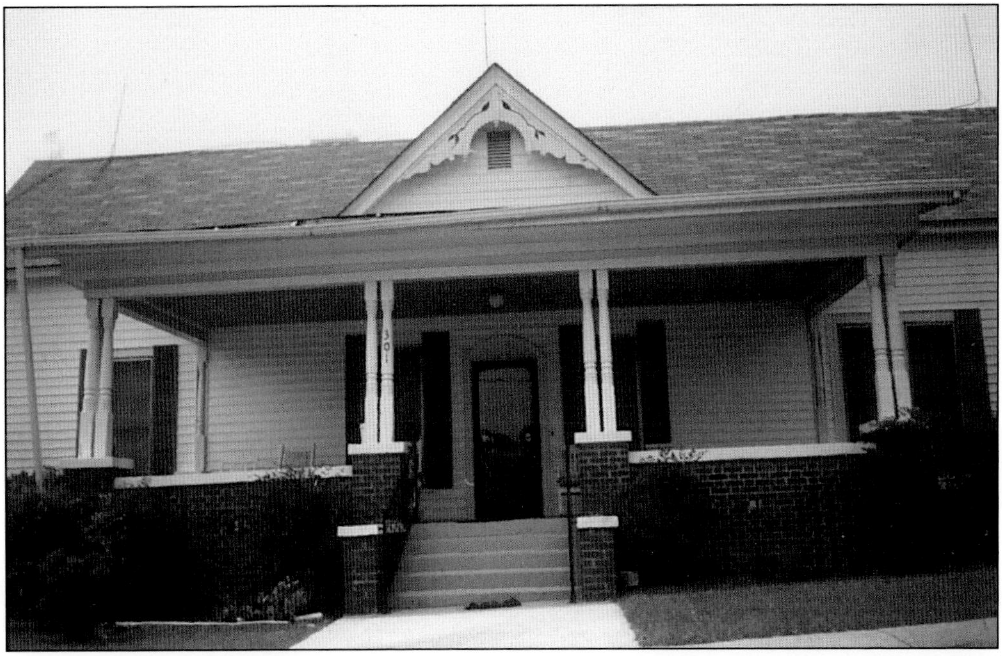

301 North Isabella. Built in 1902 by Mrs. Mangham, its last owner Mrs. Elizabeth (Sis) Ford Leary donated the property to the Barnard Trail Chapter, NSDAR, and the Worth County Historical Society at her death.

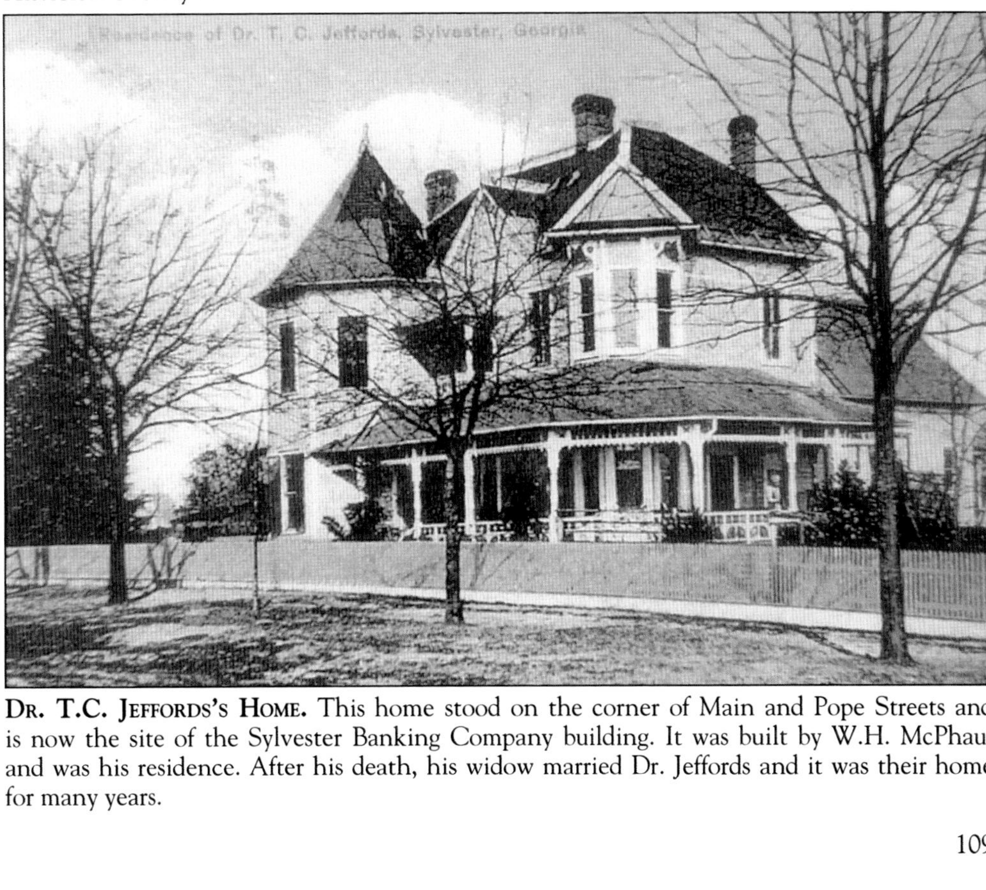

Dr. T.C. Jeffords's Home. This home stood on the corner of Main and Pope Streets and is now the site of the Sylvester Banking Company building. It was built by W.H. McPhaul and was his residence. After his death, his widow married Dr. Jeffords and it was their home for many years.

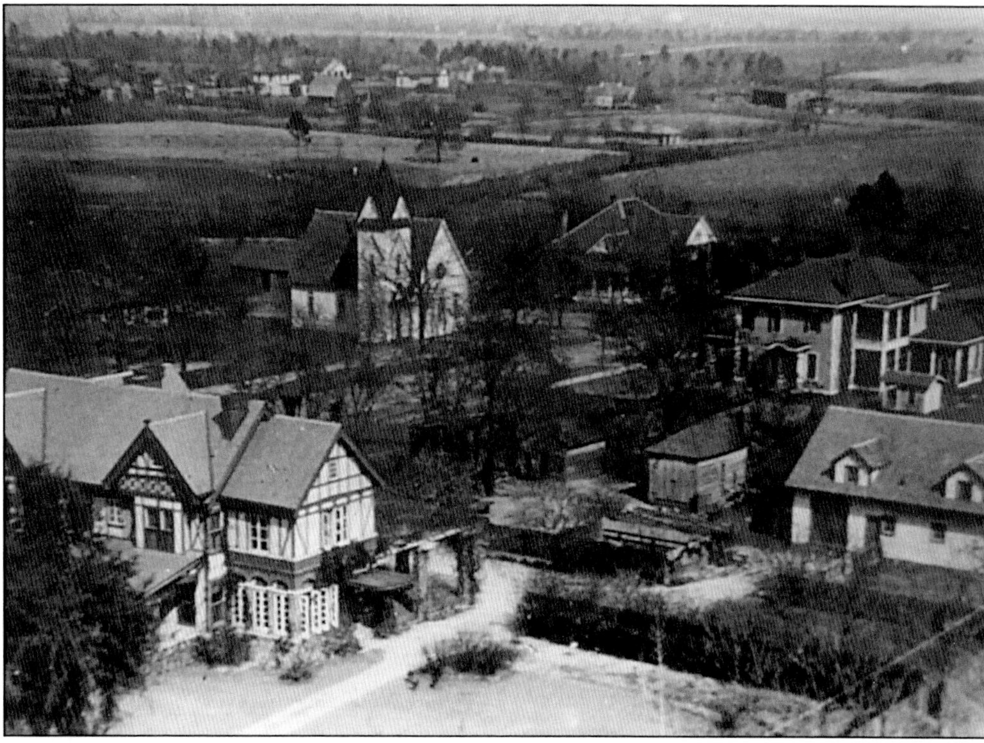

Aerial View of Main & Pope Streets. Taken from the Courthouse Clock Tower, this view shows the W.A. Johnson House (Banks Funeral Home), the M.H. Westberry House (Sylvester Woman's Clubhouse), and the First Presbyterian Church (later the public library after its move across the street).

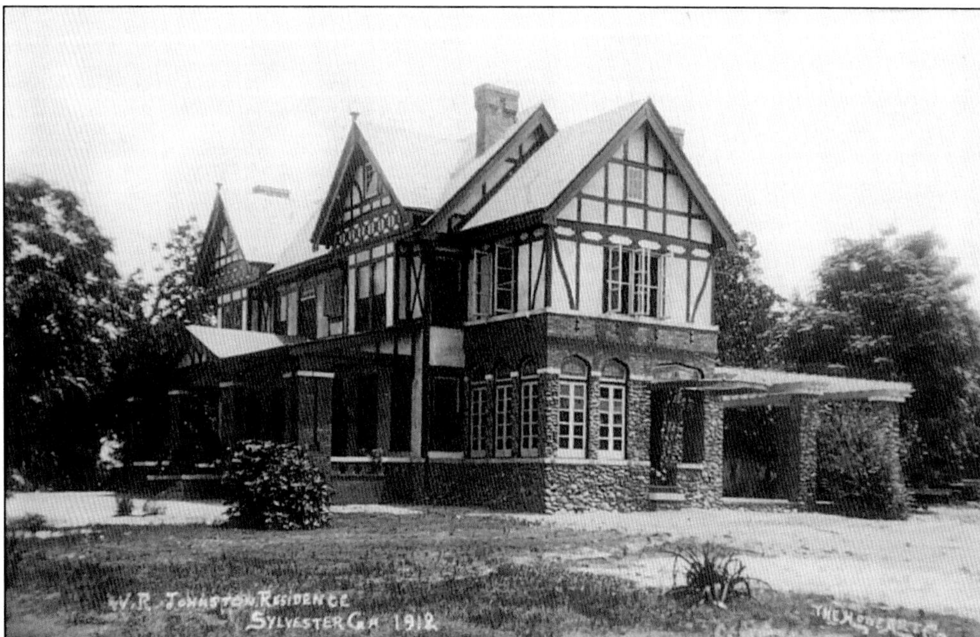

W.A. Johnston Residence. Built 1911–1912, it is now Banks Funeral Home.

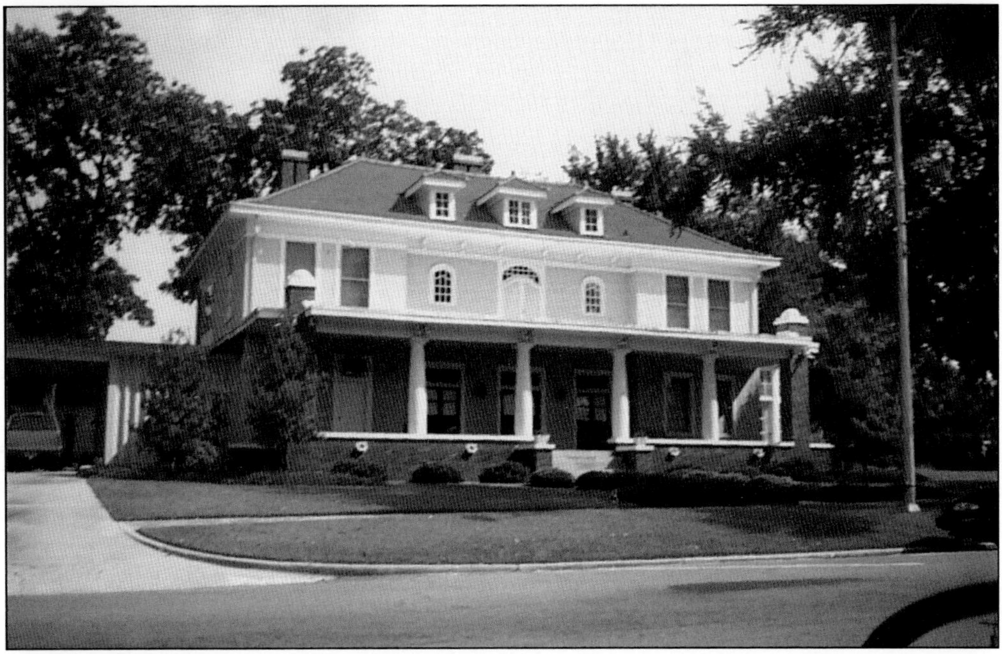

101 East Pope Street. Built by G. Floyd Alford in 1912, it is now the law office and residence of Clarence A. Miller.

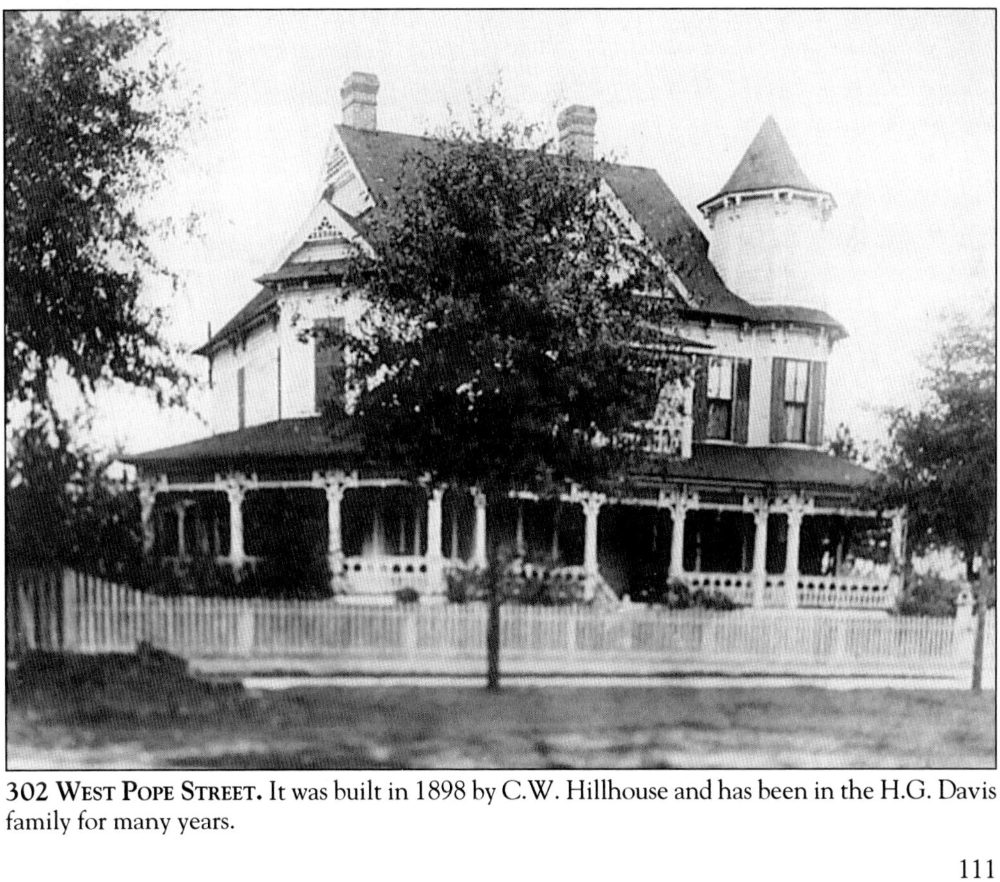

302 West Pope Street. It was built in 1898 by C.W. Hillhouse and has been in the H.G. Davis family for many years.

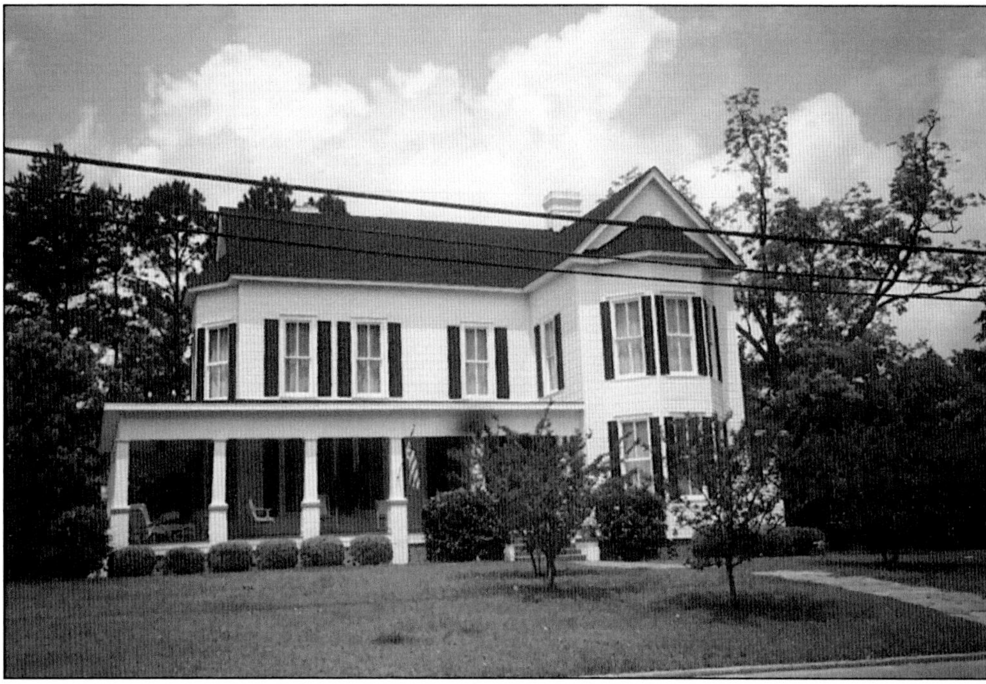

501 North Isabella. Built by Contractor John H. McPhaul for T.J. Pinson in 1898, this house has been in the D.L. Gammage family since 1939. At the same time, McPhaul was building a home for T.J.'s brother, Jesse. W. Pinson at 505 North Isabella. Both used the same house plan.

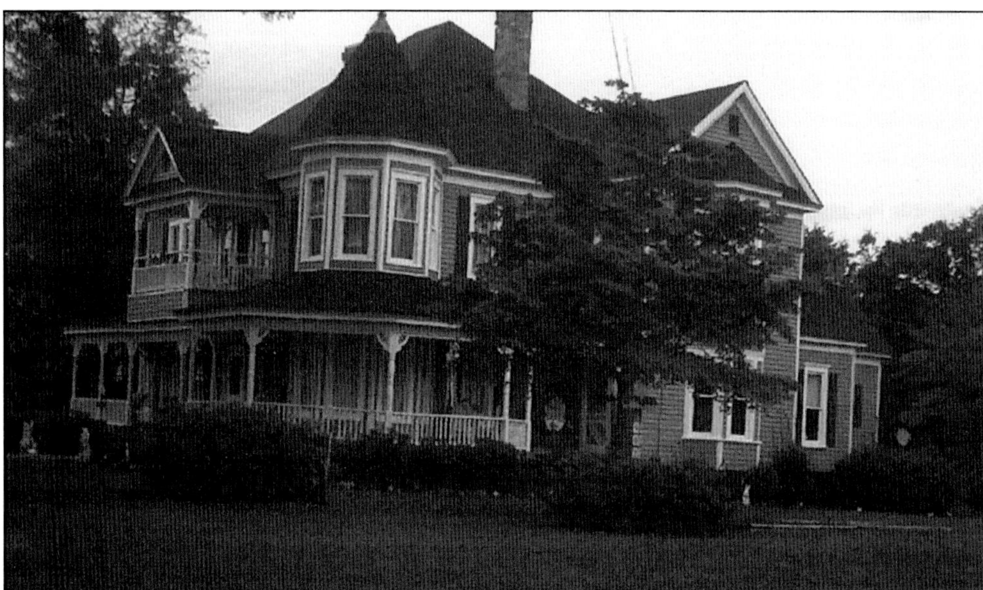

902 North Isabella. Gary Green Ford II built this house *c.* 1900 for his second wife, Annie Heard. It has also been the home of Preston Powell and Col.W.J. Crowe.

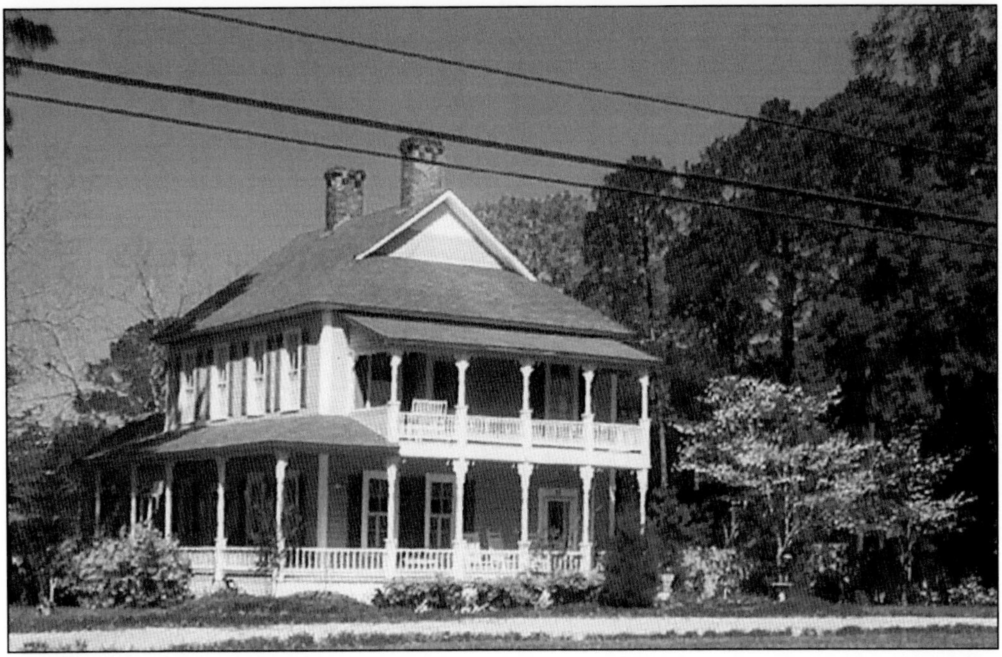

803 NORTH ISABELLA. This house was built in 1902 by J.N. Welch and immediately sold to Mrs. Rowena Ford. It remained in the Ford family for many years.

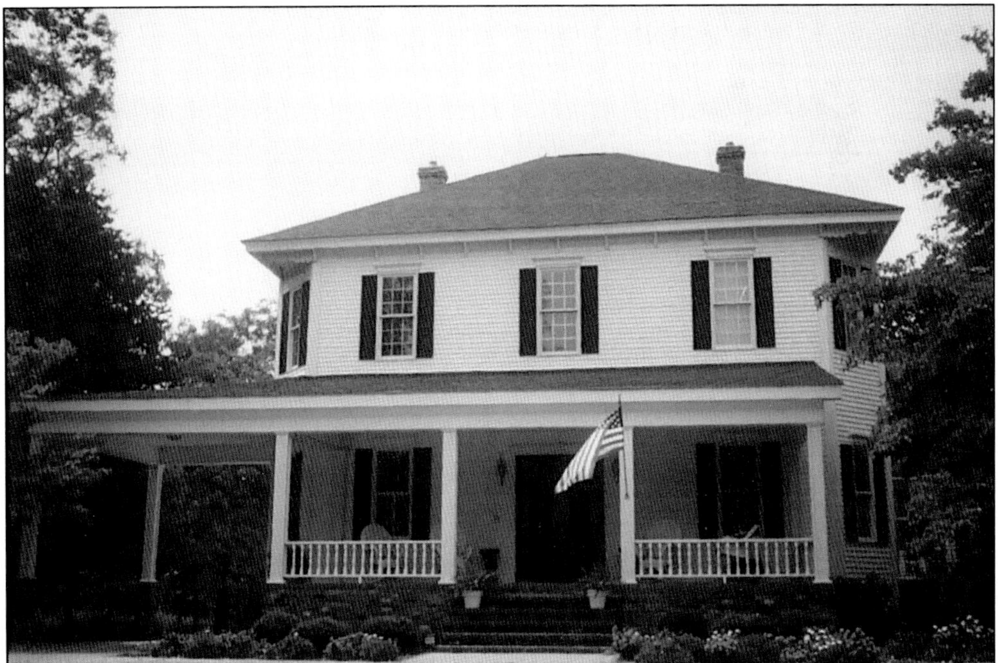

901 NORTH ISABELLA. Sylvester's first physician, Dr. M.J. Crockett, built this home in 1903. It is now the home of Hal and Priscilla Carter.

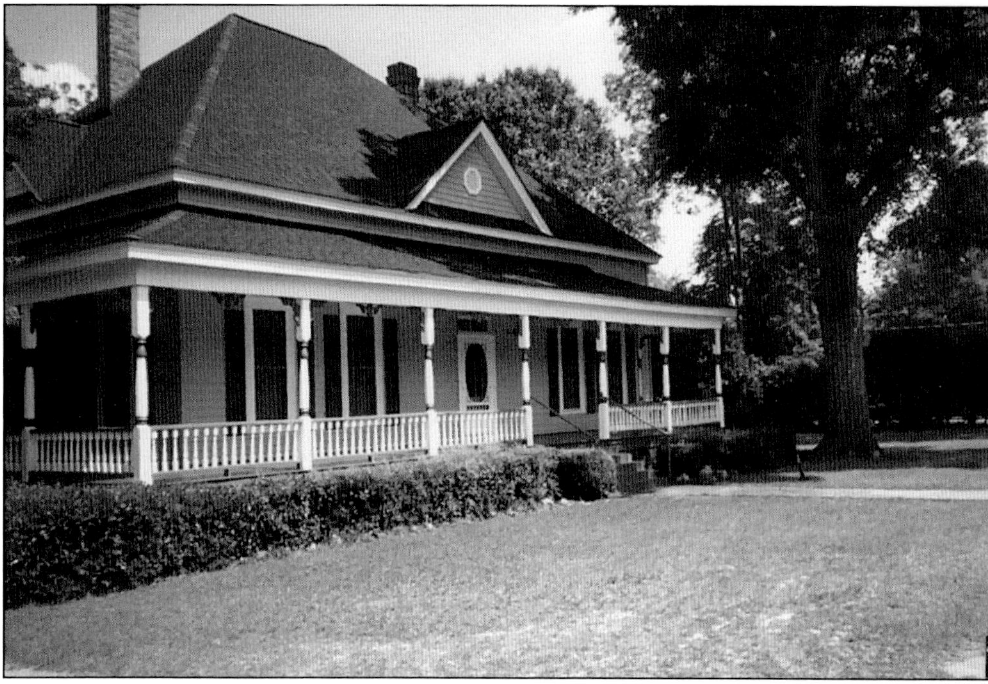

904 North Isabella. Built by Gary G. Ford II in 1905, it has been home to four generations of Fords and Dearisos.

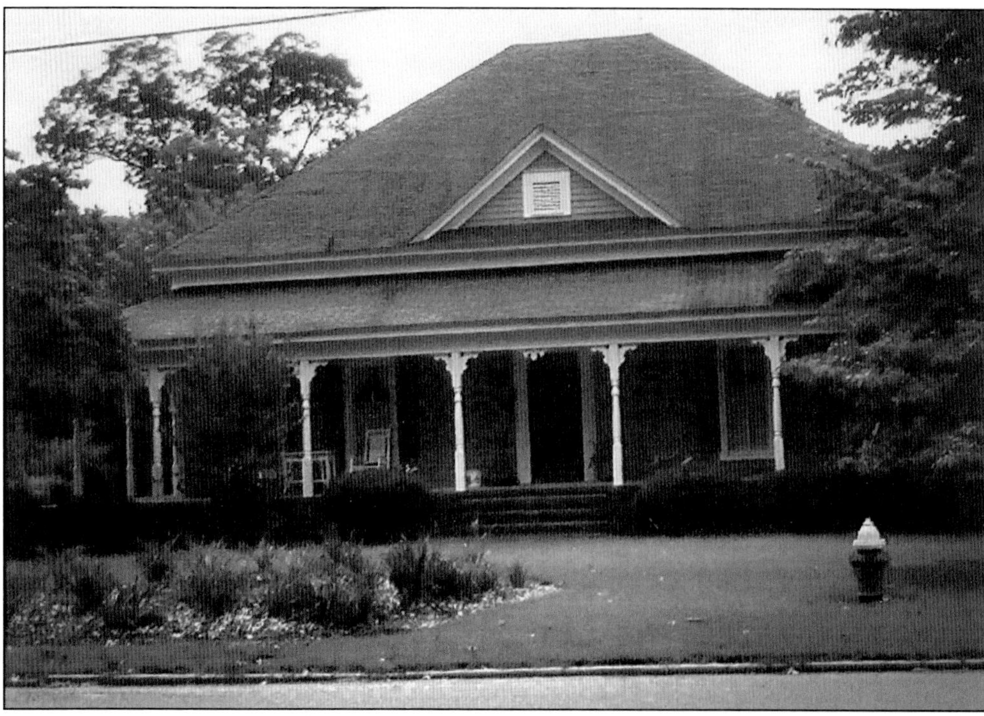

906 North Isabella. This house was built by Gary G. Ford for his son, Wm. G. Ford. 907 North Isabella Street shares some of the same features as its neighbors across the street, numbers 904 and 906.

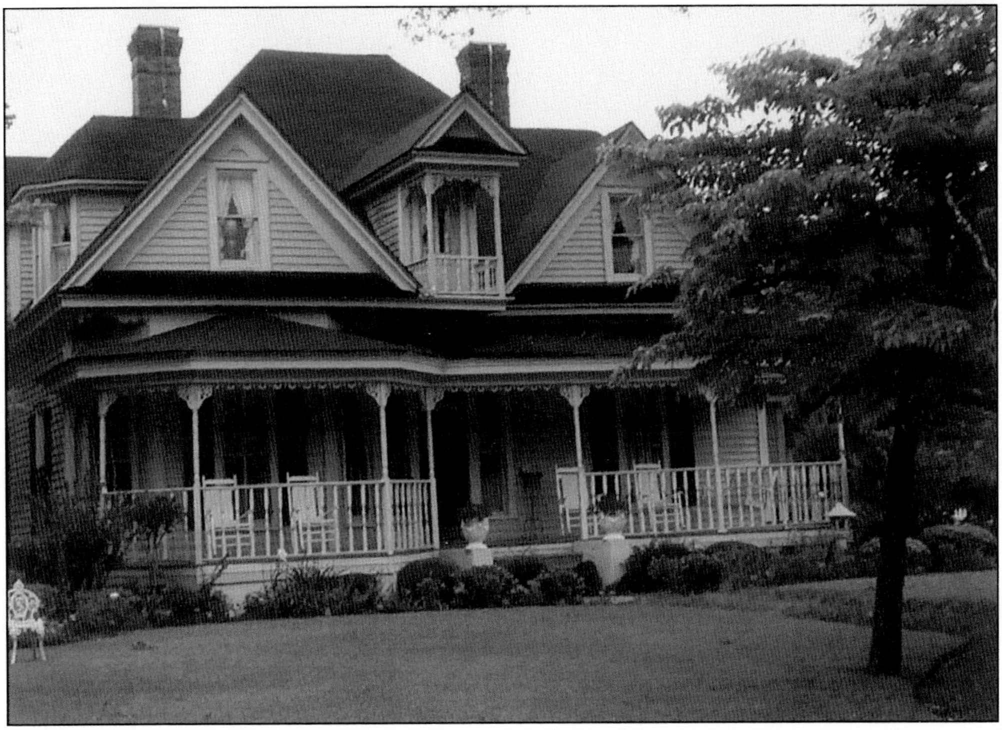

808 North Isabella. Doris Cochran's home is a beautiful example of gingerbread trim and turn of the century architecture.

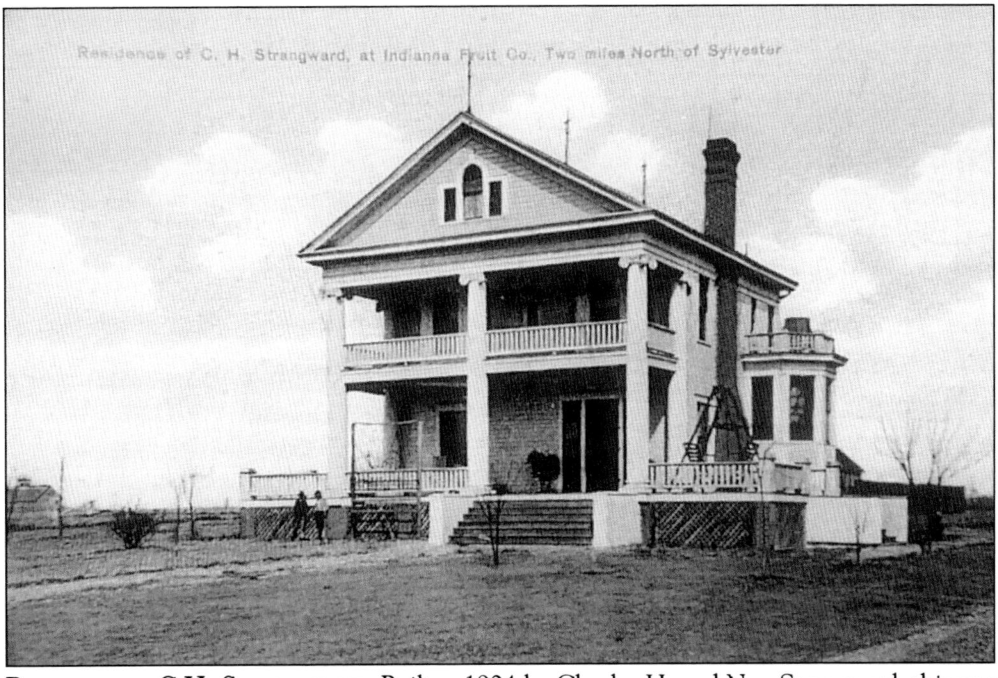

Residence of C.H. Strangward. Built *c.* 1904 by Charles H. and Nan Strangward, this was their home for 65 years. He was president of the Indiana Fruit Company and the Sylvester Fruit Company.

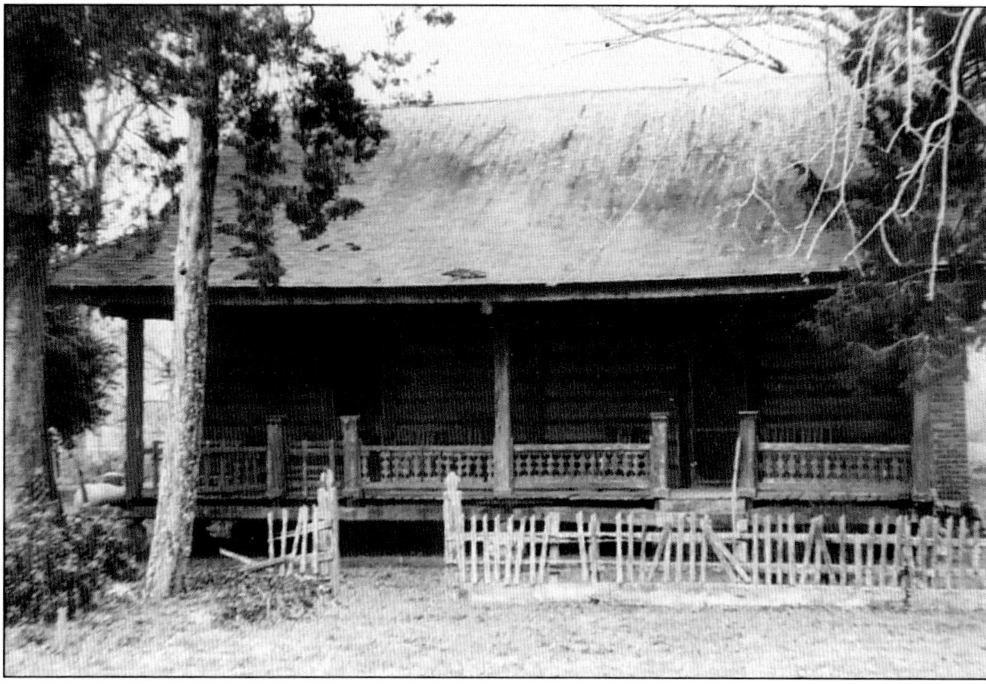

Lucy Ann Culpepper Whiddon Home. This home located near Doles is still standing.

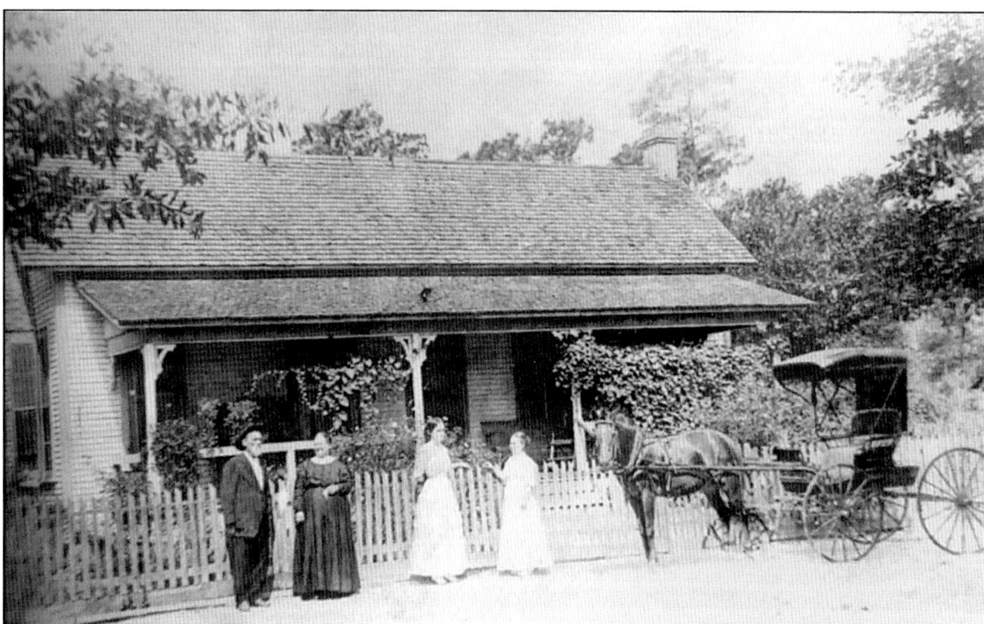

Hancock Home in Anderson City. This home has now been remodeled and is still in the Hancock family.

Eight

Clubs, Organizations, and Celebrations

Since the beginning of the county, men and women, boys and girls, have joined together sharing interests, fellowship, fraternal brotherhood, and promoting good will for the betterment of the citizens. The Fourth of July was always a time of celebration and all stops were pulled out for the 1953 Centennial of the creation of Worth County.

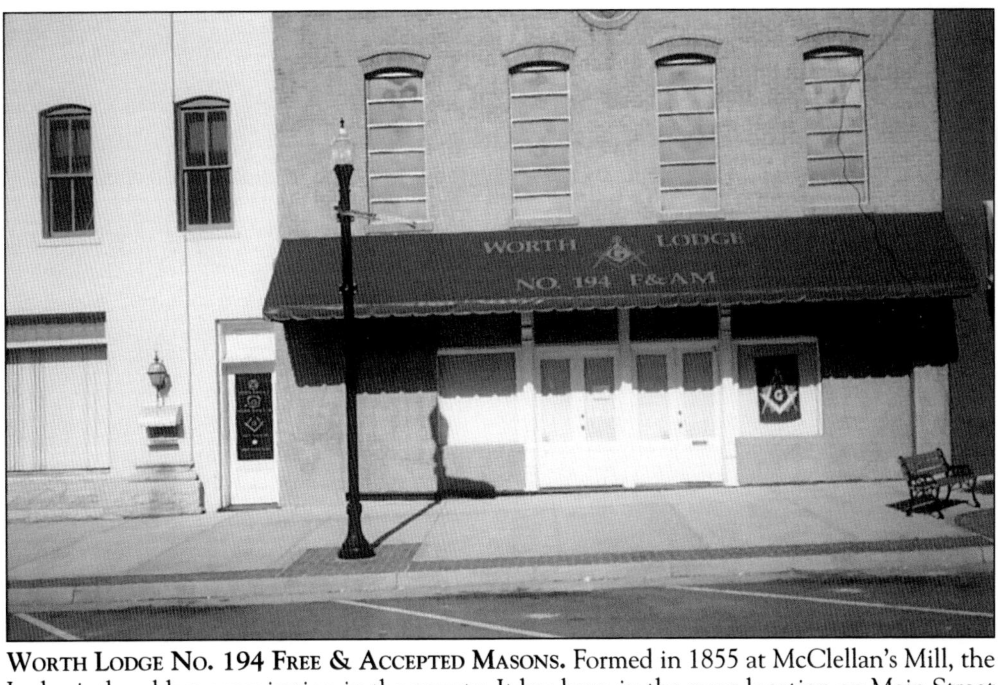

Worth Lodge No. 194 Free & Accepted Masons. Formed in 1855 at McClellan's Mill, the Lodge is the oldest organization in the county. It has been in the same location on Main Street since 1888. For years, the lodge occupied the second story only.

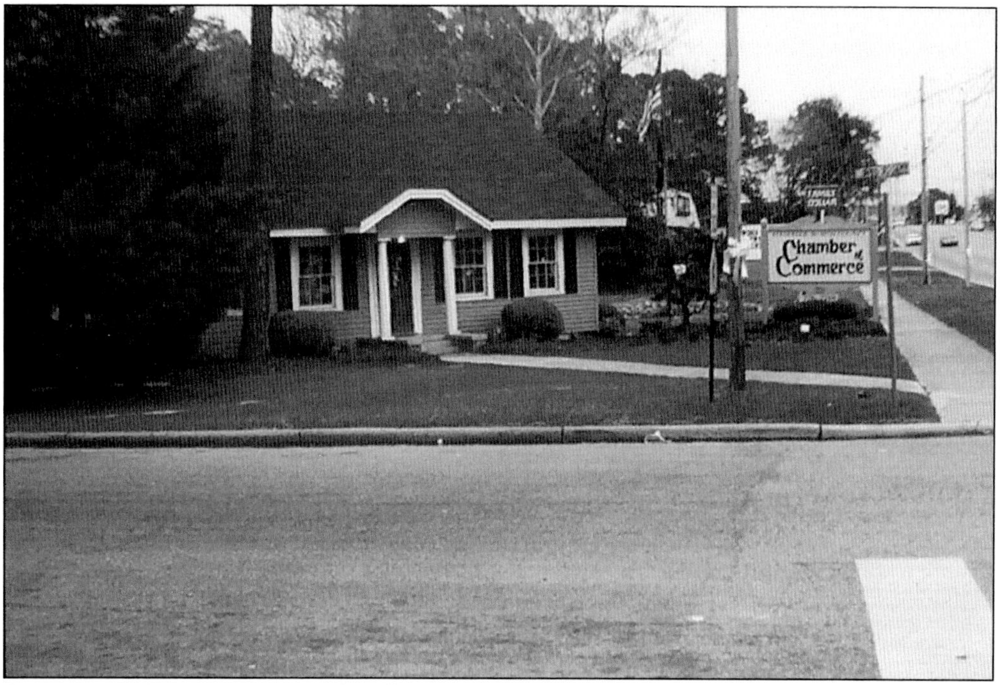

Chamber of Commerce. Located in the old American Legion building (1934) on busy US Hwy 82, it is perfectly situated to promote Sylvester and Worth County.

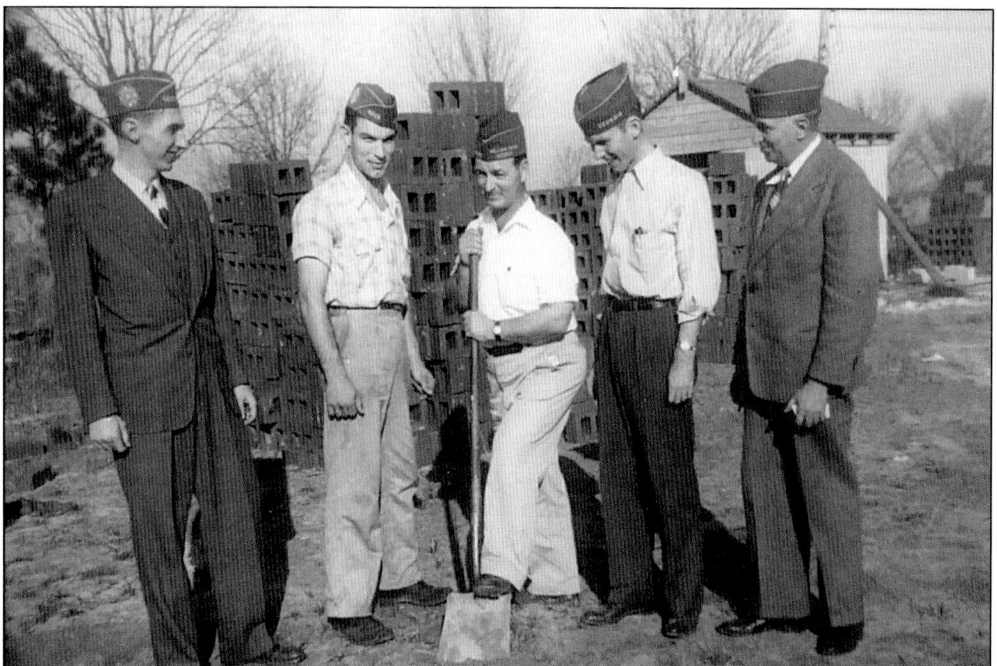

Breaking Ground for the William L. Sikes Post 4825 VFW Building. Pictured, left to right, are Bill Forehand, Cohen McKenzie, Clint Sumner, Pat James, and unidentified.

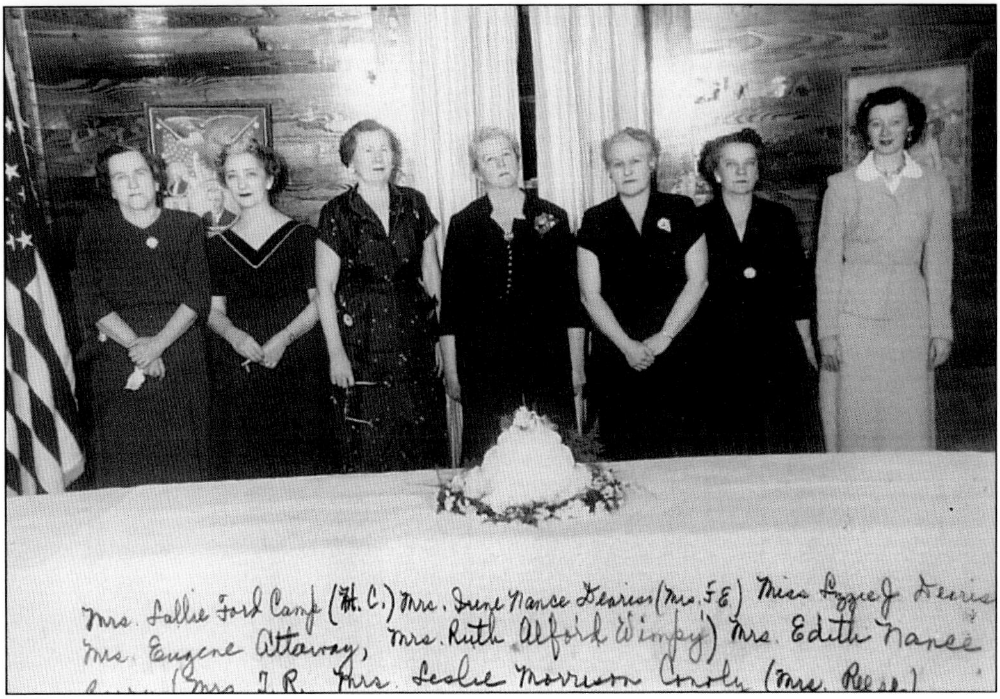

AMERICAN LEGION AUXILIARY. This auxiliary of the C.A. Brownlee Unit No. 113 American Legion was organized in 1924.

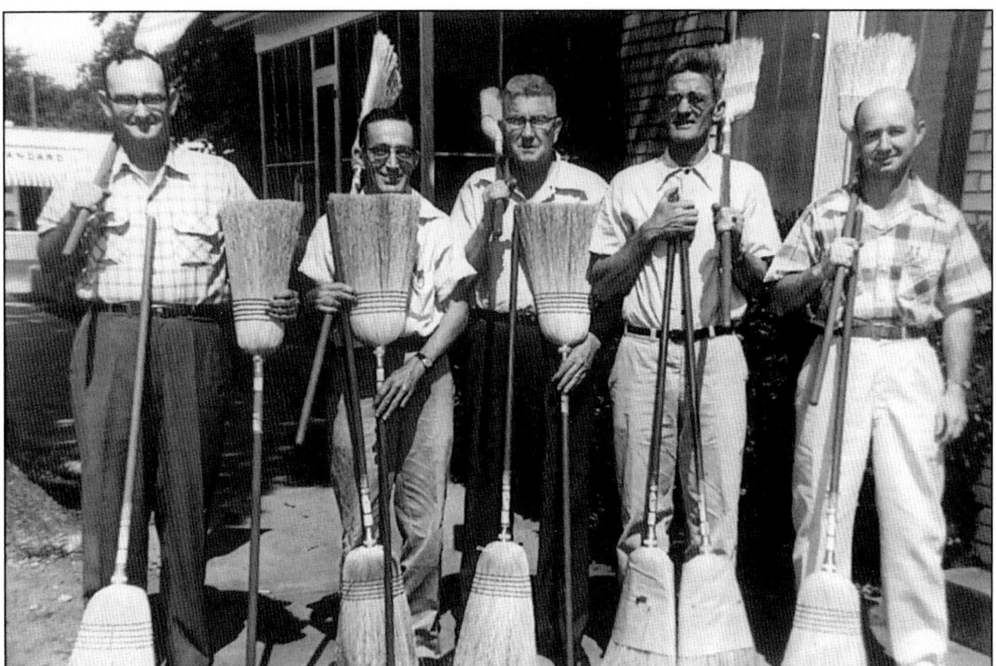

SYLVESTER LIONS CLUB. Shown, left to right, are Jack Jennings, Elzie Clayton, R.T. Land, Theron Golden, and Elmo Agoos.

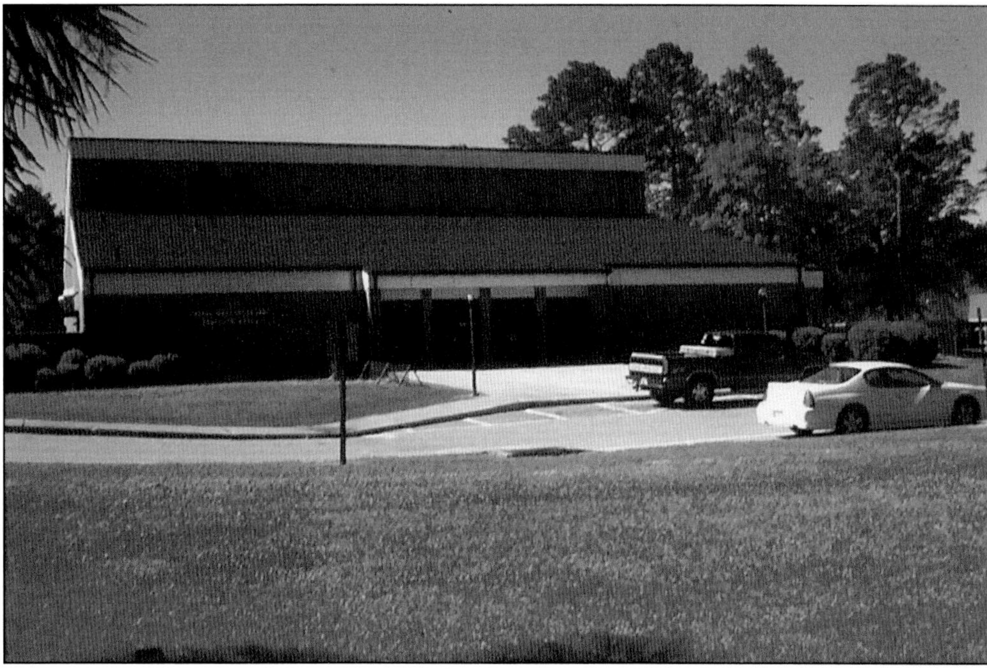

Henry Hall Woolard Civic Center. This was named in honor of the former mayor of Sylvester, Henry Hall Woodlard Sr.

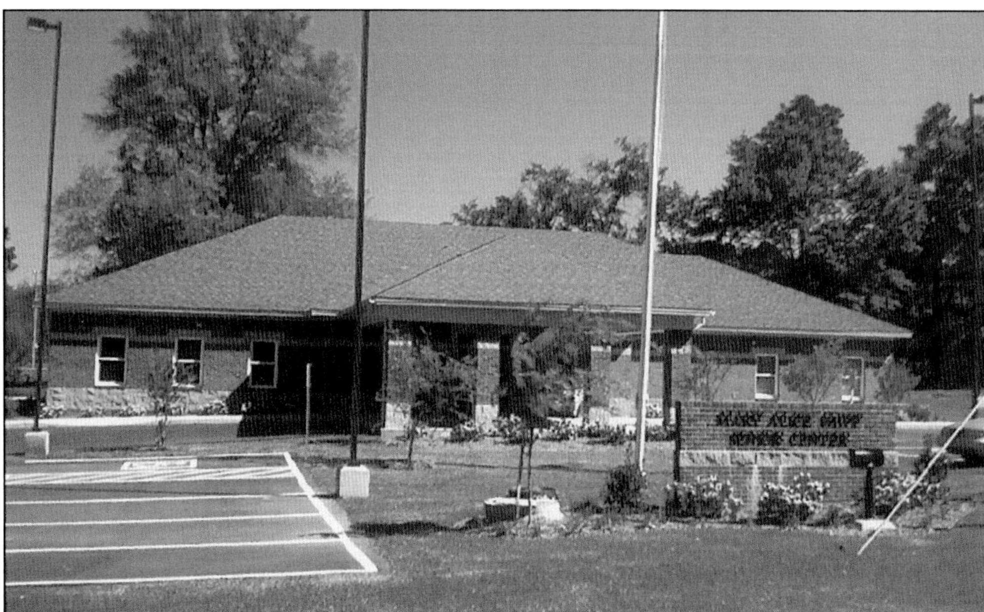

Mary Alice Shipp Senior Center, 2002. This newly built center for seniors was named in honor of longtime community activist Mary A. Shipp.

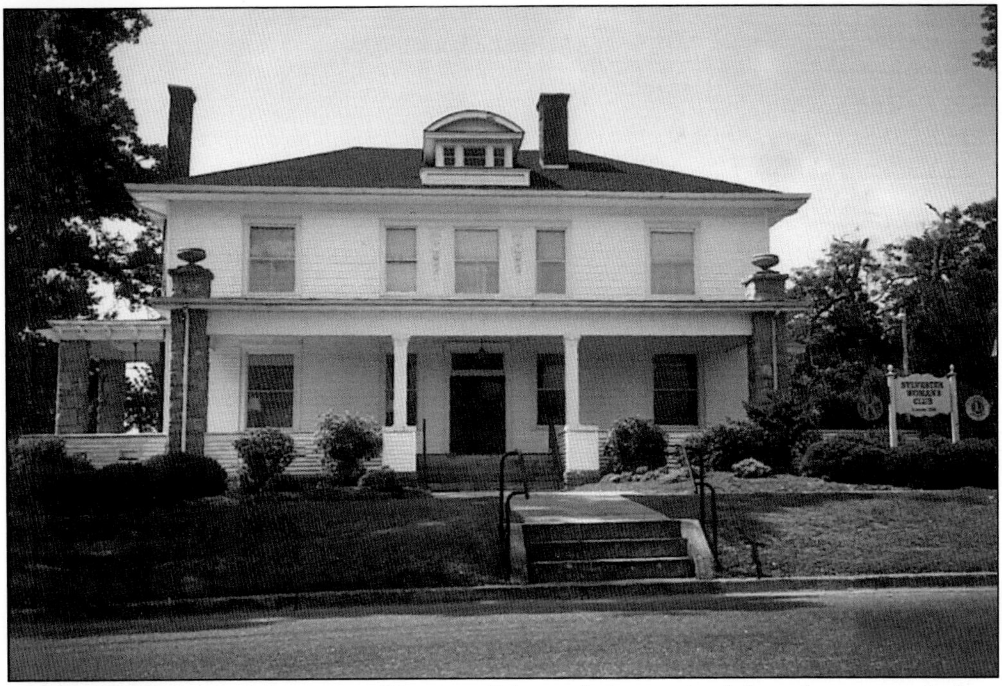

SYLVESTER WOMAN'S CLUBHOUSE. This was Sylvester's first civic club and was organized on May 13, 1908.

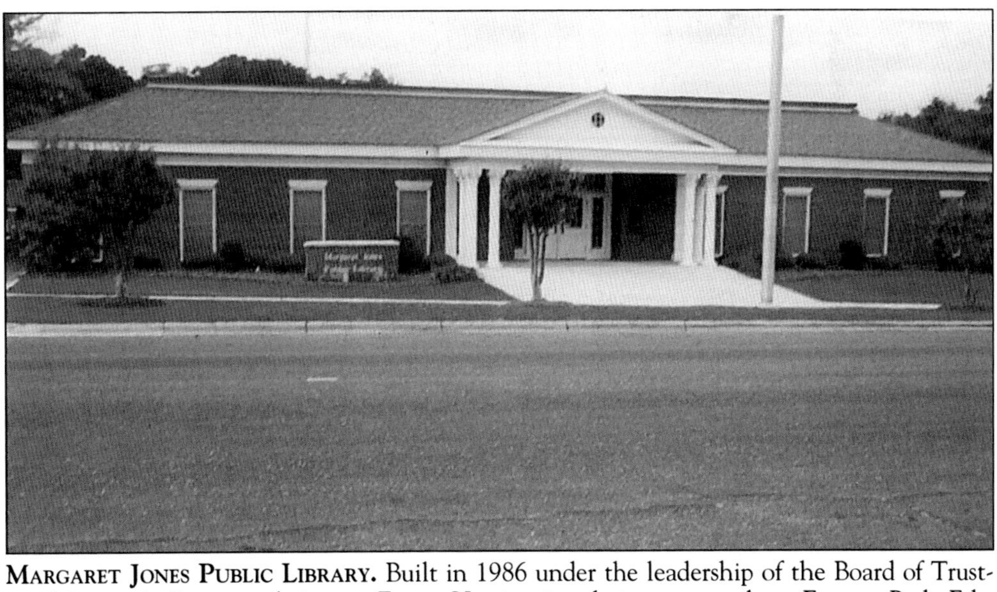

MARGARET JONES PUBLIC LIBRARY. Built in 1986 under the leadership of the Board of Trustees, Marian A. Sumner, chairman; Ernest Harris, vice chairman; members, Frances Park, Ethel Strangward, James E. "Buchshot" Whitfield, and Lamar Whittle; and librarians, Bettye G. Westbrook, and Sara Willis.

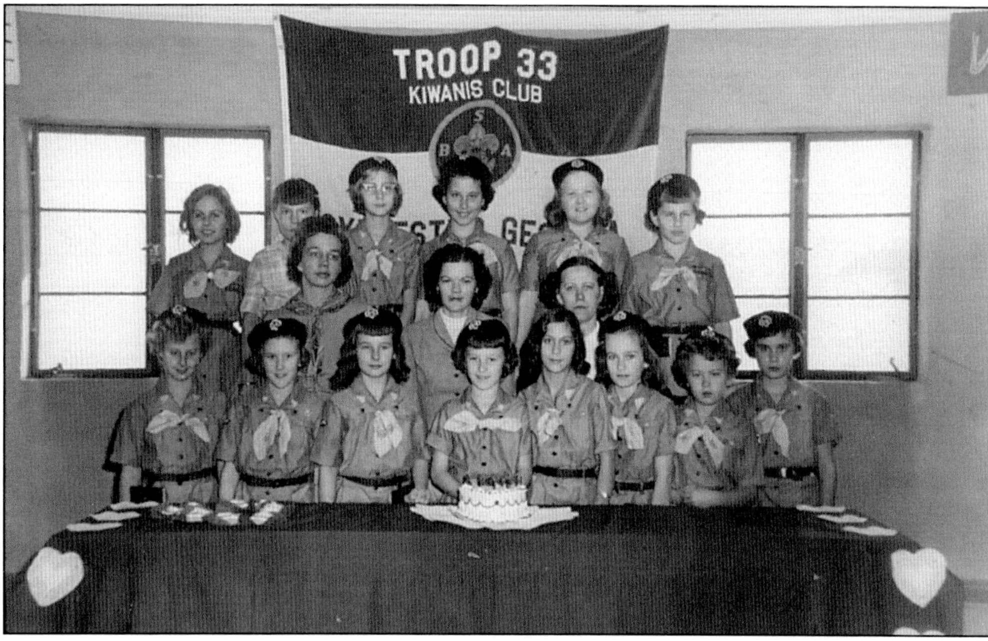

GIRL SCOUT TROUP. Pictured, left to right, are (front row) Lynn Agoos, Lynn Miller, Diane Durden, Sylvia Moore, Patricia Floyd, Anne Miller, Sharon Fowler, Jackie Golden; (middle row) Glenda Gammage, Billy Fowler, Peggy Miller; (back row) unidentified, Vicki Jeanes, Mary King Gammage, Mona Middleton, Rita Miller, Donna Durshimer.

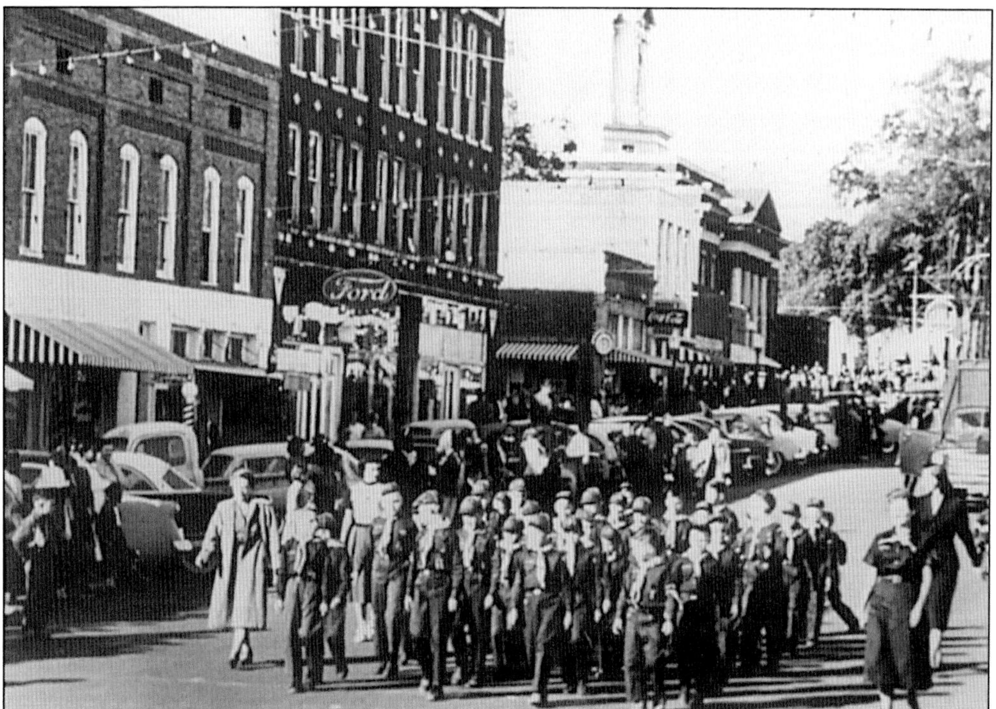

BOY SCOUTS IN CHRISTMAS PARADE, C. 1951. This parade on Main Street shows the Christmas lights in use at that time.

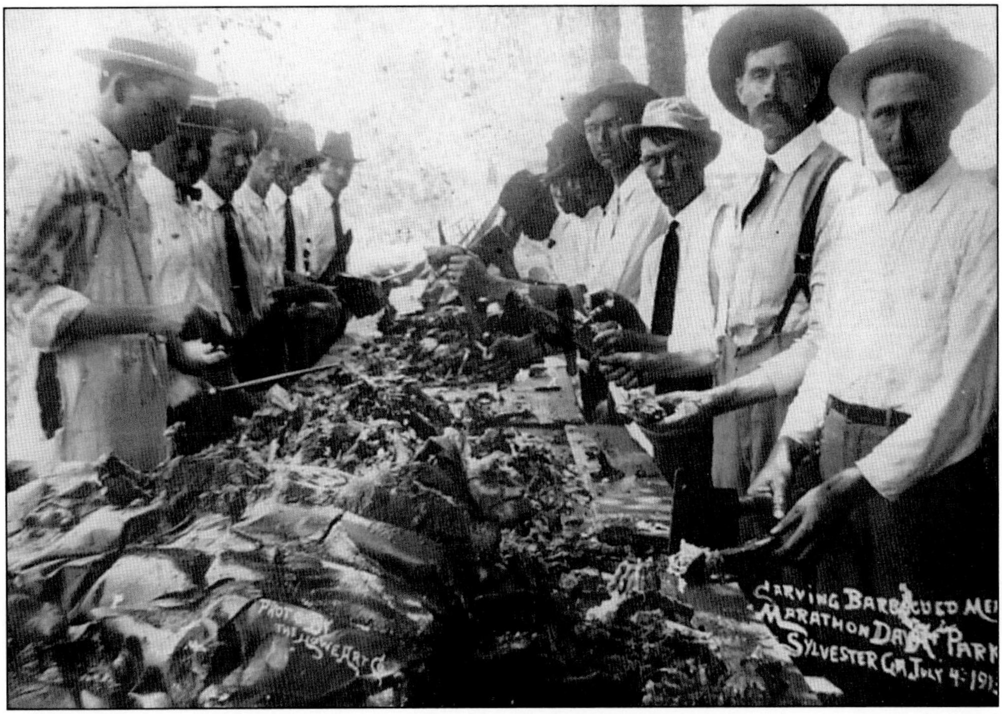

MARATHON DAY, BARBECUE, JULY 4, 1913. More than 3,000 pounds of meat were barbecued by the local Woodmen, a marathon was run between Albany and Sylvester, and Sylvester beat Baconton in a baseball game. A good time was had by all!

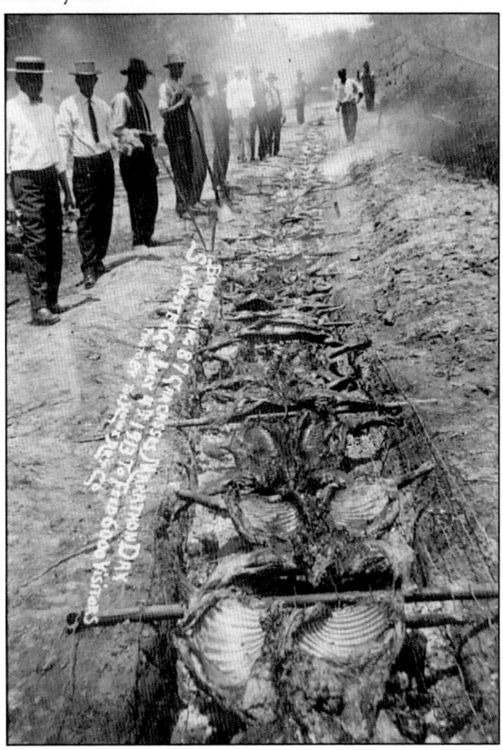

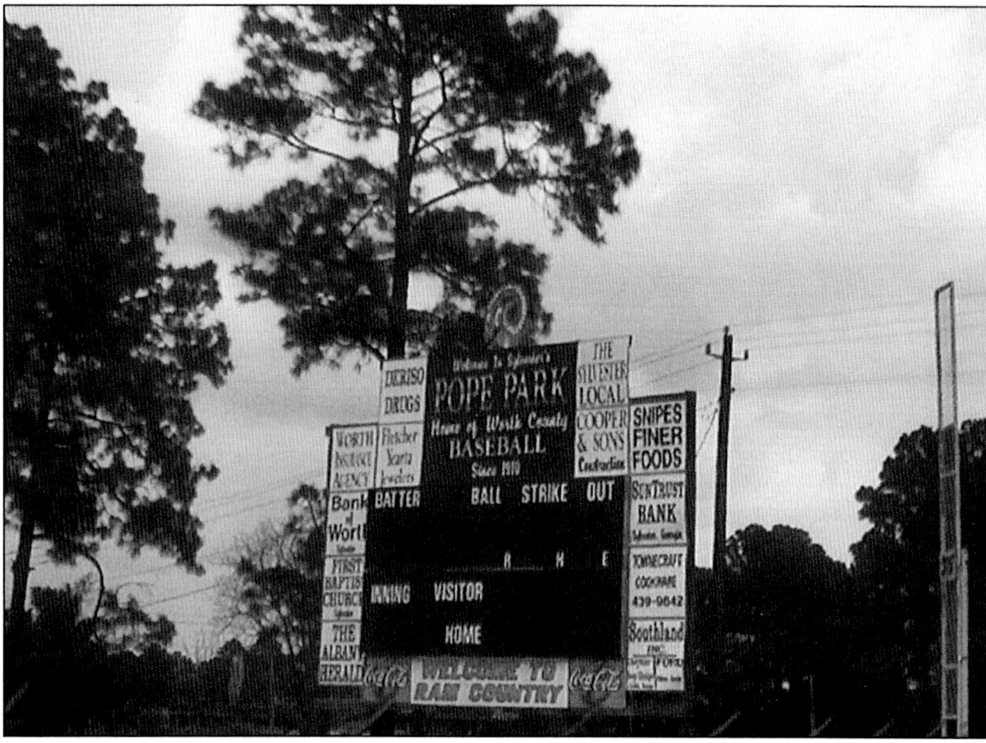

SCOREBOARD AT POPE FIELD. This baseball park has been in continuous use since 1910, the longest in the state. Land for the park was donated by Judge John Pope in 1909 with the eastern portion used as the ball field.

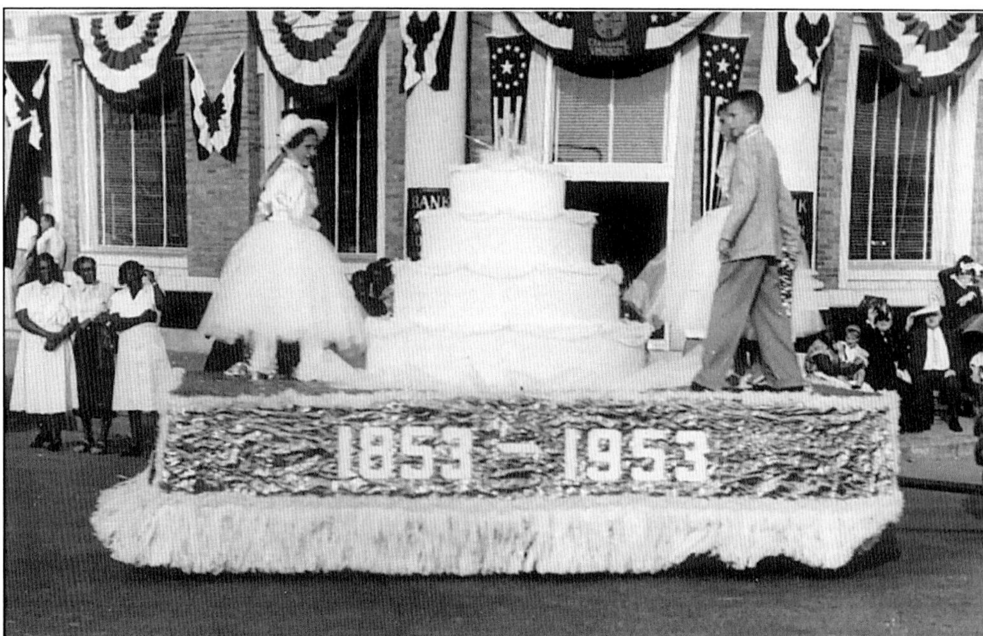

1953 CENTENNIAL PARADE FLOAT. This float is passing in front of the Old Bank of Worth County and represents a cake celebrating 100 years.

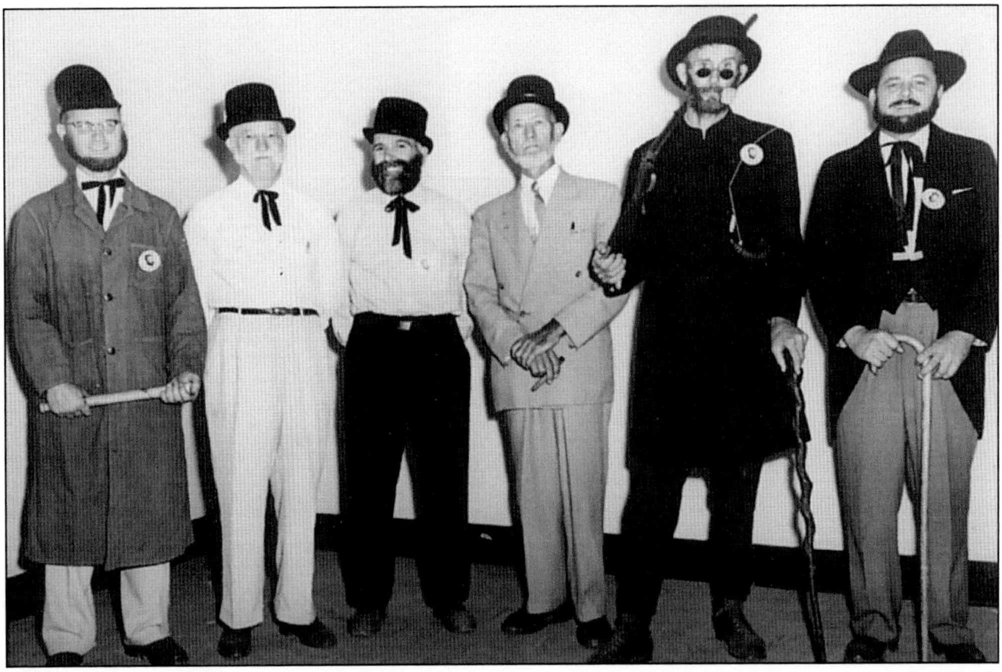

Brothers of the Brush. Those pictured, from left to right, are Theron Clements, unidentified, Pat Collins, unidentified, A.A. Mauldin, and Harvey Simpson.

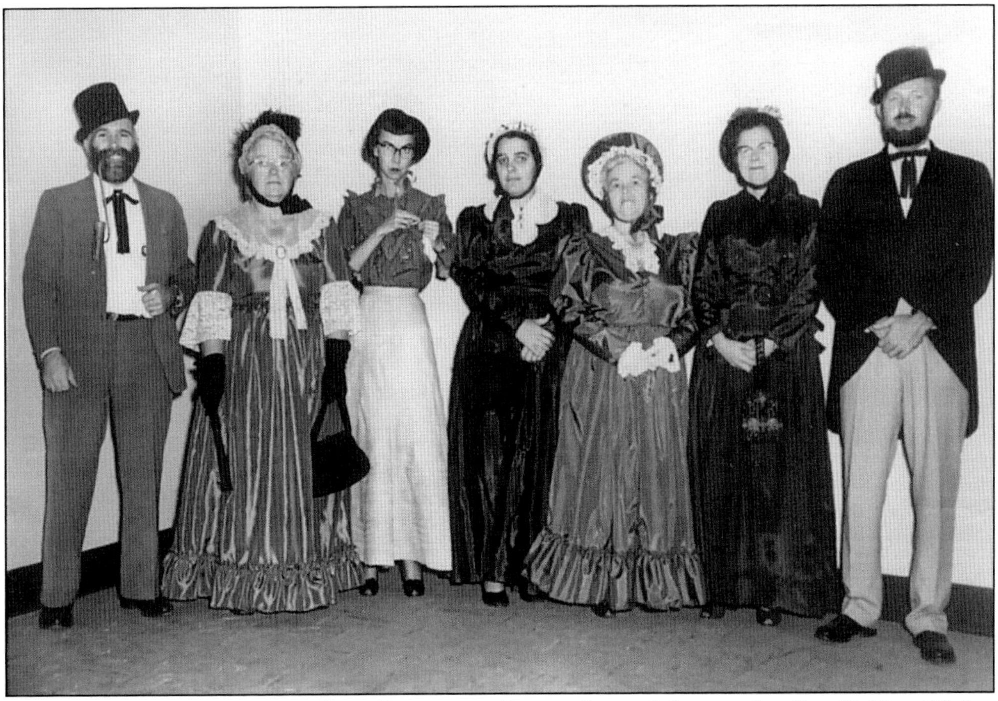

Ladies of the Swish with Two Brothers. Pictured are, left to right, Pat Collins, Helen Alford Mann, Lilla Trammell, Henrietta Wilder, Julia NeSmith Jeffords, Lizzie J. Deariso, and Cecil Johnson.

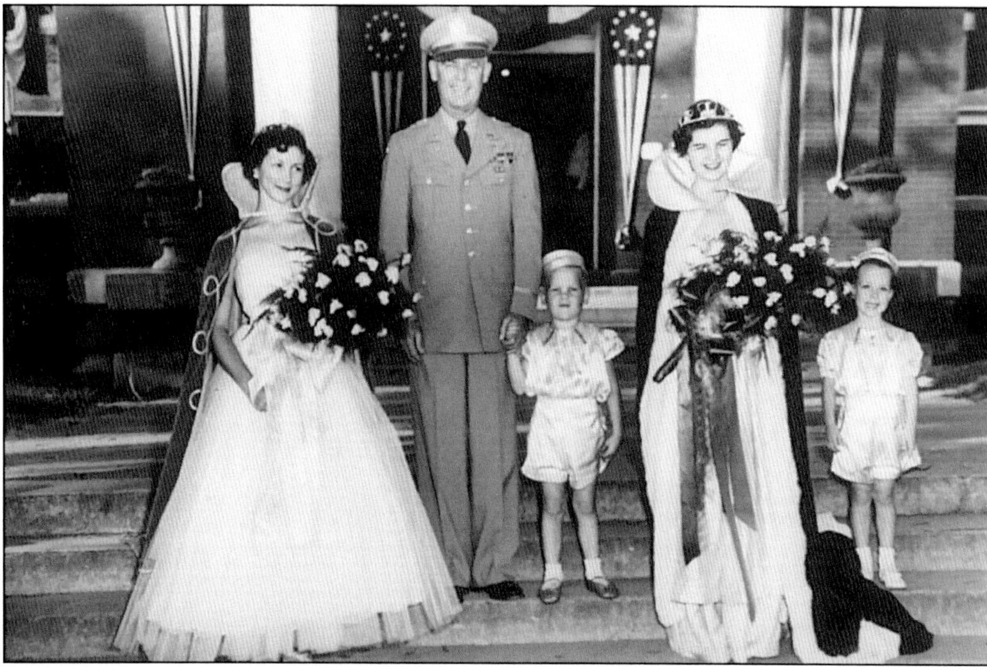

Centennial Queens and Their Court. Left to right, are Betty Sue Carter, unidentified male, Zan Tracy, Evelyn Burkett, and Beverly Sumner.

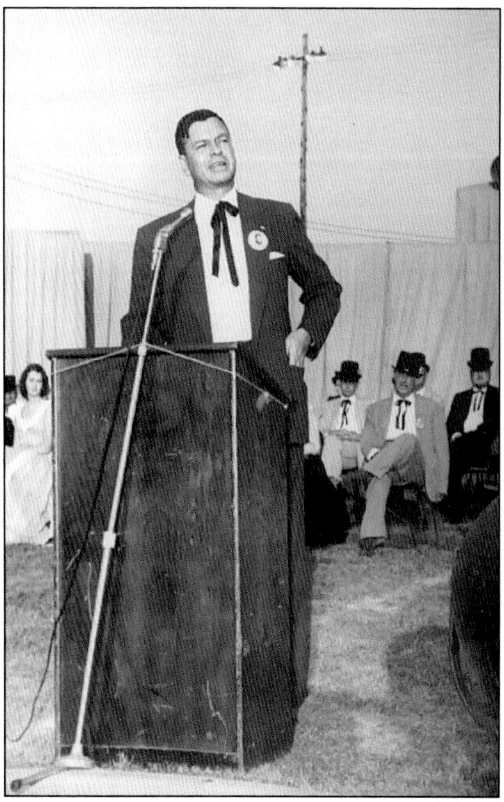

Gov. Herman Talmadge Speaking at the Centennial. The governor spoke on Wednesday, October 21, 1953. The week-long celebration included many dignitaries including the governor of Georgia.

School Days and Golden Rule Days. Teacher Mary Hillhouse and Pupil Carol Woody are showing what school was like many years ago.

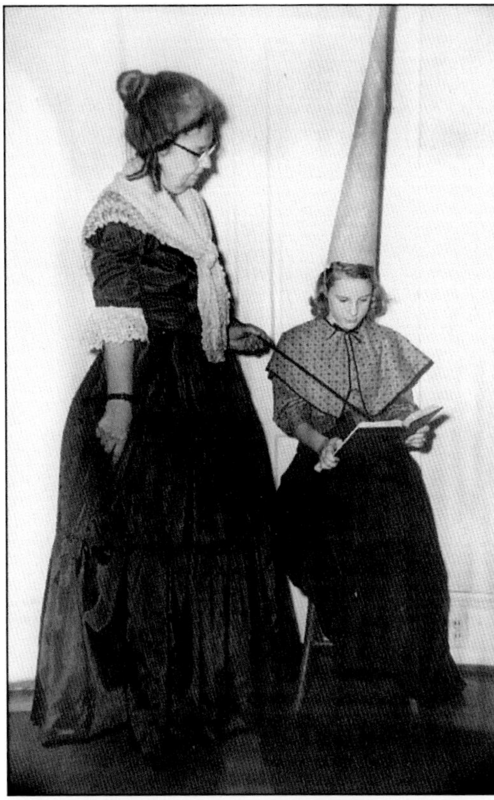

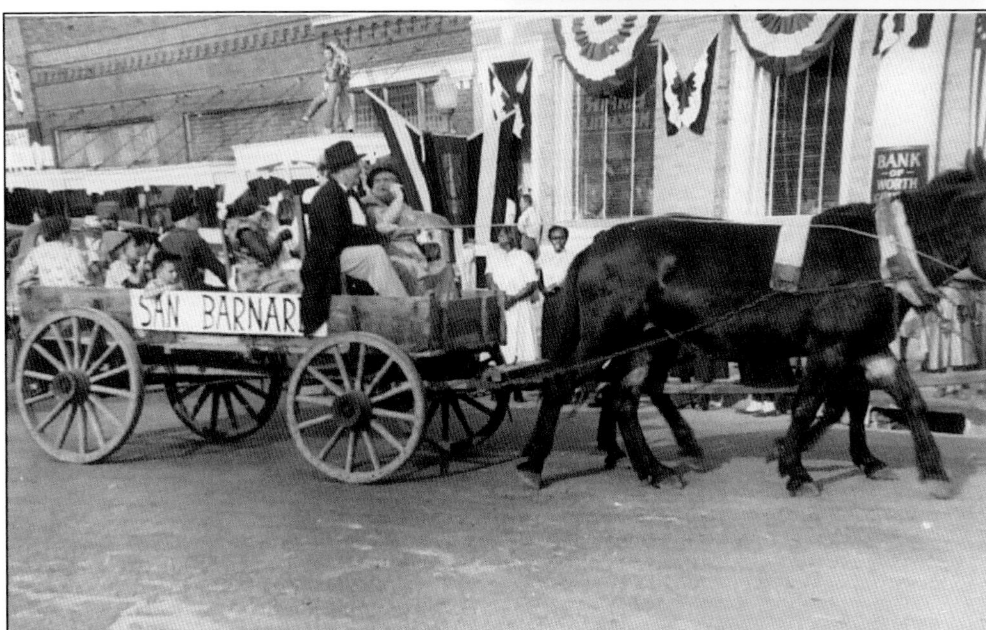

San Barnard Wagon in Parade. San Barnard was the first county site after the county was organized in 1853. It was a summer resort for Albany and was located approximately where the Isabella Cemetery is now. When Isabella was chosen as the county seat, it was deserted.

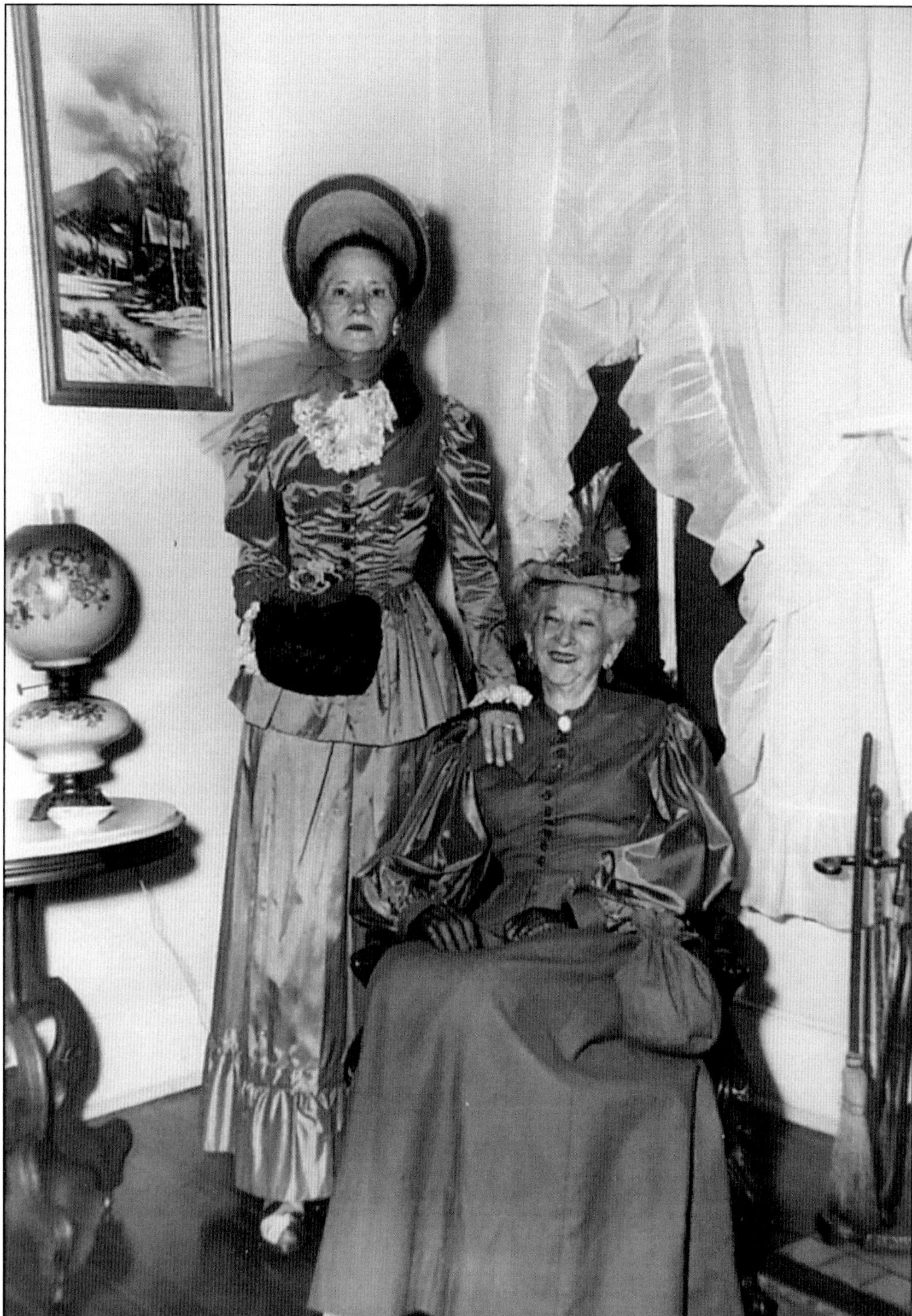

Emma and Lizzie Sumner in Their Centennial Finery. As daughters of George and Georgia Ford Sumner, Emma and Lizzie farmed a lot of land with their father and left large bequests to Pinson Memorial Methodist Church and Worth Lodge No. 194 F&AM.